WOMEN
ON BOARD
CRUISING

Questions! Doubts! You have so many before you set out! Well, just when you'd thought there was no one out there who understood you, along comes this awesome book, filled with warm women's voices offering clever advice, and helpful been-there-felt-that reassurance. It's like sitting down with a cup of tea and a support group of experienced fellow cruisers who can't wait to show you the ropes, and how cruising changed their lives and priorities.

– BERNADETTE BERNON, *BoatU.S. Magazine*, and *Cruising World*

From Mamas to tomboys, princesses to presidents, Women On Board Cruising opens a porthole for an inside look at how boating can create lifechanging experiences for women from all walks of life. North, South, East, West...these are ladies from all corners of the U.S. and Canada that share the passion of cruising. With humor, emotion and unique insight, Women On Board Cruising covers tips, information and great stories empowering us all to say, "I can do this."

– CHRISTY MARTIN, *Life on the Water Magazine*

It is such a wonderful cross-section of women on boats - The stories address the common questions we all have; I well remember I had the same concerns and fears when my husband and I left our "security" to go cruising, and wish I'd had a book like this to ease the way for me. I really think this is a must-read for anyone who's considering going cruising, men and women alike. These stories offer insight into and solutions for so many of the perceived "cruising problems" and show women that they're not the only ones who have ever worried!

– CAPTAIN PATTI MOORE, *Sea Sense–Women's Sailing & Powerboating School*

ALSO PUBLISHED BY FAVORS VENTURES

When the Water Calls... We Follow

*Twenty-five
Different Perspectives of
Long-Distance Cruising*
by
Veteran Women Boaters

FAVORS VENTURES, LLC
Traverse City, Michigan

Women On Board Cruising
Copyright © 2010 by Jim & Lisa Favors. All rights reserved.

No part of this book may be reproduced, stored in a retrieval system or transmitted in any form or by any means, electronic, mechanical, including photocopying, recording or otherwise, without the prior written permission of the publisher, except by a reviewer who may quote short passages in a review.

ISBN: 978-0-615-36348-6

Published by:
Favors Ventures, LLC
P.O. Box 584
Traverse City, Michigan 49685

Cover and book design by
Design Favors – info@designfavors.net

womenonboardcruising.com
favorsventures.com
favorsgreatloopblog.com
favorsweb.com

Questions regarding the content or ordering of this book should be addressed to:

Favors Ventures, LLC
231-642-7625
info@favorsventures.com

Printed in the United States of America

For Jim, my captain
and the light of my life.
— LTF

CONTENTS

INTRODUCTION............................ 1

1. Cyndi Boschard Perkins............... 3
2. Diane Stockard Wade.................. 13
3. Patti Salvage........................ 25
4. Ginger Austin........................ 41
5. Charlotte Snider..................... 49
6. Judi Drake........................... 63
7. Linda Thomas......................... 75
8. Pat Ehrman........................... 85
9. Carol Gordon......................... 99
10. Pam Harris.......................... 105
11. Liz Stagg........................... 115
12. Lisa Targal Favors.................. 125
13. Ellen Langer........................ 145
14. Susan Armstrong..................... 153
15. Jan Nelson.......................... 159
16. Barbara Benjamin.................... 169
17. Linda Brennan....................... 181
18. Leslie Firestone.................... 187
19. Angela M. Metro..................... 195
20. Sharon Larrison Stepniewski......... 201
21. Doris Prichard...................... 209
22. Darcy Searl......................... 219
23. Elvie Short......................... 227
24. Barbara Doyle....................... 233
25. Nancy Ojard......................... 239

The more one does and sees and feels, the more one is able to do, and the more genuine may be one's appreciation of fundamental things like home, and love, and understanding companionship.

— AMELIA EARHART

INTRODUCTION

While traveling on our boat *Kismet*, during our many years as long-distance cruisers, my husband, Jim, and I have had the good fortune of meeting countless amazing women boaters who posess varying backgrounds, strengths and abilities. I began to notice in my conversations with many of these women boaters, the topic would inevitably turn to the things we would have done differently had we had more information about this type of lifestyle before actually living it. Sometimes, I'd hear the refrain; "I wish someone had told me about this (or that) BEFORE I started cruising." Other times I'd hear, "If I were to be in a position to advise a novice woman boater, I'd make sure she benefited from my mistakes or ignorance, my list would include..."

While I recognize it's not always the woman who's anxious about the unknowns in undertaking a long-distance cruise, in our experience it's more typically true. I think many women, who were initially hesitant before heading out on the water, were amazed at how much they liked the whole experience and actually hated to see it come to an end. Then there are some WHO have had a hard time getting over their initial fear of the unknown, and due to that apprehension, may never venture off the dock. Jim and I have also met, over the years, a lot of gung-ho male boaters who want us to talk to their partners and help get them "on board." Sometimes the men just don't understand what kind of insight the women in their lives are looking for.

I quickly began to see what a good opportunity this would be to bring these two groups of women together; women who have actual long-distance cruising experience and women who have some reservations and fears about this lifestyle. My hope was that we could help women in overcoming some of the anxiety they may hold and give them an opportunity to think outside of their comfort zones by getting inside the stories shared by the contributors. I also felt this book could be a good reference tool for a woman who eagerly wants to join a partner in doing some long distance cruising (or she might be interested in a solo trip) but just wants to do some research beforehand.

I believe this format, of many different perspectives, was the right approach for either group of readers (maybe even provide some understanding for the men who have a great desire to get their women on board). This is NOT a book on blog or log entries or trip itineraries. The contributors were not required to have completed their trips to submit a chapter for inclusion in the book. Any type (sail or power) of female boater, with long-distance cruising experience, of any kind, was invited to participate. I asked a large part of the cruising community I knew personally (there are a few included in the book who were referred to me by women I knew) to share their own personal experiences, trials, tribulations, humor and tips on long-distance cruising with those less informed. And share they did!

Long-distance cruising is a life-changing event. I would hate for any potential woman boater to miss an opportunity for this type of adventure due to lack of information or fear of the unknown.

Cyndi Boschard Perkins

Vessel: S/V *Chip Ahoy* – 32-foot DownEast Sailboat
Residence: Houghton, Michigan
Homeport: Portage Lake Waterway, Michigan
Freelance Articles Website: sailingbreezes.com

To quote Chaka Khan, "I'm Every Woman," the one puking in the bailing bucket and the one artfully guiding her 19,000-pound sailboat through a tight canal. The on-top-of-it long-distance cruiser plotting safe anchorages and fuel stops – and the klutz who bruises her ribs on the way down the teak companionway steps to get another cup of coffee. I'm the brave voyager who challenges the wind, and the wimp trembling in a thunderstorm.

Dear Women On Board, you are "Every Woman" too. Whether you are just starting out or taking boating to a new level, the way that you rise to this life-expanding adventure will define who you are as a person.

Keep the rose-colored glasses handy because living aboard will bring you moments of sheer ecstasy. However, if you go into the adventure expecting all sweetness and light, you will quickly be disillusioned. Far better to just admit that the "Oops" moments come right along with the "Aha's" and keep your sense of humor handy at all times. In a little Tiki bar down in the Florida Keys, my husband Scott and I nearly choked on our tap beers while listening to a couple bragging about how they had never run aground. Oh really? We have run aground too many times to count, a number of times of which we laugh about every time we tell the stories. Our mistakes as well as our successes have taught me more than any university ever could.

My years on the water have been incredibly humbling. For all I have learned, there is so much more that I still need to learn. I still suck at tying knots. I don't enjoy racing or even heeling. The other day we had some friends out for a sail and I revved the engine speed without putting the boat in forward gear. Duh! The lesson here is to go forward with new adventures, even if you end up performing really embarrassing or amateur maneuvers in your efforts to have a good time on your boat. As long as you keep safety in mind and follow the correct rules of operation for your boat, there is no situation that you can't get out of while keeping the boat and yourselves safe at the same time.

You will learn some fascinating stuff traveling on a boat. Along with bird watching, shell, insect and fish guides, be sure to stock the diesel or gasoline engine repair manual and a full schematic of your plumbing and electrical systems. Safety rules must be one of your first areas of learning, along with basic navigation, which is simply a matter of where are the green buoys and where are the red nuns (the pointy ones) and how to stay well to the middle of the channel so you don't run aground. Figuring out how to read the natural and manmade markers on commercial and recreational waterways can and should be an obsession. Trust me; it is as much fun as cruising Route 66 in a vintage Mustang.

Boating opens you up to extraordinary experiences you have never had before. Dare to experiment. Allow yourself to try new things. For example, I am not a socializer. Hosting people on the boat felt strange at first, but without workaday worries, it was quite pleasant, even when it involved throwing a shrimper, while in North Carolina, off the boat after he drank up all our beer. Most boaters enjoy offering advice that tells you flat out where to go or not go. Consider the source, but heed the advice. Conversely, you will have delicious private time alone to read books, craft, listen to good music and breathe; exploring any hidden interests that life on the water brings out in you.

The practicalities of life on board require a sense of humor as you figure out new routines for cooking, cleaning, eating and sleeping. For example, it is always wise to scout out a marina bathroom before you gather up your towel and shower bag so you can bring along the appropriate cleaning supplies or coins. Yes, I did say coins. You may actually experience the joy of a coin-operated shower. One couple we met had actually stripped down and lathered up before realizing they needed to purchase tokens from the front desk to activate the water. A broom is also handy for wiping out spider webs in a neglected shower room. Many seasoned cruisers find out when the bathrooms are cleaned and time their showers accordingly. Life aboard accents the joy of little things and a hot, clean shower ranks high on that list.

Venturing out into open water offshore may seem daunting to some, but there is a real freedom to be savored in traveling in the "Great Wide Open." There may be shipping traffic, but there are no stop signs or markers to worry about, and that is why many boaters, male and female, adore that unfettered state of sailing along with Mother Nature away from the sight of land where most people never go. There seems to be two schools of thought on the sight-of-land issue. Some people just can't bear the idea. I always tell them, "It's as easy to drown in a toilet as the ocean." For me, being away from land is magical. The sky looks incredible at night with no ambient light to disturb the nightly star show. Facing the endless horizon, you realize how big the world is and how small you are. It may sound corny, but the universe just makes more sense out there!

In truth, the storm stories make good magazine articles. But 99 percent of the time you will have predicted your weather correctly. You will have figured out a couple of places to duck in if things get hinky or will just stay put in a sheltered anchorage or marina because the weather wasn't favorable and you liked the grocery store, the local watering hole or the ambience. Type A personalities sometimes have a hard time adapting to the looseness of the cruising itinerary. One of the Murphy's Laws of boating is that when you have plans to pick someone up and a firm deadline is set, with airport schedules, marina and hotel reservations all neatly arranged and time taken off work, glitches come up. The weather doesn't care about our schedules or if something goes wrong with the engine or if the prop hits a rock as you are coming into the marina. For most cruisers I have met, trying to make a deadline is what kicked them in the butt mentally and physically. Cruisers greatly enjoy company. They are also super superstitious about trying to make a fast passage – such as crossing the Gulf Stream from Florida to the Bahamas – on a time schedule.

Women On Board Rule: Tell your arriving company to watch the Weather Channel or go on Underground Weather on the Internet.

Y'all need to look at the sky and wave conditions rather than worrying about when you need to be at a certain destination or back at work. Being "weathered in" is both a curse and a blessing in the cruising world. It is always a good excuse if you can't make it back to work!

Deadlines between ports must remain nebulous and patience is required. In my experience men more often than women get caught up in that "let's just go" spirit, laudable at times but at others you may find yourself restraining the impulse to smack the impatient party in the face with a fish bat. "Seriously, Scott, go look at the breakers rolling onto the beach. This is not a good day to travel across Oneida Lake with the mast down." Traveling with a racing or delivery mentality often serves captains well as far as sailing trim and efficient motoring, but the best captains are also meteorologists who tap the barometer and turn on the Doppler (i.e. any local TV station you can pull in with rabbit ears hoisted to the mast). If the forecast isn't favorable, don't go, even if you are tired of waiting to make a crossing or have foolishly committed to a firm arrival deadline for guests.

Storms aren't the thing that women worry about most.

Surveys show that our major worry is that the man who is supposed to be running the show will fall off the boat. Talking with your cruising mate about what you are supposed to do if they go in the drink can conquer this universal fear. A "Man Overboard" drill can be fun, toss something off the boat into the water and retrieve it at least once per year and practice.

Statistics indicate that it is not uncommon to find open trouser zippers on the men who drowned after falling off their boats. This means that you are allowed to advise caution if your husband, son, brother, friend or other male loved one goes forward to take a leak. Of course, we never do this on Lake Superior because it is a zero discharge zone.

Have I hammered home the point that you don't need to be perfect to enjoy living on a boat? If not, let me mention that my knees knock when we encounter high seas. I hate to be cold. I am prone to seasickness.

Here's another truth: I can't wait to get out on big water again, with no particular destination in mind. Why? It is the best, like no other way of life. I am most myself out on the water. Whether you are out for a day or two years, the relaxation level is incredible. I love the people we meet, the places we see and those euphoric hours when we flow with the universe, sails unfurled, powered by only the wind.

Amidst all this Nirvana, my observations lo these many years convince me that one of the greatest challenges women boaters with male partners face is the "Yelling Thing." Those of us who have been doing this for a while have all seen captains barking rude or incoherent commands at their partners while anchoring or coming into the docks. After almost 30 years of marriage, Scott and I still face daily challenges with maintaining calm, constant and consistent communication. Happily, the tears and the one-fingered hand gestures are now few and far between.

Lest you consider me a female chauvinist, yes I know there are strong single-handing females; one of my favorites is Tania Aebi. Nobody beats the Ontario women sailors I know for guts, knowledge and a laissez-faire attitude. They know their stuff and don't hesitate to zing snappy comments right back at their captains when the going gets tense.

By far the majority of cruising women I have encountered travel with a dominant male guiding the ship. Nurturing a loving relationship while putting up with the inevitable stresses of a different lifestyle can be exhilarating. The playing field will often be leveled because you will do dumb things and so will he. Conflicts can't drag on for too long because the typical "I'm not talking to you" avoidance typical on land is impossible in this environment. There is no walking away, sisters! There's nowhere to go! So, you have to figure out what is causing the tension and relieve it, just as you would spill some wind off an unhappy sail or adjust your engine speed and course to get into smoother water.

I take great comfort in learning that legendary sailing women have also faced yelling matches or stony silence in their boating relationships. When I first read Lin Pardey's recollections of being sent down below by Larry in the early years because she burst into tears during a terrible storm, I felt vindicated and not alone. For those of you who haven't read any Pardey books or articles, check out this sailing couple, they are awesome. Their well-chronicled sailing life has been so stellar that you would never believe they had ever had even a minor disagreement on their boat. More recently, in the June 2009 issue of Cruising World Magazine, Beth Leonard of the sailing vessel *Hawk* shared her "Storm Tactics for the Onboard Relationship," speaking openly of the breaks in confidence, clogs in communication and harsh exchanges that she and her partner Evans Starzinger experienced until they learned how to negotiate a relationship out on the water. In a million years, I would have never thought that this incredible sailing woman has a life partner who has threatened to get her off the boat and on a plane. I never thought we would have that in common.

Actually, all women do have this in common. If your mother is sick, your child has an accident, your medical tests reveal a problem, your grandchild is graduating or it is Christmas in the snowy north, every woman with a family will encounter times when you are compelled to go to them or have them to come to you. The ties of family call to us women strongly and must be answered.

Whether you are new to cruising or a seasoned veteran, you are not alone. Just because you are living a supposedly idyllic lifestyle aboard, that does not mean an absence of challenge. Any woman who gets out on the water in her boat is "Every Woman," like me, with the power to inspire and the willingness to share knowledge. If you choose to cruise, you will be amazingly braver and more resourceful than you ever thought possible.

Personally I am so grateful to the women I have met while cruising aboard our sailboat *Chip Ahoy*. They've taught me so very much, including what not to do, which is often more important than what to do. Let me get my black book out and tell you about a few of the women cruisers who have passed along a boat card. Ah, the memories.

First off, I immediately think of Trish and Ernie of *Memories*, a seasoned sailing couple from Wisconsin, former owners of High Seas Marina in Oconto, Wisconsin. We met them on our second Great Loop trip in a crowded lock. There was no more wall to tie to, and they graciously invited *Chip Ahoy* to raft up. We ended up traveling with them all the way to the Keys, stopping at every watering hole and remote anchorage they suggested. Trish taught me the importance of spontaneity, of literally stopping and smelling the roses – in their case, it was flipping the boat around to get a picture of a wading heron or plucking an apple off a low-hanging branch dangling over the riverbank. *Chip Ahoy* and *Memories* threw an impromptu Green Bay Packers tailgate party at Columbus Marina in Columbus, Mississippi, something I would never have done on my own. *Memories* also roped the crew of *Chip Ahoy* into trying new ports through skinny water, embodying "buddy boat" with gentle humor and clear directions as they led us where we never thought we could take our boat, and we enjoyed the beef jerky made aboard *Memories* all the way to the Keys.

The most iconic sailing couple I have ever met, Norm and Gerri Powell, sailed aboard *Witchcraft* pursuing Norm's pet saying, "Let's go do something, even if it's wrong." In their 70s, they cared not for publicity and graciously (but absolutely) refused to let me write a boating article about them. Their beautiful sailboat was totally modified with higher lifelines, easy on-and-off ramps to accommodate older bodies as well as the tides and was cleverly tricked out with every galley need and sail accommodation required. Starting from Oregon, they sailed from the Pacific to the Atlantic via the Panama Canal. Gerri takes everything in her stride and does not think she is remarkable. Her serenity is an inspiration. It strikes me how many cruisers have continued to travel well into their 80s. I have partied at Tiki bars with 70-year-olds who could drink me under the table.

The next name in my black book should hurry you toward the water. If you wait too long, the rewards may not outweigh the benefits.

It is OK to admit that you don't like boating or that you once did, but it is no longer your cup of tea. Doug and Helen aboard *Misty Blue II* of Midland, Ontario planned the whole Loop together. T'was not to be. Helen decided to not return after going back to Ontario for Christmas. While I had her along for our journey down the rivers on our first Loop, (I loved her clam dip, wine and love of good books that she generously lent me), it all endeared me to this sweet lady, who could also have a wickedly funny tongue even in times of stress. Her acid comment after one of their unfortunate groundings: "Doug thinks the buoys are for others and not for him."

For Helen, having to move a pile of stuff off the V-berth to go to bed at night, having to lift creaky knees to clamber over lifelines onto precarious piers and the disconnect from grandchildren's activities was finally too much. While she fully embraced the trip down America's rivers with us, she was also brave enough to decide that enough was enough. In addition, she courageously urged Doug to continue the trip on his own because she wanted him to fulfill his goal.

Then there are the hard-core sailing women. Of those I am privileged to know, most hail from Ontario. They are matter of fact about the ways of the lake (up there Superior lays down mostly like clockwork at 7 p.m.). They always seem to know what they need to take with them to cover any emergency or entertainment need. They sauna, drink their Caesars at happy hour and fearlessly navigate their way through whatever current crisis happens to pop up. They make sport of minimizing crisis. Find the tools and know-how that you need to get the job done, and then relax. I aspire to be like them someday.

Many women in this world do not know how to relax. A two-week vacation is not enough. Learning to relax takes at least a month, and it is an art. Venturing out on your boat as a live-aboard cruiser offers an opportunity to truly relax, to base your life on the simple things. Although shopping is "provisioning," kitchen is "galley," and bathroom is "head," in many aspects living aboard is no different than living in a "normal" house. There are cleaning, cooking chores and plumbing, electrical, cooling, heating and lighting systems to keep in good working order. The women who have inspired me focus on strengths rather than weaknesses; each has specialties in general maintenance and operations categories. As you gain confidence in your boating skills, you will discover your forte. It may be manning the engine or trimming sails, or perhaps programming the GPS, radar and autopilot, just three of the many fascinating and useful electronic gadgets that are standard equipment on most cruising vessels. In any event, being a helpless female isn't an option if you are intent on becoming a true cruiser. Varnish queen, galley chef, deck monkey or helmsman – if you give your all to your boat, it will give back to you threefold.

Whether you are roped into trying it for a weekend, or you are already working on cruising as your lifestyle, please remember that almost every woman on board that you will meet is sharing similar joys and travails. Every woman who enjoys life on the water is your resource. We are a sheltering community sharing everything from laundry soap to spare engine parts. Don't be shy about asking a fellow woman boater how she handled a situation, and do not be intimidated if she starts spewing a wealth of information that you cannot even begin to absorb. We are a clique of sorts, but we are not cliquey. All are welcome.

You are not alone. You are Every Woman. You'll make that big leap onto the water and into a new way of life.

Five Need-To-Knows:

1. I should begin with the number-one safety tip of "one hand for you and one for the boat," but being an eight on the girly-girl scale, let me start with fashion and beauty, i.e. why you should feel guilt-free about packing. My husband rolls his eyes at the amount of shoes I carry aboard. I make no apologies for needing black, blue and brown flip flops, basic white sandals, red jeweled dress sandals and three or four pairs of tennies. A few Christmases ago, to my delight, my husband presented me with sea bands in all colors to coordinate with any outfit.

   The point is to plan ahead if you occasionally wear make-up, dye your hair, array yourself in finery for special occasions, or do any of those non-macho things that women do. If during your travels you stray near a store that has what you need, stock up on face cream, razors, lotion or your favorite brand of conditioner. It truly is the little things in life that make cruising more pleasurable. When you are waiting for a lock to open or chilling in the anchorage, go ahead and shave your legs. I do.

   Vanities aside, there are other reasons to pack more than you think you will need. Even those headed south cannot plan on always being warm. My friend Bonnie gave away all her winter clothes, swapping jeans for cargo shorts when she left

Michigan to go cruising. Ditto my sailing buddy Janet from Sleepy Eye, Minnesota. Believe me; do not give away coats, pants, hats and gloves. There is frost in Mobile, Alabama in November and Florida is subtropical, emphasis on "sub," in the winter months. You won't be wearing a sundress every day just because there are palm trees and dolphins in the neighborhood.

A heater comes in handy. If you underestimate the amount of clothing needed, it can be a lot of fun to indulge in a low-budget splurge, hitting resale shops for turtlenecks, tights and jeans. Layer wisely and stay dry.

2. When a crisis calls from the home front – and they always do – do not feel surprised to be slightly resentful at being yanked back into the rat race. Always have a get-home rescue plan if your family ties require it. You may be days away from any type of modern-day transportation or simply out of cell phone range at times.

    When you have children and grandchildren, mothers and fathers at home, being so far away from your loved ones can be disconcerting. Considering in advance how you would handle specific situations will alleviate some anxiety.

3. Observe the weather. Read the clouds. You may not be up for shooting the sun with a sextant, but you can study wave patterns or check out the barometer as a storm front is moving in. One of the delights of cruising is foregoing a climate-controlled environment where one doesn't notice prevailing winds, tide times or wave heights.

    Attuned to the weather, cruisers shelter in many delightful harbors for longer than planned and sometimes face daunting conditions if signs are ignored and decisions made without considering what Mother Nature is trying to tell us. The truth is many of the daunting conditions can be easily avoided by keeping an eye to the sky.

4. Money is not cast away as easily as dock lines. You can be very economical while cruising, but you will still require a solid financial plan. Set a budget while allowing some luxuries and preparing for unexpected emergencies.

    If you are truly filthy rich, ignore this advice. If you are merely well off or somewhere in the blue-collar range, pay attention. Boat problems and fixes tend to range in terms of thousands not hundreds. Your money flow will also tend to be different, hemorrhaging cash in certain ports followed by mile upon blessed mile where no amount of money is spent because it will not solve your problem and there is no one to help you but yourself. The latter is incredibly liberating and the former can provide you with many good meals and libations if you learn to plan accordingly.

5. Take a boating course. Advice to self. The women I have talked to and read about who have done so swear that it gave them a new confidence and freedom. You can learn as you go, as I have done with some success, but that instruction from a talented teacher is a step to be considered and can be incredibly liberating.

   I am living proof that you can get out on the water without special training – although in my family swimming lessons at the Catholic Club in Toledo and a boating safety course were standard issue because we spent all our time living and playing on lakes. Yet, I can't help thinking how much fun it would be to flip my husband out by single-handing as he does, confidently piloting, docking or anchoring the boat unassisted.

As you may have guessed, I enjoy reading articles and books authored by sailing couples. My latest hot read is *Middle Sea Autumn*, by Carol and Malcom McConnell, passage-makers across the Atlantic. In this book the intrepid cruisers travel 2,500 miles on the Mediterranean from Gibraltar to a new home in Greece. The co-authors credit her "native caution" balanced with his "instinctive risk taking" for guiding their boat and their relationship through so many challenging passages, many accomplished in the dark. The couple increased their expertise in the comfort zone of traditional roles such as engine repair for Malcom and cooking/provisioning for Carol. Carol piloted the boat through several dicey harbor entries, where spotting lights and steering the correct degree toward unlit cans made all the difference. Once in port, exploring the town is always entertaining, whether in Greece, or Gibraltar, as the McConnells chronicled, or in my case Watertown, New York at the head of the Erie Canal, the Florida Keys, or the Bahamas for that matter.

The McConnells embody other inspirational cruising couples I have met through the years. They strive for "relaxed partnership" and "non-competitive cooperation." In the veritable nutshell, achieving true harmony with your loved ones – and with the universe – is what living life on the water is all about.

Cyndi Boschard Perkins has been a Michigan boater all her life on the Great Lakes and smaller lakes. She has been a sailor for 15 years. In addition to

Women On Board Cruising

exploring Lake Superior and Lake Michigan, Cyndi and her husband, Scott, have completed two 6,000-mile journeys around America's Great Loop aboard their 32-foot DownEast sailboat *Chip Ahoy*. She looks forward to using her passport for more far-ranging adventures in the future.

Cyndi can be found on Facebook if you would like to be her friend (lol): facebook.com/cyndiredshoes? To read Cyndi's freelance boating articles, simply Google Cyndi Perkins, *Chip Ahoy* or visit sailingbreezes.com

*Footnote: *I'm Every Woman* was recorded by Chaka Khan on her 1978 debut solo album (Warner Bros. Records); written by Nickolas Ashford and Valerie Simpson.

Diane Stockard Wade

Vessel: M/V *Bella Luna* – 40-foot Cape Dory Trawler
Residence: Leasburg, North Carolina
Homeport: Morehead City, North Carolina
Blog: bellalunalog.blogspot.com

Thinking back on it now, I believe my story actually began several years ago with a profound, stark, and sober realization – the realization that my time here on earth is so precious and so very fleeting. Up until then, I hadn't really given it that much serious thought – I was always so busy – continually on the run. Here I was approaching my 60th birthday, and I had been married to my husband and best friend, Louis, since the age of 21. I had spent my 20s, 30s, and 40s carefully rearing our two wonderful daughters, lovingly caring for countless pets, cheerfully volunteering for various organizations and faithfully following a jam-packed schedule of traveling, almost every weekend, with my husband and daughters. We were fortunate, by living in North Carolina, to have easy access to nearby lakes and beautiful beaches on our coast. We were continually blessed with a good eight months of really pleasant weather.

We were always outside, as our family loves the outdoors and especially the water. Almost every weekend we would head to the water – constantly towing a boat behind our car, which was always heavily laden and packed down with children, coolers, dogs, fishing poles, toys, etc. We would trudge home after an exhaustive, yet fun-filled, weekend only to wind up repeating the same scenario just five days later. Friends would continually comment that they didn't know where we found the energy to do so! But the water always called us, and besides, we loved every minute spent near, on, or in it. However, as I aged, I was finding myself running out of steam and I was, naturally, always exhausted.

Underneath it all as I look back on it now, I was churning in a restless stew – but in those three decades, I just hadn't figured that out yet. With a growing concern, I was beginning to hear the clock ticking.

My 50s were spent watching our girls graduate from college, helping them with their weddings and joyfully welcoming four precious and beautiful grandchildren. My immediate family of four had exploded to a family of ten in that decade – how proud we continue to be of them to this day. Also, how busy with their lives we quickly became – I now wore two additional hats: grandmother and mother-in-law! Meanwhile, another decade had passed and the clock was still ticking. Time was really picking up speed – "Didn't we just have Christmas?" I seemingly said over and over! As we approached our 60th birthdays, both Louis and I realized just how fast that clock really was ticking too. All of a sudden, both sides of our parents were gone, and we were now the ones sitting in the chairs "front and center" in all family pictures! Yes, a profound, stark and visual realization indeed. Yet we both prayed that with good luck and God's blessings we possibly could have another 10-15 (or more!) years left to enjoy good fortune, health, energy, agility, enthusiasm, strength and hopefully, good sense. We both, me especially, yearned for a new adventure – something we had never done before – something mutually enjoyable, challenging, adventurous, exciting, but mostly just plain fun. But what and where would it be, we wondered. Well, as luck would have it, Louis began reading and hearing about this thing called the "Great Loop." It is a circular boat trip around the Eastern United States from Florida to New York, up the Hudson River, passing through Vermont (or an alternate route through the Erie Canal), two provinces of Canada and through the Great Lakes. Then it wound south through the interior parts of America from Chicago to Mobile, the Gulf Coast, and the Florida Keys – all within mostly protected and safe waters. Almost immediately, we both said, "BINGO!" We thought it sounded perfect for us – it involved water, boating, new friends, new ports, new adventures, and a yearlong dose of fun. It would take us out of our comfort zone and throw us into a new lifestyle. We would have only one area of responsibility (our boat), and we wouldn't be running up and down the road every week trying to do it all – a true chance for us to slow down and escape the complicated life we had carefully built for ourselves. For me especially, our timing could not have been better. I was ready and raring to go!

We joined the organization called America's Great Loop Cruisers' Association (AGLCA) and immediately started reading and studying anything and everything related to this 6,000-plus-mile, yearlong journey. The more we read, the more excited we became! We bought the largest boat we had ever owned – a 1994, blue-hulled, 40-foot Cape Dory power trawler. We fell in love with her immediately at first sight and renamed her *Bella Luna* after our mutual affinity for stargazing and the memorable movie *Moonstruck*. It was October – we had only six months to get ready to leave on our journey – we wanted to leave in late April.

Diane Stockard Wade – *Bella Luna*

Talk about the clock ticking! Louis quickly immersed himself in mechanical and electrical issues on the boat plus getting the bottom painted, zincs changed, and the propellers finely calibrated. I worked on interior teak cleaning, shopping for items that we would need and tried to update our interior's 14-year-old fabrics. Although a true "team," we each knew our strengths – he had his list and I had mine. He carefully found all our maps, charts and GPS "chips" that we needed for the full trip, and I began stocking the galley, twin staterooms, two heads and saloon. We bought boat passes ahead of time for our travels through Canadian waters. In those hectic and sometimes frantic periods leading up to our departure, we bought and outfitted a dinghy, got our passports updated, and got full check-ups for our dog Buddy and ourselves. We got an official Coast Guard inspection done on our boat and dinghy – complete with stickers. We asked one of our daughters to help us set up a "blog site," we set up Skype (very important when you have grandchildren), we got a Verizon wireless card for our computers, added a cell phone booster up on the flybridge for Louis's phone, and bought a satellite TV for our boat. We gave away all our houseplants, had our mail forwarded to one of our daughters and were able to get most all our bills automatically drafted from a bank account – which took some time to successfully set-up. Our daughter showed us how she could take the bills which could not be automatically drafted and scan them on her computer, then e-mail those bills to us for payment. We bought "Forever Stamps." We emptied our freezers, began closing up our home for an indefinite period and began harassing our land-loving friends with stories of what we would be doing for possibly the next year and a half. Some were incredulous and others seriously thought we had lost our minds or that we would never complete our journey. In fact, we were later told that some friends even made bets on when we would turn the boat around and come home!

All during that time, Louis and I were like two children the night before Christmas – we could hardly contain ourselves and sleeping those nights was all but impossible! As the weeks passed, like squirrels getting ready for the winter, we furiously put more and more things on our boat – the waterline all but disappeared on her hull! As we had read in various periodicals and witnessed yearly, most "Snowbirds" and Looper boaters moving north would be coming through our area of North Carolina in late April or early May. As we thought of more things we would like to get done before we left, we were determined that we would be ready to leave with them – somehow.

Two of the best things we ever did before casting off our lines for good were:

1. **We went to the three-day Spring Rendezvous of AGLCA in Charleston, South Carolina.** In Charleston we met, networked, socialized and enjoyed the company of most of the wonderful people we would be traveling with for the next year.

We took several very informative and helpful classes that were held during the Rendezvous on pertinent parts of our upcoming voyage that were of interest to us. Much to our joy, we also found out there would be over 60 boats doing the same trip as we were planning! We also realized that we quickly needed to get our own "boat cards" – everyone there had those cute and informative businesslike cards, and early on we found out we really did need these "memory-joggers" to carry with us.

We bought a white AGLCA burgee to fly on our bow – the best insignia our boat could ever have entering a marina – a true "welcome mat" which was recognized by other boaters throughout our entire journey. We realized too that we had joined a loving, experienced, supportive and ever-so-helpful fraternity of like-minded people – all eager to cast-off from the everyday world for new adventures. What a fun and energetic group of people we were going to be cruising with – they all called themselves "Loopers." Very quickly, we realized we needed to put more cases of wine on the boat than previously planned – a lot more! Looking back on it now, those three days spent in Charleston were so very fundamental in the enjoyment and comfort of our trip.

2. **We spent almost two weeks staying on our boat in the marina before we left for good.** Both Louis and I had spent the majority of our lives on various smaller boats, so neither of us was the least bit uncomfortable with "overnighting." However, we had never taken any leisure time getting to know our own *Bella Luna*. With all our "trappings" on board with us, we were squeezed in like two sardines. We spent some leisurely days right there in the marina getting to know our boat, seeing friends, and resting our bodies before the marathon trip.

We quickly came to realize that we really didn't need on board nearly as much as we had originally thought – our second stateroom was packed to the gills, making it impossible to use it for anything other than storage. Thankfully, we still had our car parked behind the boat, so we began to off-load as much as we thought reasonable – mostly clothes, shoes, and galley odds and ends.

We also realized we needed more freezer space – trying to keep frozen foods plus ice ("It's five o'clock somewhere!") in our saloon's small refrigerator/freezer unit was all but impossible. Louis fortunately found an area on our flybridge where a small 110-volt chest freezer could easily be placed, so he ordered it and installed it within a week.

In those two weeks of painstakingly staying still, we actually wound up having three "going-away" parties bestowed upon us – much to the chagrin of our friends and the marina staff, who all must have thought we would never leave. Plus, Louis was enjoying the fuel economy of those days sitting still!

Well, leave we finally did – mid-May. We threw off our lines without any hesitation or trepidation, knowing full well that we would not travel in rough or inclement weather nor would we take any unnecessary chances otherwise. We were not in a hurry, not on a schedule, and we were adamantly sticking to it! Our buddy boat *Sunshine*, from Wilmington, North Carolina, left early with us on that calm and beautiful morning. We would travel with them on and off for most of our entire year's journey. The blog I kept tells the route of our trip and our various experiences over the 11 months. Before we left, we chose to take the longer Loop – going up the Hudson River to Lake Champlain then down through Montreal and Ottawa – making our trip over 300 miles farther than two-thirds of the other Loopers doing the trip – so if interested, you can read our blog of what, where, and when. But mostly the blog was just my journal – my thoughts and impressions. There were other bloggers who did a much finer job than I – more informative, more creative, and more accurate – I just wrote as to how I would like to remember it all in my "old age." Wrongly and sadly, I did not take the time before we left home to learn how to place our many pictures there, but in the very near future, I plan to revisit my blog and add them accordingly. My brother so graciously wants to print and bind the whole thing up for us, plus have copies made for all our children. I hope that when our grandchildren are our age, they too will want to take a "special journey" of their own!

Our travels that year took us to the most amazing and beautiful places. We met the most wonderful, informative, positive, helpful and pleasant people all along the way. I have always and now firmly believe that people on and around the water are simply the best! Day after day, we enjoyed a carefree freedom from the daily mayhem we were trapped in and a leisurely lifestyle few people our age can seldom experience. We saw hidden beauty only seen in fantastic pictures: of spectacular sunsets, remote mountains, animals, fish, and birds. We saw New York, Montreal, Ottawa, Chicago, Mobile, Miami, Charleston and Savannah (to name just a few) from another angle – from the water – WOW, what a fantastic view! We experienced and greatly enjoyed Grafton, Illinois during the flooding of the Mississippi River while we were sequestered there for 12 days in our protected and very safe marina as the waters rose 23 feet!

In Florida, we saw a launching of NASA's Space Shuttle from just a few miles away; we saw migrating stingrays and white pelicans; we saw brilliant shooting stars and spectacular sunsets. Later, we saw four Trident nuclear submarines; we saw wild ponies, manatees, eagles, alligators, white pelicans, spoonbills, jumping carp, and nesting turrins. We marveled at the almost silent wind generators behind Atlantic City. We thoroughly enjoyed the beauty of Canada and its gracious and welcoming people – the Chambly, Rideau, and Trent-Severn Waterways there were small, charming, and extra special – so different from ours here in the States. We ate the most delicious (and often unfamiliar) meals; we went to local farmers' markets almost weekly and endless ice cream shops almost nightly; groups of us would stuff ourselves, like teenagers, into cars sharing rides to local stores and attractions. We waved at countless trains, ferries and strangers.

We went to bed early, slept soundly and rose the next morning itching with energy and enthusiasm – what new and exciting thing would today bring? With seemingly no worries or responsibilities except the "here and now," we often acted much younger than any of us actually were – always laughing and enjoying the wonderful company of our new family of friends. I absolutely cannot fathom why any woman would not have gladly stepped into my shoes.

With all that said, we have been on land now for three months. After having had the time to think through our whole year, from my experience alone, I would like to offer these few suggestions as helpful hints to other women:

1. **We learned from our AGLCA Rendezvous that Louis would be called the "captain" of our boat, and I would be called the "admiral."** Although he was at the helm up on the flybridge most of the time and I was below in charge of lines and fenders, we both equally shared in the decision making of our trip. Most always, if one of us disagreed with the other, that topic was nullified. Every morning before we began to travel, we would know where our destination for that evening would be and we would try to be either anchored or tied into a marina by 3 p.m.

2. **Buy a small pocketsize guidebook of birds.** We saw so many different kinds and were constantly referring to a friend's copy. Also, have two good pairs of binoculars on board, one for the captain and one just for you. The self-stabilizing ones are the best.

3. **Have a "white" noise machine in your stateroom.** With sound traveling so easily over water, many times the noise of neighboring boats hampers your getting to sleep – I fell in love with mine!

4. **Take a trip home if needed.** If you have a cell phone and a computer (especially with Skype), you should not get homesick. It was only after having been gone six months that I felt the urge to go home and physically get hugs and kisses from our children. When that was accomplished, I couldn't wait to get back to the boat!

5. **There is no need to carry a bunch of cash. ATM machines are everywhere – even Canada.** We figured that around 90 percent of our trip was paid by credit cards. Louis has lots of "points" built up on his Cabela's Visa card now – he is a happy camper and eager to go shopping!

6. **Don't worry about trying to pack everything you think you will need, be it clothes, linens, canned food, or even paper products.** Most every marina can make a car available to you – either their courtesy car or access to a rental – and there are Wal-Mart stores everywhere. West Marines are too! Someone is always going to a Wal-Mart – they mostly have it all. Grocery and liquor stores were not hard to find either. So pack lightly, you can always buy (or borrow) what you don't have. And we found we needed very little – we would wear the same four or five sets of clothes, wash them, and put them right back on! Everywhere we went was ultra-casual and "Crocs" make wonderful boat shoes. We were usually following fabulous weather, so an abundance of cold-weather clothes was not needed.

7. **Early on during our journey, a group of us "girls" decided we wouldn't wear make-up – except for lipstick.** What a freedom we few shared and enjoyed for a year!

8. **Most marinas have "book exchange" libraries – ones where you leave a book and take another.** Don't burden down your boat with excess books like I did in the beginning – swap and enjoy!

9. **We had our landline home phone "call forwarded" to Louis's cell phone.** Also, Verizon offered a Canadian add-on plan for $20.00 a month. As we were approaching the border, it was simple to activate this plan and then two months later cancel it once we were back in the States. We never missed a call from home.

10. **Loopers love a party – anytime/anywhere. Several times a week we would gather on the dock for "docktails" and appetizers or potluck dinners.** It was always a much-anticipated special time with special friends. We were having so much fun every evening that several times Louis even remarked to everyone gathered on the dock, "When we get home, Diane and I are going to have to join two new organizations: Weight Watchers and Alcoholics Anonymous!" A sad-but-true statement for most of us Loopers.

11. **Start saving quarters now – easy to do.** Most marinas have very nice laundry facilities, but all require quarters for both washers and dryers. Also, buy a sturdy, square, folding, and collapsible rolling cart, to carry "dirties" back and forth. That cart is invaluable in grocery shopping too – especially for heavy canned goods and bottled drinks – a must-have for your boat. That cart was the most useful thing aboard for me.

12. **Carry about $200.00 in five-dollar bills for "boat tips."** Keep them handy for exceptional dock service. One very nice young man helped us into a particularly difficult slip in the pouring rain and gusty wind and we actually gave him $10 – helped ease his pain a lot!

13. **Zip-lock bags became another best friend.** Use them in every available space on your boat. Also use the green plastic bags for fruits and vegetables – they really do work! If galley space is an issue, I found the brand of Corelle dishes stack in cabinets much easier and tighter than other brands. We used paper products a lot, but every now and then it was nice to actually eat on "china!" Write the name of your canned goods on top of each can so that when stacking them under seats and such, they will be easily identifiable. At the same time though, try not to carry a lot of canned goods – it was shameful how many cans we carried all 7,000 miles and never used!

14. **We, unlike a lot of others, almost exclusively used our own shower on the boat.** Although most every marina had very adequate and more-often-than-not very nice bath facilities, we just felt more comfortable using our own. Good, clean water was never an issue for us – it was available at every stop. However, if we were anchoring out for several days, we were naturally very conservative with water consumption. Louis put

an extra filtered-water faucet at our galley sink – we used it for drinking water and making ice. We probably anchored out a fourth of our trip and we never got anywhere close to running out of water at any time.

15. **On the topic of anchoring out, we really did enjoy it every time!** On the Loop, anchorages are very plentiful and so beautiful. The *Skipper Bob Publications* boating guides do a wonderful job of guiding you to every good anchorage in his detailed guidebooks. Many boaters do not like to raft together, however, our groups always did. You do not find the strong tidal currents in fresh water (which was over half our trip), so rafting together was easy, plus the social advantage of having everyone closely tied together made for some really fun evenings on the hook.

16. **We found it more comfortable to travel during the weekdays and rest/stay still on the weekends.** Weekend traffic on the water is often very congested. It also leans towards the more inexperienced boaters going way too fast and leaving us rocking badly in their big wakes. This is in addition to all the weekend jet skis, which seemingly continue to use no common sense when passing boats like us. They appear to have no fear at all.

17. **Realize that sharing a confined space 24/7 is going to be challenging at best.** Every single person on our trip felt like choking his or her mate at one time or another! Both Louis and I each had our "moments" several times, but thankfully, we were aware of each other's needs and wishes and we worked through those brief times. We had been together for over 40 years and thought we knew each other inside and out – not so. Finding a delicate balance is a must, plus long walks and a glass of wine help with most situations! Thankfully, we can (and do) continue to laugh about those moments now.

18. **We started our journey with our ten-year-old black Labrador dog Buddy. We never hesitated as to whether to take him along with us or not – he was a major part of our family, and he was definitely going with us.** Unfortunately, he became terminally ill with a massive inoperable tumor and we had to put him down in Canada. It was a heartbreaking decision – his loss to us was profound and lingers to this day. However,

having started our trip with him and then losing him three months later, I can now regrettably say it was a more enjoyable trip without him. We were able to anchor out without having to put the dinghy down and the hassle of going ashore several times daily for "potty detail." We were able to take tours and whole-day excursions on land without the worry of having to get back to the boat in time to get him to the nearest grass. Our boat was much easier to keep clean; sadly, our boat became bigger too. For animal lovers, I am singularly the most proud of the blog post in honor of him. You can find it under bellalunalog.blogspot.com. Scroll down to the entry titled *Buddy Wade*, which was published in July.

19. **We found our month-long time in Marathon, Florida to be absolutely wonderful and filled with beautiful sunny days.** With easy access to a Publix grocery store, a Home Depot, a movie theater, many restaurants and cute shops all nearby, two liquor stores, barbershops and hair salons and a weekly farmers' market – we had it all! We had a two-mile loop right behind the boats which we would walk every morning. We took a respite from our travels and stayed there for five weeks and found that being in one place for that length of time really gave us a chance to unwind. We all caught the delightful and much sought after "Key's Disease" – which is a perpetual state of laziness. We really used our bicycles and dinghy there too, plus, being in the Florida Keys in February was a whole lot better than the weather back home! We enjoyed it so much that in fact we are planning to go back by boat this coming winter and hope to stay for at least two months!

20. **Love your boat** – we did and continue to do so.

After getting back home, most friends have asked us the same three questions. The first one naturally was, "What was your favorite place?" We would quickly answer, "Everywhere!" – simply because it was impossible to single out or narrow it just to one place or one particular time. Most friends thought we were sick of boating so they would ask us the second question, "Are you going to sell the boat?" Louis and I would answer without hesitation, "Nope!" Then they would always ask us, with a smile on their faces, "Would you do the trip again?" After looking at each other and smiling, and before taking another breath, we would answer almost in unison, "You bet we would – in a heartbeat!" You see, for us it really was the trip of a lifetime, a culmination of wishes and dreams, and a welcomed breath of fresh air into our lives. "What a ride!" another Looper and dear friend said, and we continue to say it to this very day. In fact, that just may be our epitaph – it is definitely under consideration. I have a sign on our boat which reads, "Life is not measured by the number of breaths you take, but by the number of moments that take your breath away." I found and bought that sign halfway through our trip and believe in its sincerity and therapy.

After almost 7,000 miles, 163 locks, and 11 months, that pretty much sums up our most recent experience of being on the water. We now proudly fly our gold Looper flag signifying our huge and major accomplishment of completing the Loop. I would like to think of that special year as a beginning for us, a year of coming closer together as a couple; a year of making new lifelong friends who we now consider "family;" a year of wonder, glory, pride, beauty and excitement; a year full of challenges and adventure; a year of getting out of our protected and safe comfort zones; a year of exploring at least half of our country; and a year of learning how exceptional the people and this country of ours truly are. It was the year we dared. Having a year away from family and friends gave me a lot of time to rethink my life from here on out. As a result, I found that I have truly wizened as a wife, mother, sister, grandmother, and friend. With so much sadness all around us seemingly popping up weekly, I have learned to focus on the important things. I have learned to be selective and almost greedy with "my" time. I have found I need very little to make me happy – I truly enjoy the things money cannot buy – the simple things. I don't feel guilty anymore when some things don't get done either – and I am truly at peace with myself for feeling that way. So, as long as Louis and I stay healthy and our children don't disown us for being away so much, we will hopefully keep on cruising – there are still so many places we want to see and haven't. Being such seasoned boaters as we are now, we would be crazy to stop – after all, we would really like to believe we are just getting started!

Though I continue to still hear that clock – it is a much sweeter sound now. Tick... tick... tick...

Diane Stockard Wade was born in Raleigh, North Carolina and has lived her entire life in her home state. She married her college sweetheart, Louis – they just celebrated their 40th anniversary. She is proudest of her two beautiful daughters and four precious and adorable grandchildren. She has been an active volunteer all her life – but now considers that chapter in her life finished! Her hobbies include reading, playing bridge, theater, movies, music and entertaining friends. The "saltwater girl" and the "freshwater guy" plan to keep on cruising for several years – as long as they can often say, "The good Lord willing and the creek don't rise!"

She extends her sincerest appreciation to Lisa for allowing her the opportunity to put her all thoughts down in print.

Patti Salvage

Vessel: M/V *Salvage Crew* – 48-foot Jefferson Motor Yacht
Residence: Birmingham, Alabama
Homeport: Lake Guntersville Yacht Club, Tennessee River
Website: salvagecrew.com

"Well it's not just a daydream if you decide to make it your life" – a lyric from *She's On Fire* recorded by Train for the *Drops of Jupiter* album.

Maybe it all starts with the fascination we all have with water. To be on it, in it, or around it has a positive effect on most people. It can be tranquil or exhilarating, but it is always fun. When we were kids, it seemed the most natural thing in the world was to swim until we totally exhausted ourselves and our skin became shriveled up like a prune. As adults, we will pay a premium just to have the view. After cruising for the last ten months, I have come to the conclusion that there is not a bad place to be on the water. It is all beautiful and the ever-changing view from my favorite chair is always a million-dollar view… of the water. As we have moved around on the water there have been towns I liked better than others, marinas with more or less facilities, days with fairer skies than others, and many challenges, but I have not had a day on the water that I did not absolutely love.

My husband Brad and I retired two months before we departed on the "Great Loop." This plan came together over a period of years. As a real estate broker in a large office in Birmingham, Alabama, I was used to a pretty fast pace. Any time Brad referred to "retirement" I would respond with "Retire and do what? We are both going a thousand miles an hour with our hair on fire. How do we stop?" The Great Loop boat trip was the bait that Brad dangled out there in front of me to get me to retire.

Women On Board Cruising

We had a condo on Orange Beach in Alabama, and a 23-foot cuddy cabin boat. We enjoyed running the beaches and the Intracoastal Waterway (ICW). The beach umbrella just didn't hold the same appeal for us once we started boating at the beach. We even began to limit our restaurant choices to the ones that had docks so we could get to them by water. No trip to the beach was ever complete without a visit to West Marine. When you own a boat, any size boat, a marine store is always on your to-do list. It doesn't take me very long to look through a marine store, and being an avid reader, I usually drift toward the book section. It was just by chance that I picked up a book entitled *Honey, Let's Get A Boat...* by Ron and Eva Stob. It had never occurred to me that one might be able to circumnavigate the Eastern United States by boat. I bought the book and was thoroughly entertained as they told their engaging tale of being boating novices while doing the Loop.

Wanderlust is defined as "a strong desire to explore the world." I have that. If you give me the choice of going somewhere that I love or seeing a new place, I will always choose the new place. I am always happier when I have a trip planned. So, the Loop was right up my alley. I come from a family of adventurous souls by most people's standards. The kids in my family flew airplanes, scuba dived, rode motorcycles, parachute jumped, and flew gliders. Our parents taught us that we could accomplish anything we wanted to do if we went about it safely and got proper training.

In 2004 Hurricane Ivan – dubbed Ivan the Terrible – struck the Gulf Coast of Orange Beach, Alabama in September with great force and caused horrific damage. Although not totally destroyed, our little "get away" would not be usable for a very long time. We got an unexpected offer and sold it. Time for a new direction! What a coincidence, we had just discovered that we had a new interest in buying a much bigger boat!

Shopping for a boat was entertainment in itself! Every weekend would take us to a new and interesting place to look at all kinds of different boats. It got us to thinking about what we would need if we were actually lucky enough to get to live this dream of doing the Loop. We certainly did not have time for "three-foot-itus" (the common practice of buying and selling boats every year or two to buy one three feet longer). We were too close to retirement for that.

Luckily, we ran into a sharp boat broker who listened to our plans and told us just what we needed. We purchased our 1988 48-foot Jefferson on New Year's Eve and started the new-year with the goal of learning as much as we could about our boat and long-distance cruising.

Alexander Graham Bell said, "Before anything else, preparation is the key to success." We definitely believe that to be the case. We initially took our boat, which we named *Salvage Crew*, to Chattanooga, Tennessee on the Tennessee River, where my sister and brother-in-law had been big boaters for years. They were excellent tutors and we were eager students. We began to take short trips that were great learning experiences and helped us determine what electronics, furniture, and other necessary systems we needed to upgrade or add to make our vessel worthy of safe, easy, cost-effective, long-term cruising.

We also realized the need to improve our minds and become more knowledgeable about boating. Local Power Squadrons can be helpful with this point. We had an opportunity to go to a USCG Captains School, so we took advantage of that chance for each of us to get our captain's licenses. There have been many instances in our travels when that knowledge has been helpful. Sometimes it still surprises us when we know the answer to a puzzling boating question. We look at each other and say, "Wow, we already know this!" Sometimes, however, knowledge and application can differ considerably. Luckily, our private pilot's training helped us fill in the gaps. There are many similarities in flying and boating when it comes to navigation, weather, and some basic engine knowledge.

We became members of America's Great Loop Cruisers' Association (AGLCA) and also attended three of their twice-yearly Rendezvous. We signed up for the daily e-mail forums where Loopers share information about what issues/situations they are currently dealing with on the Loop. We found many publications and waterway directories that held a wealth of information for us. Still, there are two books you will always find on our bridge, *Chapman Piloting & Seamanship* and the Bible.

I made my major commitment to the trip two years later during the Christmas holidays. Brad loves people and is very social. I always kid him about the fact that when we pull up to a new dock, he is off the boat meeting everyone, shaking hands and kissing babies before we can even get the boat secured to the dock. I will ask him, "Have you heard that they need a new mayor here? Are you running for office? How many votes did you get today?" As he makes his rounds on the docks, he frequently announces that "Life Is Good," which it surely is. His Christmas gift from me was 125 bright yellow T-shirts in all-different sizes that proclaim:

The Brad Salvage
2008
"Life Is Good" Tour
Sponsored by Miller Lite

When he opened his gift of T-shirts to give out to our friends upon departure (later to many people we met along the way), he knew I was committed. From that point on, I had lots of questions.

How will we pay our bills? Who will take care of our house? How will I get exercise living on a boat? What shall we do with our cars? What clothes will I need? What if I get seasick? How will everyone survive at home without me to take care of them? Will I get bored? How will I feel about the few times we will be out of sight of land? Where do we have our mail sent? How will we know what condition the sea is in before we venture out? Can I live in a limited space with my spouse without murdering him (divorce is not an option for me)? I had all these questions and more.

Some of our friends thought we had lost our minds when we told them what we were planning. They were hilarious with some of their questions. I am not sure what their perception of the Loop was, but when I told them we would be gone for a year, I think they pictured the explorations of Magellan! "What will you do out in the middle of the ocean for weeks at a time by yourselves and how will you eat?" My answers were: "I'm NOT going out in the middle of the ocean for days at a time, and I'll buy food at grocery stores and eat in nice restaurants, just like I do now!"

Luckily, I was not really a pioneer and was not going anywhere long-term cruising women had not gone before me. The answers to all of my questions had already been worked out, and I simply had to discover where to find them. There are many publications, websites and organizations where you can benefit from the knowledge of others without reinventing the wheel. That's a good thing to know and remember.

Finally, the big day came. We had provisioned, packed, plotted and planned and now we were off. What an exciting day for us when we cranked those 3208 Cats (Caterpillar engines) and heard them purr! We roared off down the river like our Cats thought they might be cheetahs! Warp speed for us is 12 mph. Day by day we have met the challenges and overcome the fears of this new lifestyle. And we love all the new doors it has since opened up for us.

While I miss my four children and their families, my siblings, parents and friends, there are a couple of things we have done that eases the pain of separation.

Of course, you want an excellent wireless program with a large network, both cell and broadband. Skype (requires a built-in or external webcam) is a wonderful program for your laptop that will let you see the grandchildren while you are talking to them. It makes me feel a bit like Jane Jetson, but when my youngest grandchild took her first steps, I got to see them. In addition, I posted a daily log on the website I set up. Initially I just thought it would be a good and efficient way to make sure I was staying in touch with everyone. It actually ended up being so much more to me. When I sit down to write and post pictures of the things we see every day, I actually feel as though I am talking to them. A lot of my family and friends have commented that they feel closer to me than they have in years because I talk to them every day through my website. There has been an unexpected "website bonding!" Who knew computers had a warm fuzzy side?

Another unexpected fulfillment from doing a daily travel log on my website was hearing from people who happened onto the site by chance and took time to e-mail and tell me how much they enjoyed it, or took time to comment on some place we were visiting. Many said that they were reading it daily and living

Patti Salvage – *Salvage Crew*

vicariously through us until they could do the trip themselves. I had to admit to them that I had done the same thing for two years before we actually departed on our trip. It is a good way to get an idea about the lifestyle, and it sure makes it more fun for me to do the website when I have people responding to it.

One afternoon in Green Turtle Cay in the Abacos Islands, Bahamas, I was sitting on our aft deck reading when two ladies walked down from the hotel and out onto the dock of the marina. The tone of their voices changed as they passed the stern of *Salvage Crew*. They were excited about something and I got up to see what was going on. They came over and said, "We can't believe it's you! We're from Houston, Texas and we've been following your travelogue for months and we knew you were in the Abacos somewhere, but we never dreamed we would get to meet you in person." They amazed me as they asked pertinent questions obviously remembering many of the details of our trip. You might have thought we were Brad and Angelina and they were the paparazzi (but on a much smaller scale of course)! After a pleasant chat, they said goodbye and moved on farther down the dock. All of a sudden they saw *Good News*, who we had been traveling with for several months. It started over. "Oh my gosh, is this Mary and Andy? We're so excited to have run into all of you!"

I found that I thoroughly enjoy walking new areas around the 120 different marinas and towns we have stayed in so far. Even though I am getting exercise, I will admit that I have put on some weight. In my prior life, I managed to eat sensibly four days a week and not worry about it so much on weekends. Now all my days are more like holidays and weekends. I probably wouldn't know what day of the week it was if it wasn't printed on my hormone pills. There are also always other Loopers and boaters around. They like to meet for "docktails" at 5:30 in the afternoon, and somehow appetizers have become a standard. Appetizers? That's something we rarely ever had at home! Suddenly we began to understand why one of the Loopers who had just "crossed his wake" (completed the Loop) was heard to say, "I'm rushing home to join two new groups, Weight Watchers and AA." Oh my, Brad and I may be fitting into this Looper stereotype too well. Sometimes it seems like we are "eating our way" around the Loop. Well, what's wrong with that? We may never be this way again, and we want to "taste and savor" local cuisines.

On the water, "every day is an adventure and every meal a feast." Finding grocery stores and nice restaurants has not been a problem, overindulging sometimes is!

You don't have to leave your hobbies at home. I know one cruiser who brought her sewing machine and enjoys letting her creative sewing juices flow while they are underway. I have a healthy herb garden but really admire another cruiser who has a six-foot tall tomato plant on her boat. I suggested to Brad that we stake one to the radar mast, but he overruled in favor of working radar! I should have waited until he was hungry to ask. At lunchtime, the thought of a homegrown tomato sandwich may have made that decision more tenable.

I had actually planned to work on my photography while traveling, read more and learn some new computer software programs. I had many lofty goals I thought I might accomplish while cruising for a year on our Loop trip. I found that there is not as much spare time when cruising as one might think. Did I really need to worry that I would be bored?

To begin with, when cruising, I don't want to miss a thing. I find it fascinating to be on new water where there is a surprise around every bend. For example, we have two friends who were traveling together on the East Coast ICW when an atomic submarine surfaced between them. I certainly would not have wanted to miss that!

There are also many responsibilities for the crew that can fill your time. Someone has to monitor the weather, study the charts, chart the course, enter the data into the chart plotter, hang the fenders, set the lines, wash the salt off the boat, make the marina reservations, maintain the engine, check the fluid levels frequently, keep the ship's log, go sightseeing, check e-mails, work through locks, decide what excursions are worthy of your time, take the pictures and write the travel log, plan the menus, do the laundry, buy the groceries, fill water and fuel tanks, prepare for "happy hour," cook the food, study the waterway guides for pertinent navigational information, pay the bills, arrange for mail to be forwarded, and coordinate plans with friends. I am pretty sure I have left out some things!

Well, nobody ever said boating was for sissies! And YES, it is fun! If it ever feels intimidating or gets to be a little bit overwhelming, I just remember that we only have to do one day at a time. If I concentrate on the one day that I plan to move the boat only about 40 miles, it puts things back into prospective. And, hey, you can always decide to take a day off and do absolutely nothing except enjoy where you are. We are still trying to get a handle on this new "retirement" thing when it really is OK to have a day of just doing nothing. We loved our life when we were working, but time is one thing that working robs from you.

It is quite a shock to realize I don't have to "rush" through a grocery store. The whole concept of having a more relaxed lifestyle has helped us in boating, and boating in turn has helped us have a more relaxing life. When approaching a dock that you have never been to before, it takes a moment to figure out the effect of currents and wind. Early in our trip, Brad missed a tricky approach and was beginning to sweat a bit to correct. Then we realized, we had all day, all week and month, as well. It took us three thrilling tries to get the best angle and approach, but we did it. After all, we are no longer in a hurry.

There are many choices to make on the Loop! We came to the conclusion early on that we would not be able to do everything that we wanted to do. All the wonderful side trips we had read about sounded so enticing. If we tried to do them all, we would sacrifice the quality of where we were because our pace would have to increase.

Also, beware of deadlines! We boat for fun. That means we never choose to cause ourselves any discomfort. Sometimes that equates to sitting still on the dock on days that have less than favorable conditions. One thing that can put the pressure on is having a commitment to be in another city, which has you traveling on days when you really shouldn't. You may find yourself in uncomfortable situations that could have been avoided. Most boats I know have the "Admiral's Rule" in place. It basically states that the admiral (usually the head female on board – in our case, me), after careful consideration of weather, wind and wave conditions, has the final say in whether a boat shall leave the dock on any given day. If she isn't pleased with all the conditions presented, the cruise is postponed to the next favorable day.

Clearly defined responsibilities simplify life. We have one cruising friend who divides the chores into "Pink Chores and Blue Chores." Sometimes there are "crossover responsibilities" like when something goes bump in the night. I'm not the designated mechanic, but I am the light sleeper. So, when I hear a "new" or "unusual" sound coming from the bowels of the boat, I am right on it. Even at 3 a.m. I can be found with a floor hatch up and my head hanging down listening for 30 minutes. Hear that? There it goes again. In one instance, we finally figured out that it was a water pressure pump overworking because we had left a faucet dripping.

We are all talented at different things, and it took us a while to settle into a routine of who should do what. But after a while, we were working together like a finely tuned machine. Of course, it helped when Brad realized the pecking order and that when mutual agreement could not be reached, my rank immediately escalated to admiral. Everybody knows that when the admiral isn't happy, nobody in the fleet is happy (in other words, the crew might as well just go ahead and walk the plank).

It is true that boating can be hours of relaxed enjoyment punctuated occasionally by moments of intense anxiety. Strong winds, high seas, swift currents and skinny water can bring on those moments; all enhanced by tight maneuvering around other vessels or fixed objects. As in flying, there are at least two critical times on every trip, the departure from a fixed point and the arrival at your destination (which is also a fixed spot). Both give an opportunity for sudden deceleration syndrome.

While I drive the boat a lot, Brad is the ace when it comes to close-quarters maneuvering in adverse conditions like high winds, swift currents and heavy boat traffic. A successful docking should be more than, "A controlled crash into a dock not leaving marks on either the dock or the ship!" That's the nautical equivalent to the old pilot's adage, "Any landing you walk away from is a good landing." I hope that we have honed our skills as we have traveled. But boating can also be very humbling. Just when you think you have mastered the fine art of boating, some circumstance will surely happen to make things "interesting" again.

I have a better natural sense of direction and enjoy the navigation responsibilities more. Brad is a neat nut and sometimes feels the need to vacuum in the middle of a cruise day. Hardly ever having that urge myself, I play the part of a good wife and obligingly lift my feet. However, if Brad were given a cooking chore, we would all starve. I guess a shift in that responsibility could be the solution to our "water weight" (temporary weight you gain while living on the water because everything tastes so dang good here).

The inspiration to cook fabulous meals has been a surprise. I have that gourmet kitchen at home that was rarely used to its potential. On board, I have three words for you. Seafood! Seafood! Seafood! I have a cookbook called *Seafood Twice a Week*, but I am thinking of writing my own called "*Seafood Twice a Day.*" This is our kind of eating! Buying live lobster off the dock for $3 each in the Bahamas, learning to shuck oysters in Apalachicola, Florida, enjoying the superb North Carolina shrimp, Chesapeake crabmeat and scallops, and making friends with tournament fisherman everywhere who would gladly share their catch has inspired me to new heights of my culinary skills. I have been delighted to find that almost every town has a farmers' market at least one day a week. However, I may be impaired when it comes to fixing a complete meal. Boating friends are big on dining together, and many nights you are responsible for only your specialty dish or two as a contribution to a fabulous meal. I have so many wonderful new recipes now that have been shared by participating dinner companions. Meals will probably seem very mundane when we return to our regular "life on the hard." We have become accustomed to dinner being our evening's entertainment, especially when it is served along with the interesting stories of new friends.

Boating friends! What a great bonus to long-term cruising! The boating community is a small one. Boaters are the best people in the world. I always say, "No matter where you are (land, sea or air), if you need help, the person who will stop and offer it the quickest is probably going to also be a boater." And you might say that even though the "highway is larger – the rest stops are fewer." You pass the same people along the "blue highways" over and over again. What a thrill to pull into a marina and recognize the boat name of someone you enjoyed knowing a few weeks before at another stop. There are such interesting people out there and everyone "has a story." As the long-term boaters move along their path, always in search of the perfect weather or new adventures and for the most part finding it, you will have an opportunity to form friendships that will last a lifetime. We have. Of all the benefits and rewards of this lifestyle, the relationships built along the way are the best. We feel so blessed.

We met some Loopers from Gibraltar. They had their Broom, an English-made boat, shipped to Fort Lauderdale, Florida to begin their Loop. We saw them on and off all the way up the East Coast. It was lovely to hear their clipped English accents on the radio. One day there were five boats in a line headed north on the ICW when suddenly their boat, *Final Decision*, made a complete 360-degree turn in the middle of the channel. We were all watching to see what the problem was when he came on the radio and excitedly explained that, "they had just spotted their first crock on the bank in the wilds and it had sent them into quite a twit." Situated on a point in Yorktown, Virginia, there is a huge monument commemorating the historical site of Cornwallis' surrender to General Washington at the end of the American Revolutionary War. As we reached this point, we saw *Final Decision* anchored. Later we ran into Terry and Sue on shore and we kidded them with, "How many times do we have to run you Brits off this point?" They loved visiting all the historical sites along the way. We later ran into them again in Canada.

Our country's history began around its perimeter, by the water. We are fond of history and have so enjoyed the museums that abound on the rivers and waterways that we have traveled. Tracing events, industries, regions, and people who influenced our past has been fascinating. To stand on the very spot where our forefathers stood while forming the framework of our great nation is very awe-inspiring. Circling the Statue of Liberty during the Fourth of July holiday week brought tears to our eyes and will be something we will never forget.

Experiencing the contrasting regions and communities has also been fascinating. From the Tennessee River, Florida's Panhandle and "Forgotten" west coast, the Keys, the Bahamas, big cities on the East Coast, the little towns in the Chesapeake Bay, the Jersey shore, New York Harbor, Hudson River and hamlets along the Erie Canal, to the Canadian waters of the Trent-Severn Waterway, Georgian Bay, North Channel and the Great Lakes. Each is an unbelievable treat. The flavor of each is so different.

What a delightful surprise to stumble onto a jewel such as Tarpon Springs, Florida, the "Sponge Capital of the World." Some explorers from Greece settled here in 1890 because it is one of the few places useable sponge is found. There is a large Greek population to this day and the sponge industry is still alive and well in Tarpon Springs. We learned all about that industry and we ate every meal in a different restaurant there. Cook? Are you kidding? These are the people who invented feta... how could we even think of having a cold turkey sandwich on the boat for lunch? English is practically a second language there. Sometimes we couldn't understand a thing they were saying. It was all Greek to us!

Through the various museums we visited on the Loop, we learned new respect for industries like sponge diving, boat building, shrimping and crabbing. I think it was somewhere around Venice, Florida that I became absolutely fascinated by the mullet fishermen. I sat for long periods of time watching the slicker-clad craftsmen. They obviously work very hard, but they are also artists of sorts. Even before daylight, I could hear the "clack" of lead weights hitting the deck of their small boats. They would stand poised on the highest point of their boat while balancing on a moving deck, holding a ring in their teeth as they layered their nets on both arms and waited for the perfect moment to cast them into the water onto a school of mullet. The nets would land on the water perfectly spread out and absolutely flat. Manually hauling them back in; they would shake the fish from the nets into the bottom of their boats. If they had a good haul, the word would spread and there would immediately be a dozen more boats all maneuvering around the same small area. The strength it must take to do this repeatedly is unbelievable. I gained new respect for these fishermen who work behind the scenes. One doesn't always think of these guys when we sit down to an excellent meal of seafood, but we probably should.

Marinas are ever-changing communities in themselves. Boats are coming and going constantly. Your first contact is with the staff, and then you meet your dock neighbors, and before long you know the names of all the cats! There are always helpful people around to share the local scoop! If you have a need, the wonderful marina staff will usually help you solve it. Need a car – take our "courtesy clunker." Want something to read – visit our swap-a-book library. Suddenly you find that you are part of that community, at least temporarily. We loved every marina we stayed in. Some marinas are chosen because of their proximity to your course, some because they are close to the historic or entertainment venues of the nearby town. Deep ports for easy transit and other amenities also play into your decision of where to dock. Cruising guides can tell you a lot about the different marinas. We chose one marina in Thunderbolt, Georgia simply because they were known for delivering fresh Krispy Kreme donuts and a *USA Today* newspaper to the boats at their docks every morning. Yum!

Most marinas will accept mail for you prior to your arrival, supply a list of services in their community (including restaurants that will pick you up or deliver take out to you), share local knowledge of the waters and go far and beyond the call of duty for their transients. Their customer services are touted up and down the waterways. Guess what? Boaters talk, e-mail, post to websites and blogs. They share information constantly.

Elizabeth City, North Carolina does a great PR job with their "Rose Buddy" program. You must visit there at the south end of the Dismal Swamp. There is so much history and Americana to experience there as well as a wonderful museum across from their complimentary city dock. We had to stop there because we had heard so much about it from other boaters. It started years ago when two local retired gentlemen started welcoming the visiting boats at the free town dock. They would bring newspapers to the men and roses out of their own gardens to the ladies. They would host a wine and cheese gathering in the afternoon at the dock as a symbol of the town's hospitality. The old gentlemen have since passed away, but the town now has a rose garden at the dock dedicated to the original "Rose Buddies" and the town's people now carry on the tradition.

We have been constantly amazed by the wildlife. The incredible aerodynamics of an eagle's flight can compare only to the fluidity of a dolphin's roll. There are many miracles of Mother Nature here on the Loop. What an unbelievably intricate ecosystem God has created for his world. We have seen manatee, sharks, giant sea turtles, bird species too numerous to mention, alligators, beavers, woodchucks, deer, wild horses, American bald eagles and laughing gulls. I surprise myself with how excited I can get when we spot the different species of wildlife.

I think I love the dolphin best. I was thrilled every time I spotted them. Many days we would see a pod and they would run alongside the boat, putting on quite a show of jumping and slapping the water with their tails. Sometimes there would be so many that I would wonder how they kept from running into each other under the surface of the water. It must get really crowded down there. Wiggle room only. We had heard that they respond to a woman's voice, so many times I would run out on the bow and sing to them. It is entirely possible that I ran some of them off, and it was not uncommon to find myself hoarse after an hour or so of special time spent with my dolphin friends and Barbra Streisand show tunes.

Occasionally since moving north of the Mason-Dixon Line, someone takes note of our Alabaman "southern drawl." When asked if the "mocking" of our accents bothers us, we always answer with, "What accent?"

We were having dinner with one of our new friends from Canada, eh? We asked her why all her sentences sounded like questions, eh? She rebounded with, "My attention span is almost long enough to figure out what words you are saying, eh?" Point taken!

While on this adventure, I wondered how well my spouse and I would enjoy "living large in such a small space." I had heard of couples getting off the boat and heading straight to their divorce attorneys. Yikes! One might consider a long-term boating experience as a redefining moment in a relationship. It rates up there with marriage, childbirth, becoming a grandmother and retirement! I have learned that my life can be different now and it is not just OK, it is a good thing. Change is the only time we have an opportunity to make things better – more like we want them to be.

OK, we will admit it! As romantic as living aboard a motor yacht can be, occasionally, living in tight quarters with no escape from your loving significant other might wear and tear on your nerves no matter how madly in love you are. Some of the other cruising wives and I were discussing that just the other day. Here was my analogy, and everyone agreed it hit the nail on the head. I said, "Sometimes it seems to me as if Brad were the captain of the Titanic, he would rather just go ahead and hit that iceberg than to hear me say one more time, 'Honey, you do see that iceberg, don't you?" Apparently it is possible to get too much of a good thing! I had to admire how a fellow admiral had her captain trained. We noticed her command of the situation when she handed him his windbreaker and he asked, "Honey, am I cold or am I going somewhere?"

Another boating couple we know had special shirts made to wear while locking through. Her T-shirt says, "Stop Yelling at Me!" and his says, "I'm Not Yelling!"

Women On Board Cruising

Boating attire! Ladies, leave the "Bling" at home! This is a cruise and I am a princess, but this is not a Princess Cruise. My captain likes me fine in cut offs, even at the captain's dinner table. I have become quite proud of my Timex watch that lights up and the Croc sandal tan lines! To my knowledge I have not yet been accosted by the fashion police, and I basically agree with a friend who said, "Honey, if I can't get it at Wal-Mart, I must not need it!" Honestly, you will be able to find anything you require, but somehow it is a simpler life and you might find that you require less. I did.

Another practice among boaters is the exchange of the "Boat Card." That's what we have now instead of the traditional business cards we had in our former, professional, lives. It is really a calling card of sorts and provides information about our names, boat name, cell phone, e-mail, website and any other information we want to share. Boaters exchange these all along the waterways, and we make notes on the back of them to remember places and occasions we spent with new friends. When you are long-term cruising, you are visiting so many places sometimes it is hard to remember details. It is nice to have a system that will help you remember people, places and events. This has absolutely nothing to do with our age! Rather it is about the number of wonderful people we are meeting and the many good times we do not want to forget. It is such a thrill to be a member of this "special club!" Our network in boating has become larger than Verizon's!

As mentioned before, we named our boat *Salvage Crew*. It seemed fitting because our last name is "Salvage." Commercial traffic always gets priority while transiting the waterways. Occasionally we have gotten preferential treatment from a lockmaster that thought from our name that we were commercial traffic. Honest mistake! Who are we to question the authority of a lockmaster?

There are wrecking and salvage laws still on the books in many states. A grounded vessel still falls under those laws in some states and can be claimed by the rescuing vessel in some instances. In the Keys we came back from Hawk's Channel while traveling on the outside into the ICW at Channel Five and headed north to Miami. The water is very skinny on the Florida Bay side of the Keys, and we came across a sailboat that was grounded outside the channel. The sailboat captain hailed us on the radio and asked us to give assistance by towing him off the shoal. It wasn't something that we could even attempt because of our four-foot draft. But when we called him back on the radio and identified ourselves as *Salvage Crew*, we suddenly heard a note of panic in his voice, he immediately came back on the radio and said, "No, no, no! I don't want that! I do not need your help." Because of our name, he thought we were interested in taking over his boat! We laughed for several nautical miles! As we were on a rising tide, I am sure he was able to push off the shoal before high tide.

Looking back, I can honestly say, "We've come a long way, baby!" For the most part, we have been lake boaters, so, initially open water crossings caused me some level of anxiety. As I am writing this today, we are doing a six-hour crossing of Lake Ontario. I no longer sleep fitfully the night before a big open water crossing because I have gained confidence in myself, in my husband, and in our boat! Our crew will make good responsible educated decisions about when and where to travel, and I trust that our boat will perform as expected. Always remember that your ship can handle a good bit more than your crew can. So, we go by the crew's standards of acceptance.

Our first experience with this boat in salt water was when we exited the Tennessee-Tombigbee Waterway and entered Mobile Bay in Alabama. We were delighted when our boat did not disintegrate from beneath us like our freshwater boating friends had warned. The bay was calm and with a sigh of relief, we said, "This is a breeze." Obviously, we could easily handle salt water and a busy ocean port full of traffic. Ah, but we had not yet been truly tested!

We docked at Dog River Marina on the west side of Mobile Bay for some boat maintenance. It was time for *Salvage Crew* to have a little work done on her bottom (yes, she is of that age). They lifted her from the water and placed her on the hard, a most unnatural state for her. But some discomfort must be tolerated in order to "put things right" again. You can relate, right, ladies?

Some cruisers say, "You can't trust Mother Nature and NOAA (pronounced Noah – a marine weather forecast station) is a liar!" When we left the western shore of Mobile Bay, fate was not shining on us quite so brightly with two to four-foot seas and a gusty wind. The chop (not to be confused with swells – think CHOP, CHOP) was hitting us on the beam and being quick studies, we figured out what needed to be stowed away when we cruise in open waters. Some lamps fell over, books slid off shelves, and the sofa walked across the saloon floor and tried to go downstairs to the aft cabin. Luckily, it would not fit through the door. We added non-skid furniture coasters to our Wal-Mart list and started trying to figure out what speed and angle was most beneficial to our progress. Every little victory adds to proficiency.

Another "learning" experience was crossing the Gulf Stream from Fort Lauderdale to the West End, Grand Bahama Island. The forecast was a textbook perfect day for crossing with seas at one to two feet and winds less than ten mph with no northern components. In actuality, we had some four to six-beam seas that had us rocking and rolling like Elvis for a few hours! It was completely doable, but it was not at the comfort level I had hoped for. You must hold on while moving around the boat and sometimes scooting on your butt is the best way to travel within your vessel. Could someone please tell me where to find some "sea legs?" At lunchtime, I made a good call by deciding not to open the refrigerator door. I could have had a mess to clean up if a wave chose to pitch the contents onto the floor at that moment. So, I grabbed a sleeve of crackers and a jar of peanut butter and scooted back up to the flybridge. I sat on the floor carefully spreading crackers one at a time while holding the peanut butter jar between my knees to keep it from rolling away. They were delicious! We handled the crossing just fine and were not really alarmed at any point.

Seasickness was not a problem, which is great because the only sure-fire remedy is sitting directly under a big oak tree and that's just too high a price to pay if you want to be an adventurer. Although I know it can happen to anyone, having a purpose and being focused on something else probably helps in avoiding the problem. Even though I had that thought prior to departure, there was never a day when it actually crossed my mind again. The conditions that day became a point of reference for us to go by in the future. Calm seas never made a skillful mariner!

The rewards of making the crossing over to the Bahamas were many! It was also the most cost-effective portion of our trip because we enjoyed longer-term slip rates. The water there was so clear and so blue that sometimes you couldn't tell where the sky ended and the sea began. Marine life abounded, and we enjoyed using our dinghy as our preferred mode of transportation. The food was fabulous and the fresh seafood plentiful. We loved island hopping by day and listening to local island bands playing island music by night. We loved living on island time. I know that we have never been so relaxed in our lives.

We became aware that there is a subculture of people from Canada, the United States, and points abroad who trek to the warmer climates of the Bahamas for the winter months every year. Much like the snowbirds who travel to our Alabama and Florida climates, we became part of the group called "seasonal residents" of the Abacos. If you choose to be part of the organized society there, you can easily join a group at the marina that schedules walking trips every morning, water aerobics, luncheons, socials, dinner parties and such. Every morning there was a "Cruiser's Net" broadcast on the VHF radio that gave us the weather forecast and a report of what was going on that day on every island in the Abacos.

It was a fabulous two months for us and the only time we paused for that length of time on our Loop. As the seasonal residents departed, boat horns would blow and the people lining the dock would call "See you next year!" It was hard to leave. The last few days we were weathered in at the West End of Grand Bahama Island waiting on the sea to calm down so we could cross back over to the States! Stranded for a few extra days in the Bahamas, slap us if we complain! I know where I will be thinking of next February and March.

All of our boating skills have improved as our trip has progressed. I have become a regular Dale Evans when it comes to throwing lines. We arrived at one marina and the dockmaster had us aft-in to a slip with no finger piers, only pilings (Mediterranean style). As we maneuvered, he called out to me, "If you can lasso that first piling as you pass it, I'll buy you a six pack of beer." I nailed it from ten feet out and moved up to mid-ship with a spring line and asked if anyone cared to wager a bottle of champagne. No takers. Dang it! I nailed that one too. The dockmaster brought my beer to me and said he had been issuing that challenge for two years and that was the first time he had actually had to pay up!

Handling the day-to-day situations on your boat will make your competency and confidence level rise like the tides. You will become so comfortable that there will be a day when you realize that your boat has truly become your home. At one point, we started referring to the boat as "home" and our "address" in Birmingham as "the house." I guess that makes us officially "Live-aboards!"

We have been fortunate so far with the weather we have experienced on our trip, kidding each other about "traveling in a weather bubble." Regardless, we think life is about learning to dance in the rain. Many boaters have experienced their most bonding and memorable experiences when they have weathered floods in the Erie Canal or been delayed on the Mississippi waiting for the water to ebb. We have a whole group of friends who love to tell amazing stories of how they earned the nickname "River Rats" while experiencing the flooding of the Illinois River during the aftermath of Hurricane Ike.

While there is a new adventure waiting around every bend, we sadly note that the trip is also a series of doors closing. Leaving things behind can be difficult for all of us. I miss the dolphins that no longer run beside our boat; we left behind the clear blue waters of the Caribbean in the Bahamas when we moved on and headed north. What happened to the magnolias that bloom all they way up the East Coast, and when did we see our last white sandy beach before leaving salt water? The beautiful manatees, marshlands, osprey and fresh seafood specialties of an area, all left behind as we moved on. More importantly, the friends you have made along the way at some point have to go in different directions with their own agendas. While we look forward to what is in front of us, we try to remember the wise words of Dr Seuss: "Don't cry because it's over, smile because it happened."

We met wonderful people and will stay in touch with many of them. Reunions are already being discussed. Mary and Andy Sarver on *Good News* were heading to the Bahamas about the same time that we were. We stayed in touch by phone and e-mail so that we could meet up to do the crossing together. We both left Fort Lauderdale about the same time as buddy boats one morning around 5:30 a.m. and traveled across the Gulf Stream. Upon arriving in West End on Grand Bahama Island we met them for the first time and found that we had much in common and were very compatible. We have traveled and laughed together, and they are family to us now. We know they are family because we traveled together for over six months and they have seen us at our best and at our worst and they love us anyway! They are Michiganders and will leave us soon with their Loop completed! We will smile because it happened!

Apparently, I am somewhat of a worrier. With all the fears of cruising the Loop behind me, I now worry about what the heck we will do when the Loop is over for us! Cruising has proven to be such an enriching endeavor and every day has been exciting, fulfilling and such a blessing. Would someone just shove some shrimp in my mouth to keep me from blubbering on? Wow!

Our expectations were high and they have been exceeded. We made a great decision when we decided to aim the pointy end of our boat south down the

Tennessee-Tombigbee ditch and join the fall migration of boats that were on the Loop. Ah, the sweet smell of diesel fumes in the morning to accompany my first cup of coffee. I will miss that.

The Great Loop
It is a reward, a dream we had for years.
It is an escape, to transition into retirement.
It is a goal, and even though we are retired, we still need those.

Note: If you would like to follow our adventure day by day, we invite you to visit our website and travel log (salvagecrew.com).

Patti Salvage, a native of Birmingham, Alabama, retired from a successful career as a real estate broker with RealtySouth. Instrumental in building a company that was acquired by Home Services, a Berkshire Hathaway Company, her background is in sales, marketing and marketing management.

Travel is a passion for her and she hopes to add many more interesting places to her list, which already includes many European countries as well as Africa. A private pilot, certified scuba diver, and now a licensed boat captain, she enjoys her ten grandchildren and has not decided what her next adventure will be, but she is sure that there will be some boating involved.

Ginger Austin

Vessel: M/V *Stargazer* – 34-foot Mainship Trawler
Residence: Muskegon, Michigan
Southern Homeport: The Glades Marina – Caloosahatchee River, Florida

"More guts than brains." I think that this is the only description I can give that best describes me. I'm not selling myself short because I say that about myself; I know I'm smart, at least I got through college three times; i.e. I have a BA, MA, and MSW, but what has this got to do with long-distance boating? I think it has to do with the fact that I like to learn and I have an ego that says, "I CAN learn," and that is where the "guts" come in. I was raised in the 50s and 60s on a peninsula in Michigan surrounded by water and parents who loved sailing. We had a collection of boats from a 28-foot sailboat to a 28-foot cruiser, and smaller craft. My father, who was a dentist, even built a 12-foot scow in our garage, and one of my pre-teen pleasures was helping him. We were four children within five years of age of each other, and we were constantly in or on the water. As a family we were risk takers. An example of this risk-taking behavior was when my folks took us to Cuba in 1952 at five to ten years of age, where we lived on an island alone with a houseboy for two weeks exploring the surrounding areas with machetes like the Conquistadors.

After going to school, getting married, raising kids and working, I finally retired, and my partner Laura and I discussed what we wanted to do in our first year of retirement. We'd been together for 11 years and all our five children were self-sufficient, so we had no at-home obligations. Our parents were all deceased, so we didn't have this issue to hold us back either. I suggested we purchase an RV and see the United States, but Laura suggested we use what we had to take a trip. What we had was a 24-foot Maxum Cruiser.

The Great Loop is a circle route by water, which started, for us, in Muskegon, Michigan on Lake Michigan. From there we headed south through the Chicago River and down the river system to the Gulf of Mexico, around the coast of Florida then north on the Intracoastal Waterway to New York, up the Hudson River, the Erie Canal, the Trent-Severn Waterway into Canada and back again to where we started in Lake Michigan. Friends of ours did this trip in a 27-foot cruiser in 1986. This was close to the time the Tennessee-Tombigbee Waterway was opened, enabling the Loop as a viable possibility.

Everyone we talked to said we would kill each other by the time we got to the Tennessee River; we didn't have any experience with this lifestyle, and Laura couldn't swim. In reality, we knew nothing about this trip at all. I thought what a wonderful challenge it would be to take on this potentially dangerous yet exciting venture. This would take some real planning, but we had a year to plan before retirement was at hand.

One challenge that had to be addressed early on was Laura's inability to swim. She tried and tried until I finally asked her if she could wear her life jacket whenever she was on deck. She agreed to this, which made her fear of drowning much less. She quickly managed the ability to swim very well in her life jacket and was confident doing it. She later became a world-class competitor in getting her life jacket on and off in just a few seconds.

We also needed to address how all this travel would affect our beloved miniature poodle, Copper Top, and what his needs would be on the trip. More about Copper Top later.

The idea of meeting up with bad weather, high waves and wind did not appeal to me. I wondered what would happen if one of us became sick or died, what would the other do? We sat down and talked about all of our combined fears of catastrophe and discussed possible solutions for them. By facing them head on, it took most of our fears away.

We resolved not to go out in bad weather and to go into a dock the minute bad weather came upon us. Our cruising paths didn't lead us out to sea very often, but mostly along the shore or on the more protected rivers. When we did have to make a big hop over open water, from shore to shore, we picked the days and times ourselves after gathering as much information as we could to make a good decision we would not later regret.

Laura took on the role of galley slave, housekeeper, and first mate very willingly. I became the skipper, navigator, safety officer and chief mechanic because I was the only one with any boating experience. All the defined roles felt acceptable to us except I also remember feeling that I still had a lot to learn and little to fall back on except for those years of being on the water in Lake Michigan.

Because of the Internet and the America's Great Loop Cruisers' Association (AGLCA), I found books and websites to order charts and navigational aids. So, armed with my new knowledge sources, I studied every minute at night and on weekends, and I talked to every skipper I'd ever met to learn what I could. The charts alone were daunting. Just to begin I needed lower Lake Michigan, Chicago Harbor, the Sanitary Shipping Canal, the Des Plaines River, and the Illinois River, among others.

With help from AGLCA and the stores that sell charts, I figured out what we needed and ordered them, along with a few books on navigation. I then started to see that I had my work cut out for me. I spread the charts back-to-back on the floor from the kitchen through the living room to the bedroom and back again to the kitchen to make the whole loop. Then the studying began, trying to figure out how 50 nautical miles would make a boating "day", and where we would end up each day... and this was just for the first two weeks!

Laura worked on food and storage problems, comfort needs, clothes and ways to communicate with her kids and grandkids. We both worked on outfitting the boat and obtaining a dinghy and safety equipment. In September of the year we retired, we were finally ready to go.

It was hard leaving. We were both frightened of the many unknowns that consumed us, and we were concerned about leaving our loved ones behind. I was insecure about my boating skills and overwhelmed by all the complexities of this type of a trip, and Laura, of course, was afraid of storms and drowning. I also hated the idea of drowning and vowed to myself that we would not leave the dock in bad weather. Initially we both experienced sleeplessness and basically we were terrified – no more comfort zone for us.

When we got out into Lake Michigan, we felt relieved to be on our way, and after two or three nights of anchoring out, our confidence grew. Reaching Chicago, Illinois meant no more high waves to be concerned with, and I finally relaxed when we arrived at the free wall in Joliet, Illinois. Joliet, a warm and welcoming community, offers boaters free electric hook-ups and quality drinking water on the wall of their park, right on the river. This is where we met our first buddy boaters, people traveling in the same direction who want to pair-up or sometimes trio-up. Our new buddy boaters shared dinners, laughs and each other's lives so much so that over this short period of time many of us have become friends for life.

A short aside is to tell you about our buddy boaters John and Anne, who were both born in England and now lived in Canada. He was a retired physician, and she, his office manager. They had been married since they were 17 and 19 years of age respectively. We love them both dearly. John is a brilliant guy who possessed many of the electronic skills I did not, and consequently, I learned a lot from him. Traveling became easier with the buddy boat system, as there were two crews and two captains to discuss what the next day would bring and what problems the boats might encounter.

Laura and I also had a growing problem that started to get in our way and became quite annoying. Our boat, which was quite small, became increasingly overloaded. It seemed like almost daily Laura would accidentally hit me in the head with her elbow while reaching for something as she moved around the boat or did her chores. However, we seemed to be adapting to cruising, and our new roles became more familiar and defined the farther we traveled.

Since I had more boating experience, I had to teach Laura everything about being a first mate, and that posed a dilemma. On one hand, she wanted to know how to do it "right," and on the other, she resented me for assuming the role of boss. Finally, as we met and talked with other couples who had similar issues, we decided that the captain is not defined as one's partner or husband. Furthermore, the captain is only the captain while on the bridge, underway or docking. At these times it is crucial for him/her to issue orders for the safety and well-being of the crew and vessel.

We also noticed that while docking our boat the dockhands and skippers showing up to help started giving us orders on how to dock. I don't know if it was because we were women, or if it happened with male captains as well, although I've heard men say they've had it happen to them also. Naturally, Laura would become confused and forget the sequence of her duties as we'd practiced. I reminded her that she should listen only to my voice, and that helped her focus on our decided plan for docking. For example, it often happens that as we approach a dock, the dockhand will yell, "Throw me your bow line," and Laura now says, "No, we have a bow thruster, I'll throw you the mid-cleat line." This works out better for all of us.

When we arrived at Green Turtle Bay Marina in the Kentucky Lakes, we sent most of our extra clothes and provisions home to lighten the load, and this made it easier to move around. We wound up carrying one pair of jeans, three pairs of shorts, six T-shirts, and other necessities in small numbers and noticed that others also wore the same clothes two or three days in a row. This made laundry easier with less loads and the fewer times we had to come into a marina to do this ongoing chore.

When we got to Florida, we decided to look for a bigger boat and soon bought a 34-foot Mainship trawler, *Stargazer*. I adapted to piloting the bigger boat fairly easily by going slowly and docking even slower. We normally cruise between 7 and 7.5 knots; this speed is just right for us for enjoying the scenery and for safety reasons.

We found throughout our voyage that the more we knew about our boat and our motor, the less we were victims of overcharging mechanics. Luckily, two wonderful fellows helped me learn about the diesel engine. They also taught me to change the oil and fuel filters by myself and various other tips of engine maintenance. Whenever I talked to another captain about a mechanical, electrical or navigational problem, most would offer what they knew without hesitation, and I would also, in turn, pass on my knowledge to any less experienced captains we met. We found that the people were always helpful and giving all along the waterways. One in particular helped me to install a new water pump and

Ginger Austin – *Stargazer*

water heater. I also learned how to grind out blisters on the bottom of the hull and fill them, fair them and cover them with five coats of epoxy. The wiring was a complicated skill for me to learn, but I eventually did and re-wired the cockpit, added a horn, and worked to keep the navigation lights working. I'm still learning. As we live on the boat we, try to handle each new challenge as it arises.

The only time I felt discriminated against was in Apalachicola, Florida. About six captains got together to discuss crossing the Gulf of Mexico to Crystal River, Florida. When crossing the Gulf of Mexico a captain must decide whether she/he wants to hug the shore of the elbow first to Steinhatchee, Florida while hopping down the shoreline or venturing out into the wide, open water to one of the cities farther down the coast. I was not invited to the meeting. I wasn't even sure which boat the meeting was on, so I couldn't even crash it. I knew I had something to offer at this meeting, and I needed the learning opportunity since this would be one of the biggest, open-water crossings on our trip. I had studied the charts and weather and, because of my research, I had formed a tentative opinion. This being our first big crossing, I was very intimidated about finding my way across the open water and had originally planned on going around the bend. I was more than a little alarmed when I finally heard the outcome of this captains' meeting. They had all decided to start out at 6 a.m. the following morning to cross the Gulf in one straight shot. We had all watched the weather and it was the only "open window" for quite a while. This was the first and last time I ignored my gut feeling and went with the crowd.

I wanted to go around the bend because the forecast predicted waves of two to four feet all night. I attempted to talk another captain into breaking away from the crowd and going with us because I didn't want to do either route by ourselves. That attempt failed, and I caved in on my better judgment and joined the group crossing the wide, open water.

As it turned out, at midnight the wind changed and the waves became somewhere between four and seven feet. Laura thought we would die out there, and I was frightened but determined to hold on until we pitched over or worse. We medicated our dog and sweated it out for seven more hours. In total the trip was 25 hours of pure misery. I existed on M&Ms and coffee all night.

When we arrived at Crystal River, Florida I collapsed and slept for three to four hours while Laura talked to the others coming in after us. There were about six or seven boats in this group crossing, and the captains and crews were visibly shaken from the experience. It took us three days of verbalizing our fears to even begin to think about moving on. This experience taught me to use my own judgment in the future instead of joining the pack, this realization and decision has paid off many times since then.

On our second crossing two years later, we motored around the bend with a buddy boat, and the trip was smoother, shorter and flatter except for some fog. That was a good decision and we had a better experience.

As I mentioned earlier, we had our two-year-old miniature red poodle named Copper Top on the trip with us. He'd ridden on the boat on the Great Lakes quite well, so we thought we'd take him with us on the trip. He seemed to like being with us continually night and day after having been left at home while we worked in our careers. He also liked the routine we developed between us and began to expect certain rewards at specific times. Each morning and night when we anchored out, he would be waiting for his life jacket and the dinghy to be lowered so he could be taken to shore. There he could do his duty and smell all the unique scents onshore which were new and interesting to him.

When we weren't able to take him to shore, he learned to go on the papers we provided in the cockpit or on the foredeck. This took him a while to learn because he is shy by nature and needed darkness to do his duty. His health seemed to mirror ours and improved with sunshine and fresh air. During our trip we took many long walks, which he loved almost as much as meeting people. It was his mission to greet everyone he saw, and he helped us make new friends at every port. The color of his coat changed with the amount of sun we had, and at one point a fellow passing by us said that this was the first time he'd ever seen an orange dog. At that point he did look a little dark orange. We tried to be careful of the sun he received so he wouldn't get dehydrated or sunburned. I also made up a dog emergency kit with bandages, salve and medicine, including his monthly heartworm dose and the meds to keep away ticks, chiggers and fleas. We were fortunate and didn't need to take him to a veterinarian except for seasickness; the vet suggested one-quarter of a Dramamine and that worked well.

He had to learn new lessons like no barking at the dock and not leaving the boat without his leash. Twice he fell in the water, but we lifted him out easily, and we never left him alone on the boat without locking him in the saloon. We also carried a little holder for baggies to pick up after him when we were in the city or around a marina, and that made others less critical. At night we needed to supply him with food and water on the v-berth because it was too high for him to jump up or down to get his needs met. He thought this was wonderful as well. Even though Copper was extra work, we didn't mind the effort because we love him and there were many benefits to having him along.

After our first cruise, we noticed that Copper Top was lonely at home, so he and I went to a rescue home for pet adoption and he chose a little poodle/Bichon Frise mix named Roxy for a friend. Roxy also adapted to boating quickly, and it was just as easy to meet her needs as we had Copper's. She is more vocal than Copper Top, and training her is a little more difficult because she was a year old when we got her, was afraid of people and slow to bond with us. However, she'd been on her own for several months in the wild, so she was very brave about new challenges. Because of this, she fit right in with the rest of us adventurers.

During Roxy's first ride to shore in the dinghy, she jumped out of the boat and tried to swim in. Of course she had her life jacket on and her leash, so we pulled her leash gently and picked her out of the water, putting her back into the dinghy. She loves water and we always kept an eye on her so she wouldn't jump in and go for a swim. The pups have learned to play in a small area of the boat, and they do that frequently. When the motor starts up, they are at the bottom of the ladder to the bridge waiting and excited to be taken up top. They also sleep in their beds on the flybridge when I drive.

Having personal health issues became an extra effort for me because I needed to be out of the sun as much as possible due to my autoimmune disease. I had previously purchased clothes with sun protection built into them and tried to remain in shade whenever possible. This worked out well, even when I started to get a tan through the material and found that I didn't get sick. It may be that my disease has been in remission on the whole, aside from very short-lived flare-ups from time to time, or that my disease is not as bad as others who have it.

When I couldn't avoid direct sunlight for periods of time, I did develop symptoms of a flare-up for about 24 hours, so we just stayed where we were or went into port to wait or sleep it out. Again, this scenario happened at home as well, so it certainly didn't matter where I was, whether sick on the boat or at home, the procedure was the same.

Once during our trip I broke my ankle and needed it set. I went to an urgent care center so it could be set temporarily and was then referred to an orthopedic doctor where I got a more permanent cast. We stayed in port until I could climb the ladder to the bridge. (I can't drive from our saloon, even though we have a lower helm there, as I'm too short to see out the windows.)

Another time my knee began to swell and became red and painful. We happened to be in Annapolis, Maryland, where we found a doctor's office right on the waterfront. He performed tests and prescribed antibiotics and sent me on my way. I received the results of the test by mail. Luckily, my insurance covered most of the bills, but they gave me a $300.00 penalty for being "out of system." I have since changed my plan to avoid an extra expense when traveling.

Another personal issue that came up the first year we cruised was the unexpected death of my oldest sister. We happened to be in Charleston, South Carolina when my other sister called me and asked us to come home as soon as possible. By the next morning we were on a flight home. The marina was very supportive and cut us a deal on a two-week stay. We got a cab at the marina office to the airport and on our return from the airport back to the marina. It seemed hard to return to the boating life after the funeral, and as many of you who have experienced losing a sibling know, for me it took a very long time to absorb the truth of this event into myself and go on incorporating it into my identity and daily life. I'm sure that it's different for each of us, however.

During our first trip, our mail went to one of my grown sons. Each week I talked to him, and he told me what was in the mail. I paid my bills and did all my banking online; he sent us anything else we needed by sending it to the address of a marina we gave him, which was usually about two weeks ahead of us, so that we could get it when we arrived. The marinas are generally great about saving mail, as well as packages, for transient boaters. All of our medicines came that way along with any books, parts, or special items we ordered.

Having a cell phone and a computer, with Internet capabilities, with you handles many of the communications problems that arise while cruising. There are only a few places you can't be reached by, or reach out with, one of these devices in and around the United States. Communication services are a little different in the Bahamas, the Caribbean, and Canada, so a little research ahead of time may be in order. We now have a home base in Florida – the Glades Marina on the Caloosahatchee River – where we check in or stay for extended periods of time. This is where all our mail goes now.

Long-distance cruising has so much to offer a person. The challenges are the same for women and men in many respects, i.e. keep the motor running properly, stay on top of boat maintenance, and always work on improving navigation skills. Yet, for women, the challenge to perform these tasks is typically much harder because, more often than not, a woman has to overcome an upbringing that usually, but not always, says, "Let the man take the lead." Each woman must decide to trust in herself, her knowledge, her intuition, and her skills with or without a male around. Cruising can be life changing and energizing. It can hold the promise of meeting new and exciting people, seeing new places, and gaining new experiences. The rewards are very high, and I am truly thankful Laura and I have chosen this lifestyle for ourselves. Our grown children marvel at their 65-year-old mothers and how independent and interesting we are. They can't wait to see what we'll do next. I can't either.

Ginger Austin was born in Muskegon, Michigan and grew up boating on Bear Lake, Muskegon Lake and Lake Michigan. She graduated from Michigan State University in Secondary Education in 1966 and from the University of Michigan with a master's in Social Work. Her work experience included: Community Mental Health Emergency Services, two adolescent treatment facilities, independent family counseling, and high school social work. In 1961, Ginger was an exchange student to Germany and lived with a non-English-speaking family. She is the mother of two wonderful sons and daughters-in-law.

Over the years, Ginger has taken on other challenges, she ran a marathon and other races and walked across the State of Michigan. She currently plays French horn with the West Michigan Concert WINDS, a community band that has traveled to Europe three times to perform. Ginger is a member of the PEO Sisterhood, which offers scholarships to women for education. Among her other interests are kayaking, reading, woodworking and listening to beautiful music.

Charlotte Snider

Vessel: M/V *Foreign Exchange* – 48-foot Bayliner 4788
Residence: Toronto, Ontario
Homeport: Honey Harbour, Georgian Bay, Ontario

I have always been a very career-oriented person and worked full time as a nurse, then as a sales manager and director of marketing for a large multinational pharmaceutical company. Bob is an entrepreneur and has owned two manufacturing businesses over his career. Right after our daughter was born he muttered something about starting his first business so that in a few years we could sell it and possibly go cruising. Being quite preoccupied with a newborn baby I said, "Sure, whatever," and that was that! It sort of unofficially became a distant goal whose likelihood of being realized was so low I didn't really worry about it! For several years we were busy working, him working seven days per week and me traveling for work approximately 60 percent of the time. Andrea grew up to be quite patient and flexible, knowing that someone would eventually pick her up from school, the babysitters, the daycare or her grandma's house!

Our first boat was a 24-foot cuddy cabin runabout. We covered a fair bit of the popular waters in Ontario Canada in that boat. The Rideau River system and Georgian Bay were favorites. Quite a challenge to enjoy a vacation aboard a boat with no galley or fridge, etc. with a two-year-old in diapers, but we all loved it! We moved up to a 28-foot express cruiser and thought we really had a big boat! We spent most summer weekends and a couple of weeks of vacation on Georgian Bay aboard *Minstrel*. We were so busy working and going in different directions that we rarely drove the two and a half hours to the boat together, we would just meet up there sometime between Friday night and Saturday morning.

The cruising plan was still there but in the far off foggy future, and we only talked about it occasionally.

We both read Beebe's book on *Voyaging Under Power* and wondered if we could actually make the break from the mainstream to get a boat like he described (a boat designed for long-distance cruising, a trawler) and head out.

Friends of ours announced that they were going to get married and immediately thereafter board their sailboat to head for the Bahamas or wherever the tides took them for an indefinite period of time. Hearing them talk about their plans and watching them unravel their land-based life and prepare their boat, etc. really got us thinking even more about getting out there ourselves. Hearing of their adventures convinced us that we could do it too.

A few years later Bob decided that the time was right to sell the business he had started five years previously. When it was clear the business was sold and we would be free of it within 18 months, it became a reality. We needed to find a cruising boat and get our plans in order! I spoke to my boss, told him of our plans and requested a one-year leave of absence from my job to begin one-year hence. He immediately said I could have the leave but could not guarantee me my current job when I returned. I'll take it! (There was some concern on my employer's part as to what kind of a precedent they would be setting for others who might want to do something similar, but they did recognize that they weren't regularly receiving requests from people who were ditching their current life in mid-career, so they approved my departure.)

Andrea was in grade two at the time. When we spoke to her teacher she advised against taking Andrea out of school for the following year, "because grade three is a critical year." Oh well, we figured what she lost out on in the formal school setting she could make up for in life experience.

The search for a boat became top priority. Having done lots of reading and attended lots of boat shows in places like Fort Lauderdale, Florida and Annapolis, Maryland we knew what we wanted. We set our sights on getting a Nordhavn 46, a design very similar to that in Beebe's book, a long-distance passagemaker capable of blue-water cruising while providing a comfortable live aboard environment. It has two cabins, two heads, a pilothouse and the usual combined saloon and galley. After looking at a couple of them we settled on purchasing *Avatar*, a beautiful black-hulled Nordhavn 46 that was located in Florida. Having been owned by a retired sailor, it was rigged with a mast and two sails and had a single screw. The Florida laws didn't allow foreign-registered vessels to stay in the state for long without paying the state sales tax, so until we were ready to actually leave for our full-time cruising adventure, we had to take the boat back and forth to the Bahamas a few times in order to stay on the right side of the laws. Not too much of a hardship to have to check on her in the Bahamas every few weeks!

Meanwhile, back in Canada we were figuring out how to rent out the house and store our belongings, etc. as well as finding an educational program we could use to homeschool Andrea.

All three of us were looking forward to the cruising adventure, and it had sort of crept up on us with lots of time to gain a comfort level with the idea. Amongst all the positives we could see in the trip there were a few apprehensions, probably the biggest one for me was the fact that Bob and I had hardly spent any time together "attached at the hip" the way we would be on the boat. (Previously we hadn't even been able to coordinate our schedules to drive to the boat together for a weekend!)

We had consciously made the decision that I would not work in his business but rather continue to pursue my own career. We decided this because we had different work styles and because it would help mitigate the risk of being an owner/operator of a small business. Now that our "job" was keeping the boat afloat and educating Andrea, would we be able to do it "together?" We did have a few other concerns like: Will there be any health crises we can't handle? Will there be emergencies related to the boat... etc? We read lots of books on the cruising life and did the best we could to prepare ourselves for the "what if" situations. For example: Bob took a marine diesel mechanics course, and I gathered some basic medical and dental equipment and prescription drugs that we might need. Thanks to our family physician, who gave me the prescriptions, and our dentist, who showed me how to do a temporary filling!

Finally, the day to leave our home in Cambridge, Ontario had arrived! We left with a truck full of the "stuff" we felt we would need and drove to Fort Lauderdale, Florida, where *Avatar* was having some work done at a yard. Of all the adventures in "boatyard land" we have had over the years, that may have been the worst! Imagine arriving with a mountain of belongings during a hurricane warning to find your boat in total disarray. The electronics we were having installed weren't ready, and all the header and wall panels were still laying about with wires running everywhere and ending nowhere, absolutely no way to have access to the boat. When the yard manager said he wanted to have a word with us, we thought, "No kidding, we want to have a word with you too!" He needed to tell us that there had been a little problem, when the guys were reinstalling the washing machine they had dropped it down the beautiful teak and holly stairway, causing damage to the walls and stairs. Add this to the fact that the way the boat had been tied up, the lines had chafed the gold leaf lettering off the stern, and you can imagine this was not the glorious beginning to our adventure of a lifetime that we had planned! Needless to say, we checked into a hotel to wait for the hurricane warning to be lifted and for *Avatar* to be reassembled. Now, with much more experience, we know to never count on the boat being ready just because the yard says it will be! And we are definitely believers in doing it ourselves whenever possible; we just think of it as a cost-effective learning experience and fitness program (many trips walking to West Marine and back, schlepping stuff) wrapped into one!

We finally got out of the yard and headed up the Intracoastal Waterway from Fort Lauderdale. It was July, so we had thunderstorms every afternoon and humidity like we had never seen in Canada. As we think back on those early days, we can't believe we planned a trip that included Florida in the summer! We can't even remember what we must have paid for insurance to have the boat down there during hurricane season – we figure our minds are blocking that out!

We followed the East Coast up as far as Cape May, New Jersey that summer and then turned around and headed back south. While in the Chesapeake Bay we commented to someone working in a marina that there were far fewer boats out than we had expected. He informed us that most locals don't boat at that time of year as the weather is too hot, humid, and stormy. "So what are we doing out here?" we asked ourselves. We finally started to see other cruisers that fall as we made our way south. That winter we made it as far as Georgetown, Bahamas.

All went well, a few mechanical problems, no major medical situations, and Andrea passed grade three (yippy!). It definitely helped that Bob is an engineer and can problem solve many/most problems, and I am a previous ICU nurse, to most problems I just say, "I've seen worse – take a Tylenol." That is not to say there weren't situations that reminded us to be careful and be prepared for the unexpected.

One day the autopilot became possessed and was determined to head us into shallow water; Bob turned the breaker off and took control. On the way back from the Bahamas to the United States the seal on the transmission blew, so he caught the leaking oil in a pie plate and kept pouring it back in until we got to the States. One day in the Bahamas our friend Cathy Rae from *Evening Star* came up to our boat in her dinghy and asked what I thought she should do because she (who is also a nurse) had been bitten by a wild pig on the beach while trying to prevent him from eating a plastic bag! Now, I couldn't actually say I had seen that kind of injury before!

There are of course "real" medical emergencies. One early morning a sailboat came into our marina in Nassau. A woman got off to tend to the lines etc., but it was strange because she had a large towel wrapped around one hand. Apparently, she had got her hand caught in the wind generator the day before while offshore and had cut two fingers off. They had the fingers in a bottle and shortly thereafter she was airlifted to Miami. While in another anchorage in the Bahamas on a stormy day an older woman on a sailboat started to have chest pain. They took her off her boat and loaded her in a wheelbarrow to roll her to the local landing strip where she was airlifted to Miami. Emergencies do happen, but they happen at home too. You really see the cruising community work together when something has gone wrong, either mechanical or medical.

On that trip, probably the one thing we underestimated the most was how difficult it was going to be to be both parents and teachers. We got a great program from the Ministry of Education in Ontario. It was specifically developed for children who are not attending school because they are traveling; I had no idea our tax dollars were at work on such "frills!" The program was great because every day it told you what the parent was to do and what the child was to do and what was to be mailed in for marking, etc. The program wasn't the challenge, the relationship between the parents and the child was the problem. Andrea is a very cooperative, competent and self-directed person NOW, but at age seven she was not inclined to do what was asked of her EVERY day, especially if there was something else more interesting going on, like boats going by, dolphins playing beside the boat, etc.

When we started out on the trip we had more or less divided the responsibilities into "portfolios" as you would in a government or business operation. I was responsible for the education portfolio amongst others. I was supposed to do the teacher thing. It was just not possible. In the end we divided the subjects between Bob and me. I taught the grammar and he taught the math for example. This worked better, but it was still amongst the most difficult aspects of the trip. (Bob and I are just a bit competitive; it became a very big deal whose subjects got the better marks!) If misery loves company, we did have some comfort in knowing that most other cruising families experienced the same thing. One family with two children, living aboard their custom built 48-foot sailboat who had planned to stay out and cruise the world indefinitely, had decided to pack it in because of the problems they were having in the family over school issues. Another mother told me that schooling her kids aboard was "ruining her relationship with her children, her trip and her life." That isn't to say that schooling aboard is not possible, obviously it is because lots of families do it very successfully, but it does take planning and patience.

Any of the relatively minor challenges we experienced or witnessed were far more than compensated for by the amazing experience it was to take that cruise. As everyone in cruising says, the people you meet are one of the big highlights of the trip. The beauty of the places you see, the experiences you have and the sense of accomplishment gained by living this lifestyle is verging on addictive. And so, as that first cruise ended, we were planning our next.

After living for a year aboard *Avatar*, it was time to go home, back to work and school. The dilemma, we knew we wanted to cruise again but weren't sure when that would be. *Avatar* could not realistically come to Canada as we would have to pay 23 percent in tax and really she was too big and just "too much boat" for us to use only on our two to three week holidays. We also realized that while we loved the "beefiness" of the Nordhavn, it was really far more boat than we would likely ever need. We do not plan to ever cross an ocean or do any long offshore passages. So, our beloved *Avatar* was sold, we loaded the truck back up and came back to the grindstone. I went back to my job; yes, I got my same job back again. Andrea went back to school and Bob started another business. For six years we lived in what people around us insisted upon calling "the real world," we never really understood what that made the cruising world…?

When we were ready to cruise again, Bob managed the business from afar with the great help of some really responsible and competent employees "back at the ranch." I resigned from my job this time and Andrea got ready to do grade nine on the boat.

We decided on a Bayliner 4788 for this trip. Some of you may say, "How could you do that after having a Nordhavn?" We love the layout of this boat. What we had really learned on the Nordhavn was what was important to us and what wasn't. The pilothouse for us is a "must-have." When you cruise, you are boating in all kinds of weather. We don't like looking out from behind the plastic windows that you have to deal with in a flybridge-only style of boat. We also really like being warm and dry in the pilothouse on rotten days. There is always a cross breeze if the weather is hot. We don't ever do it, but lots of people just close up and turn the generator and air-conditioning on. The pilothouse also gives you the advantage of having "another room." If someone has their "stuff" (schoolwork, craft, maintenance project, etc.) all set up in the saloon, then other people have somewhere else to go and get away to their own space. The Bayliner has a flybridge too, but we find we rarely use it. Only on absolutely perfect days do we go up there. After many years of spending the good weather outdoors (from childhood), both Bob and I have the inevitable beginnings of skin cancer so don't want to hasten that process along by feeding our faces any more sun than necessary. We use the flybridge more for entertaining and watching the sunset than while underway.

The other boat feature that we learned was a "must-have" for us was a master cabin in the bow. We have chartered boats with huge master cabins in the stern. This offers the advantage of a large bed and great storage space. The disadvantage of this layout is that there is absolutely no "air/breeze" when at anchor. The Nordhavn had the master cabin at mid-ship, which is perfect for long ocean passages where this offers the benefit of sleeping in the most stable part of the boat while underway, but when anchoring a lot as we do, you are trying to sleep in a cabin with nothing but small port holes along the side of the boat, and its proximity to the engine room really contributed to the heat. We prefer to sleep in the bow, good breeze through the hatches and portholes when at anchor, which is what we prefer to do, and away from the engine room. Some people will say they find the noise from the anchor chain and snubber to be annoying with this arrangement, but we are prepared to accept that this may happen from time to time. If you like to cruise in cooler environments or stay at marinas with the air-conditioning running most of the time, then you may well prefer a boat with a large aft stateroom.

The other boat feature that we have learned we really "must have" is a galley "up." It is amazing how much time you spend cooking and cleaning up in the galley. Cleaning up never feels like quite the chore if you can still see the scenery passing by. It is also amazing how much time you spend preparing food and making drinks, etc. while entertaining others aboard. If the cook and drink maker is relegated to a galley "down," they really feel left out. Yes, sometimes the kitchen clutter is visible to the guests, but I don't worry about that, if they see the galley a mess, then they likely know dinner is going to be yummy!

We bought our Bayliner, *Foreign Exchange*, in Windsor, Ontario, so our second cruise consisted of traversing Lake Erie, Lake Ontario, the Erie Canal, Hudson River, Intracoastal Waterway and south to the Bahamas and then back up the same route and on to Georgian Bay via the Trent-Severn Waterway. It was a great trip, and I am pleased to report that Andrea very successfully completed grade nine having miraculously become a self-directed and driven student. The stressor on this trip turned out to be running the business while away. The employees did a great job, but still there was lots of time spent on the phone, worrying about business issues and trying to decide whether Bob needed to go home to tend to certain things or whether they could be adequately dealt with from afar.

Bob did go home on a couple of occasions during this yearlong cruise, leaving Andrea and me alone on the boat. Once we were at anchor in Georgetown, Bahamas and once we were on a dock in Charleston, South Carolina. While we were in Georgetown we had the reassurance of being surrounded by lots of other boats, and in particular our friends Jane and Dave aboard *Romana* and Gina and Woody on *Charis*. Bob put out an extra anchor before he left, and Andrea and I made sure we knew how to run all the boat systems we would need. Needless to say we didn't leave the anchorage except by dinghy! We did meet one woman in the Bahamas who was cruising around with just her two kids under eight as crew. When we commented on the fact that you didn't often see a woman alone as the skipper and only adult crew member, she assured us that she was pretty comfortable as she was a tugboat captain. Her husband is a tugboat engineer. They took turns, each working for three months at a time and then being on the boat for three months at a time with the kids while the other went off to work!

Our third cruise, which we have just completed, was ten months long and covered the Great Loop, having departed from our cottage on Georgian Bay where we keep *Foreign Exchange*. Andrea is at university now, so we did this one on our own. Our upcoming cruise will once again be to the Bahamas for the winter, with plans to spend a summer in Maine and then a summer doing the Rideau and Ottawa River systems in Canada.

We have learned lots in the time we have spent aboard as a couple and a family. While we have never really discussed a division of labor between Bob and I either at home or on the boat, we do fall into a pattern of "who does what," and I think this is pretty typical. It has worked best for us when we each assume certain roles. I am usually in charge of any galley/provision-related issues, and of course the "health portfolio." I am usually in charge of keeping the communications going with those on the home front. I may not actually do it all, but I am usually the one who says you better call so and so and check in, etc. I do the interior cleaning and Bob does the exterior. Bob is in charge of mechanical stuff. He tends to do most of the planning in terms of how far we are going to go on any certain day etc. He monitors the weather and plots the courses. We both drive the boat, but he docks it. When anchoring I put the anchor down and he brings it up while I man the helm. I think every cruising couple figures out what works for them, just like they do at home. When it comes to deciding whether to go or not when the weather is forecast to be poor, we usually do that jointly. If we are in any sort of open water, we usually don't go in winds of 20 knots or more or when the seas are forecast to be greater than three feet. With some general guidelines like this, it is easier to make decisions, especially when you have "slipped" and broken the golden rule of cruising, do not have any deadlines or schedules you can't change easily.

Before we left to go cruising I did have some concerns, probably not the right ones as it now turns out! As I mentioned before, we were both concerned about what it would be like to spend sooooo much time together. This turned out to be a non-issue; in fact it has been surprisingly pleasant! I was concerned about health-related emergencies. We have been very fortunate over three separate years of full-time cruising, some offshore to the Bahamas, to not have experienced anything that average common sense couldn't handle. We have heard of others having difficult situations, but when you think of it, these happen all the time in the non-cruising world too. It is really reassuring if you prepare in advance, take medications and some basic supplies (syringes and needles for example) you "might" need if you go to a less-developed area where the standards may not be what you are used to. If you are sticking to developed areas for your cruising, Canada and the United States for example, then there is usually medical assistance available within a reasonable time and distance. I just make sure that I always have good pain medication with us in case we have to tolerate some injury for a few hours or overnight before assistance is available. I hate being seasick! We really try not to go out in conditions that might precipitate this, and I use the scopolamine patches if necessary, but this really has been virtually avoidable.

    I was concerned, and continue to be concerned, about the situation if something happened to the captain and I had to maneuver the boat and look after him. I did worry about this on our first cruise especially. After that trip I took one of those weeklong boating courses for women only. Not only did I learn a ton and built my confidence, but I have never laughed so much in all my life! If your cruising budget and time allow, I recommend this highly. I worry about the captain going overboard and not being able to retrieve him. This would be covered in a women's cruising course, and the Coast Guard gives excellent instruction on this at boat shows etc. (The "Number One" rule to prevent this is to not allow your captain to urinate overboard, apparently this is the prime cause of the situation!)

Charlotte Snider – *Foreign Exchange*

Being caught out in rough weather is a concern for many, me included. There is such good weather and wave forecasting available now that this is really avoidable to a great extent. It is usually not a lack of information that leads to cruisers being out in bad weather, but rather a schedule that they feel they need to keep and so they venture out even if the weather is not going to be great.

I was worried about my career when we went the first time. Part of my employer's concern about holding my position was that he felt, despite my reassurances, that I would not come back. I e-mailed him regularly and kept up to date with what was going on in the business and the department because I was interested and in order to reassure him that I was returning. It seemed to work, as I got my old job back from day one of my return! With e-mail so readily accessible, it is easy to "stay connected" and keep the doors open for your return either to your pre-cruising job or at least to your "network," the friends and contacts that will help you find work upon your return.

I overloaded the boat with food and supplies on our first two cruises. For the third I had finally learned that there would be ample shopping opportunities as long as you are in Canadian or United States waters. When cruising to the Exumas, in the Bahamas, it does make sense to bring lots of stuff, as the availability is low and the prices high. (Look for "hidden" storage spots on your boat. We took down some ceiling panels and found enough space to accommodate five big plastic bins which we use for lightweight stuff like paper towels etc. We also found space behind and under drawers.) In the Abacos area of the Bahamas, you may not be able to find specifically what you are looking for on any given day, but you will definitely be able to find something that will work as a substitute. The only things I do bring lots of are items where we have a specific brand preference; we don't understand how you can live without Kraft peanut butter for example!

I was concerned about running out of fresh water during our time in the Bahamas, so Bob installed a water maker. It is really nice to have endless supplies of fresh water, especially when it is hot out! But it is not really necessary to go to this extent now, and certainly not for near-shore cruises. Water is readily available in United States and Canadian cruising grounds and even in the Bahamas, for a price.

People often ask about pirates. We were never worried about this and never had any experience of this nature. (We did not carry a gun, but did have a baseball bat.) The worst thing that happened was having a box of Q-tips stolen through our porthole in the bathroom!

The things that we did not realize would be a concern but did materialize were the schooling issue discussed earlier, and the cost of "staying in touch." The cost and availability of e-mail is reasonable now and cell phone within the United States and Canada is not bad, but the costs do rise when you leave the mainland.

Overall, cruising has been a delightful experience and has provided lots of growth opportunities for our family. There are the obvious, learning the history and geography of the places you travel and meeting people from all over the world. We have also changed in less obvious ways. Andrea is very calm, cool and collected and has a different perspective on life than she would have otherwise I am sure. She is an excellent student, highly motivated and self-directed. Both times when she went back to school she was amazed at how much time during the school day was wasted "goofing around!" I am more confident in my ability to handle different situations now, although I must say I haven't taken control of the boat as much as I should have after taking the women's cruising course. The trick seems to be to take a more active role in aspects of cruising that you hadn't previously – immediately upon your return from the course; it is too easy to let old patterns continue!

Doing "big" crossings are still somewhat nerve-racking. We find crossing over to the Bahamas or doing the Gulf of Mexico crossing are enough "adventure" for us. It is highly unlikely that we will ever do anything more than that. There is a huge sense of accomplishment for us in successfully completing those. There are other much smaller feats that give satisfaction, such as bread making, that are by no means a big challenge, but are things that I would not have been exposed to if not for cruising. Cruising does help to keep what is important in life in perspective. By doing new things that challenge us, by meeting lots of interesting people, and by realizing that it doesn't take lots of fancy possessions to really enjoy life, cruising has taught us a lot.

One type of growth that some cruisers, like me, experience and are not happy about is the expanding waistline! Unless you make specific efforts to keep your level of activity up, cruising can be a very sedentary lifestyle. Not to mention that the addition of cocktail parties on many/most nights tends to add calories quickly! When you don't have a car to use on a regular basis, you really notice that North American cities are designed assuming that people have cars. Walking is a great way to get some fitness activity into your day, but it is amazing how often the sidewalk you are on will just end and you are dumped onto a six-lane road that is clearly not for pedestrians!

The cruising life does certainly provide for lots of "Aha" moments along the way! Being inland boaters before setting off to cruise, we only knew what we had read about tides. We didn't really "get it" until we came back to a dinghy dock one day and found our dinghy totally squished under the dock! Learning how to anchor Bahamian style in wind and current took us a few attempts, but now we "get that" too. We had no idea that alcohol slugged into the gills of a fish would kill it instantly, wow that was quick! We were all totally wide-eyed and understood the meaning of "food chain" when we were reeling in a frisky fish that stopped fighting when he got close to the boat. When we lifted him up he was only half a fish, somebody else wanted him too apparently!

Bob had a real "Aha" moment when he was maneuvering the dinghy on the boat deck on *Avatar*. The davit was a strange arrangement of pullies and line – set up by the previous owner, a sailor who probably understood it! One day Bob obviously pulled the wrong line and the dinghy dropped from a height of four feet onto the deck and cracked and punctured the dinghy hull. Fortunately for us, our friend Dee, aboard *Allegria*, had all the stuff to do fiberglass repairs, so he came over and he and Bob did a beautiful repair job.

One day in the Bahamas I was cleaning up after lunch while Bob was out snorkeling around the boat looking at the starfish, etc. When I threw some wilted lettuce overboard and a bunch of barracuda came in for it, I realized it might be a bad idea to throw fish food over while the captain is in the water, duh!

We are not really "rule oriented," but we do have a few we try to abide by. Our boat has a very narrow unprotected area on which to walk from the pilothouse to the stern. Whenever anyone "goes down the side," they have to tell the others on board that they are out there so that they can keep an eye on them. When we are doing night passages (very infrequent) with only two people on board, if one is asleep the other must not go outside the pilothouse. We really try to not have clothes, shoes, sunglasses, books, etc. accumulate in the saloon. We try not to approach a dock for landing until everyone is ready – we are still working on this one! We use our kill chord while driving the dinghy. We always "set" our anchor. We always file a "sail plan" for ocean passages. We (OK, the captain) check our engine room regularly. We wear our lifejackets while locking through.

While we enjoyed 99.9 percent of the time we have spent cruising, there have been odd times when we felt a bit homesick or lonesome for some familiar things. At Christmas it just doesn't seem right to be away from home, although there are usually cruiser gatherings, which are lots of fun.

There have been times when we are out of synch with "the pack" of cruisers heading in a certain direction. After spending lots of time with others, it can seem very quiet to be cruising as a solo boat. But these times are few and far between and present a good chance to cut back on the cocktails and hors d' oeuvres for a few days!

We have had family members and friends join us on the boat; it works best if they are able to be flexible in their schedule and/or where you meet them. These get-togethers will either convince them why you are doing this or leave them saying, "Better them than me!" There are lots of opportunities to meet like-minded people while cruising. Just like at home, pets and children are great icebreakers. Being a member of an organization like America's Great Loop Cruisers' Association (AGLCA) and flying their burgee is also an instant bond with fellow cruisers. There is nothing like owning the same boat as someone else to get the conversation going either! If you want to meet lots of people, it makes sense to go where they are, if the crowd is anchoring out, you will want to as well, if they are all going to marinas, then you may feel left out if you decide to anchor.

Women On Board Cruising

There seems to be three different types of cruisers. Those who anchor out at all times. Those who seek out marinas whenever possible. And then there are those who anchor out most of the time but go to marinas every week or so to clean the boat, do laundry, etc., this is the group that we fall into. While doing the Loop we anchored 50 percent of the time (anchorages are sometimes hard to find), and while in the Bahamas we anchor 99 percent of the time. We prefer anchoring because we find it easier. There is less risk of incurring damage from docks. It is more peaceful and there is less risk of being boarded by cockroaches or mice – dare I say RATS! Not to mention that it is cost-effective and no reservations are required! Of course, anchoring does mean that you don't have a source of garbage disposal, water or power, which some people find essential on a daily basis. Obviously you have to use your dinghy more, so it is important to have a dinghy that is dry in rough weather and to have a good way to secure it to the boat. We did have our dinghy cut free from our boat while anchored in the Kentucky Lakes, but this is very rare. Dinghy theft can occur in certain areas, so sometimes it is wise to raise the dinghy at night. Anchoring is easy to learn how to do, but it does involve more than heaving the thing over the bow, and it pays to learn to do it properly, letting out enough scope, setting it, etc.

We do have a concern when in crowded anchorages that either us or other boats may drag. We try to anchor downwind from boats that look like they probably know what they are doing, have proper ground tackle and look like they probably have insurance. We try for instance to avoid being downwind from derelict boats!

While anchored in the Bahamas a boat did drag down on us, hitting us with a huge thud in the middle of the night. Amazingly the boat's name was *GHOST!* It hit our bow broadside then wrapped its dinghy davit around our bow rail. What a jumble up! The people were not on board their boat at the time. Four other captains from surrounding boats came to assist us while we were trying to push it off – tough to push a sailboat uphill! Andrea, who was seven at the time, came up on deck to see what was going on. She suggested that we just tie it up to us as if we were rafted and wait for them to come back and drive their boat off. Out of the mouths of babes! It actually was an approach that none of us had considered, but it did work quite well!

Like so many good things, each cruise comes to an end. Probably one of the things we never considered and definitely underestimated the first time was how challenging it would be to reintegrate into the land-life routine and way of thinking. Cruising changes your perspective on what is important and valuable in life. When you re-enter a corporate dog-eat-dog environment for example, it is an eye-opener in terms of recognizing that things that you once thought were important just aren't anymore. Then there are the simple things; the first time I drove to a grocery store upon returning home I left my purse in the grocery cart. I never carried a purse while cruising so just forgot all about it! After the cruising life, the hubbub and speed of land-based life seems daunting. When you return to the mainland United States after being in the Bahamas, you look at the selection in the grocery store and wonder why we need all those choices – it was intimidating! It is interesting that your land-based family and friends cannot really understand the transition that you are experiencing. But like the rest of the cruising experience from the planning, to the departure, to the return there is really nothing else like it and we wouldn't have missed it for anything!

EPILOGUE

If I had to give a few key tips for women considering cruising, they would be:

1. **If you think you MIGHT like it, you probably will!** There will never be a time when everything is in a perfect state to allow you to leave your daily responsibilities, so set a target date and plan to do it. You don't need to have the perfect boat, just a safe one that has the features you have identified as being the most important to you.

2. **Be clear about what you are comfortable with and what you are not.** Are there certain "things" you won't do without? Certain weather and sea conditions you don't enjoy? Be sure to speak up, you can always revise the list as you go!

3. **If you are concerned about your skill level, take a women's boating course if it is within your budget and timeframe.** Attend Coast Guard sessions at boat shows or Rendezvous to build your confidence at dealing with captain-related emergencies in particular.

4. **Try to strike a balance between being sure to go where you want to go and yet not losing track of "the pack" if the social aspect of cruising is important to your happiness while afloat.**

5. **Avoid making firm schedules (booking non-changeable flights for example) for yourselves or your guests.** There is nothing like an inflexible schedule to get in the way of the fun or cause you to go out in conditions you aren't comfortable with.

6. **Try to choose your boat with the cruising life in mind, you will be on the boat in all weather and for long periods of time, which means there are different criteria to take into account.** For example, if your preference is to anchor out

or you plan to cruise in the Exumas, in the Bahamas, your dinghy will become far more important than when you were doing short stints on the boat. If you want a good dinghy, your boat needs to be able to accommodate it, deploy and retrieve it easily.

7. **If you wouldn't eat it at home, don't take it on the boat!**
   I left for a 12-month cruise with a ton of canned tuna, and I brought it all home and gave it to the food bank when the cruise was over!

Charlotte Snider is 53 years old. She and her husband of 22 years, Bob, have one daughter named Andrea, who is attending university. Charlotte worked full time as a nurse then as a sales manager and director of marketing for a large multinational pharmaceutical company. Bob is an entrepreneur and has owned two manufacturing businesses during his working career.

All three of them have spent their summers around boats, on cruises and at cottages in Ontario, Canada. They started taking extended cruises 15 years ago and took three separate yearlong adventures on the water while loving each one for its unique opportunities to meet people, experience new places and grow from all the learning opportunities.

Judi Drake

Vessel: S/V Leaena – 35-foot Wooden Cheoy Lee Sailboat
Current Vessel: S/V Echo – 40-foot Columbia Sailboat
Homeport: Mystic, Connecticut
Blog: yachtecho.blogspot.com

"Let's buy a boat and go cruising." I couldn't believe those words came from my mouth, and neither could my husband, Dave. This statement coming from a girl who was born and raised in the Berkshire Mountains in Massachusetts, where boats were something you used to ski behind.

Even after moving to south Florida as a teenager, boating, especially sailing, was still something of a vague concept filled with Sunfishes, Hobie Cats, and surfing on the beach. So when I met my future husband and he informed me he had lived aboard a sailboat, an old wood Atkins double ender with his family, which included Mom (Pam), Dad (Bob), three brothers (Pete, Chris and Bruce), Needles the dog, and Periwinkle the cat, I thought he was a "little" weird – to say the least. I truly had never thought you could go down below on a sailboat. To learn that there was a "down under" environment was an amazing eye-opener.

After cutting my teeth on a couple of day sailors in the warm sunny south, we moved back to New England and purchased a Cape Dory 25 Sailboat. For me this was a great boat to learn what cruising could be. Still considered a weekender, she was a well-found boat that took us all over Long Island Sound.

When I uttered those first words about going cruising, I'm not sure that I was really serious. After much discussion, often over many glasses of red wine while enjoying the sunsets on Block Island, they did become serious. At the time, not only did we have an old farmhouse in the middle of a restoration, we were also raising my niece, Alicia.

Women On Board Cruising

The first thing we decided on was a time frame. Five years seemed about right for both of us. I hoped that would give us enough time to finish the house and get my niece through high school. I would often joke with her that when she hit 18 she was outta there! This would also give us enough time to purchase a boat and become familiar with her. Taking our time to get to know her turned out to be the best thing for me.

We found *Leaena* one cold winter day after leaving the Providence Boat Show. While at the show I boarded every "cruiser" they had, none seemed to feel right and all had a huge price tag. We decided to take the long way home and stopped at every marina/boatyard there was on the way. I was ready to call it quits when Dave coerced me into one more stop because he had spotted an "interesting" mast. When I said I would wait in the warm car, he stated that he would just take a quick peek – when I saw him jogging back to the car with a big grin on his face I thought "UH OH!" The "interesting" mast belonged to an old wooden boat, and she was a beauty. We determined that we actually had information and paperwork on her – by now we had a whole portfolio!

Let me just say that before stepping aboard this boat I had a whole list of what I wanted in a boat. She had to be at least 40 feet long, with a U-shape galley or at the very least an L-shape, a U-shape dinette, fiberglass hull and have a shallow draft. When I stepped aboard *Leaena* (named *Nautica* at the time), all of the must-haves went out the window – it was love at first sight. She was old, wood, deep, barely had a galley and had two settees. At this point, I think my husband was hoping she wouldn't survey well, as he was now having doubts about all the work she represented. You guessed it, she surveyed well.

The problem now was coming up with enough money to purchase her. The good captain informed me that if I really thought she was the one, it would be up to me to phone the broker and ask if the sellers would be interested in a partial trade. (Remember the Cape Dory 25?) Thinking I wouldn't have the nerve (maybe hoping) he figured I would only do it if I were serious, not only about the boat but also about going forward with our cruising plan. I must confess I was pretty nervous making that phone call, and when I presented my offer it sounded lame even to me. However, the fates must have been smiling, or laughing their arses off. The broker, after insinuating that it was the most ridiculous offer he had ever heard, halfheartedly presented the offer to the seller. A few days later, the call came and he informed me, almost like it had been his idea, that the sellers would indeed be very interested in a trade.

Once we bought the boat we were on our way… and, as I said earlier, getting to know the boat before we actually left was by far the single most important thing we could have done. Getting comfortable with sailing her in and out of the mooring field, slip and fuel dock was helpful practice.

I am going to say up front that I am lucky to be married to a very patient man. He has never been a Captain Bligh, not to say that we did (do) not have

Judi Drake – *Leaena/Echo*

our "moments," but those "moments" were not (are not) played out in screaming matches with one on the bow and one in the stern.

Over the next five years or so we tried to take her out as often as possible in all types of conditions. The New England sailing season is short, but we stretched it as long as we could. This helped me gain confidence not only in the boat but also in myself. I must confess there were many times I thought to myself that I couldn't wait to get back home to the warm house and take a nice long hot bath. I wondered if I would miss the creature comforts and security of knowing that if the weather was too inclement, a warm and safe haven was a mere car ride away. These thoughts did not intrude often, but when they did, I could lie awake for hours!

Dave also encouraged me to take the local sailing class. I found this class to be fun and very refreshing. If I was the one making all of the decisions, I could blame no one but myself when mistakes were made. I also took a general, dead reckoning navigation class, which was helpful in learning how to plot a course on a chart even in this day and age of electronics.

I drove all of my friends and family crazy by talking almost exclusively about sailing. Most of my friends understood, as they were avid boaters themselves. Family on the other hand was another matter. Dave's family understood and encouraged us to go ahead with our plans, although secretly I am sure they thought we were a little nuts! My family, though, was a different story.

As I said, I come from a non-boating family. My dad would come up to New England every summer, and we would often take him out on the boat. You could tell he was uncomfortable and definitely didn't have any concept of the goal we were working towards. He would jokingly inquire as to where his stateroom was and where he could put his suitcases if he came to visit us in distant lands. (Did I mention that *Leaena* was not a big boat?) We would answer right back that he could have the whole boat, and we would stay in his hotel room, wherever that might be, and take long hot showers and watch TV! We would all get a good laugh over this, and then he would treat us to a great dinner. I am sure he felt that our departure was way in the future.

We had been planning and working towards this getaway for close to four years when my dad became ill with cancer. He lived in Florida, and we were based in Connecticut. He didn't realize it at the time, but he uttered the words that gave us the go ahead. "Don't wait; go now because you never know what the future holds." We went!

Our first passage started in a frenzy. The boat was hauled out, and we were busy painting, sanding, painting, sanding and painting yet once again – the joys of owning a wooden boat. We were also finishing work, selling cars, trying to fit our wind vane, doing some last-minute provisioning, and of course attending an endless stream of going-away parties! We had set a date to leave, and as the day loomed I found myself wondering, once again, what I had gotten myself into.

Would I be able to handle the long endless days at sea with only my husband to keep me company? Was taking our old faithful dog, Sonja, the right thing to do? Was selling the house and quitting our jobs going to be worth it? Would I ever be able to make friends again, you know those types of friends you can say anything to? Was there anyone else out there crazy enough to do this other than ourselves? Did I buy too much boxed milk? The answers were, YES, couldn't have left her behind, YES, YES, YES, YES, and YES!

After the "final" going-away party was behind us, the boat was back in the water, the cars were sold, the provisioning was finished, the last visit to the vet was made, the boat was loaded with all her new equipment, the last box of milk was stowed and we finally knew that departure day was actually here. Our family and friends took the morning off from their jobs and came down and said goodbyes with last-minute advice, gifts, and a send-off fit for king. We motored out of the harbor amidst conch horns, shouts, flash bulbs and escorts in small boats, we were on our way… a short 20 miles to Block Island, where we anchored the boat and crashed!

We had spent so long working towards this day that when it came time to go we realized we weren't quite ready. We really needed a few days to organize the last-minute gifts and catch up on some much-needed rest. The only problem with this plan was it was early summer, and if you are a boater in New England, Block Island is the place to be! Of course, we ran into a few friends that we had missed on the going-away party circuit, we didn't want them to feel left out so we did what any seasoned cruiser would do – we had sundowners and made plans to meet up in tropical places. At last, departure day was here and unlike the departure from our marina with our family and friends, we sailed out through the cut of Salt Pond in the early morning sun with no fanfare.

We wanted to go to the Caribbean. We didn't have a lot of money, so we decided on an unconventional route instead. We didn't want to bop down the Intracoastal Waterway (ICW), risking the temptation to spend money on dinners out, fuel and marinas. With that route, we would have to beat our way out through the Bahamas to the Eastern Caribbean. We decided on a different route that would take us through the Azores, Madeira, Canaries, and then to Barbados all downwind, or so we thought!

As we left the harbor and raised the sails, it was hard to get out of the mindset that in another five or six hours we could be anchored watching the sunset while enjoying a cold one. When in fact, since the change of plans, it would be about 18 days before we could pop the cork off the bottle of champagne that was buried in the bottom of the refrigerator.

It was very surreal leaving the harbor. My first night at sea was one that will stay with me forever, but when the sun came up on the third day and the sky was bright red, a saying popped into my head that would prove to be true every time… "Red sky in morning, sailors take warning." If that wasn't enough, all of the fishing boats headed back towards land (civilization) should have been the next clue.

By the third night at sea I would love to say I had my sea legs, but I was sick as a dog, and speaking of dogs, I was stressed that our pooch had yet to relieve herself since her last walk ashore. No amount of cajoling could get her to go; we tried everything with no success. Our watch system was haphazard to say the least, so both of us were lacking sleep, and meal times consisted of the captain making a sandwich and swilling a bottle of water. Thank goodness Simba, as our wind vane was affectionately named, was a good helmsman.

As the sun rose higher in the sky, the mare's tales (a type of cirrus cloud formation) began to take shape as the wind built. Throughout the day we shortened the sail, and by sunset when we were contemplating putting up the storm sail, I jokingly asked the captain if it was time to dig out the drogue (a funnel-shaped device with open ends which is towed behind a boat to reduce speed or improve stability). Imagine my surprise when the good captain agreed and headed down below to begin the process of "rearranging" the stores to get to the drogue. We were both pretty exhausted by this time as *Leaena* had no roller furling and the reefing system was still being tweaked as we went along.

Let me back up to the drogue for a minute. We decided to treat *Leaena* to a new main. Our sail maker was recommended to us from friends in the marina, and he came out to the boat in the fall and took the measurements needed. Sometime during the early part of the winter, the captain went down to the shop to answer a few questions, and when he returned to the boat, he had a sheepish look about him. When interrogated by said first mate, he confessed to purchasing a drogue kit for an additional sum of money. The drogue was actually a Jordan series drogue and the kit consisted of 300 feet of line with a series of cones that needed to be sewn on by hand. The captain assured me that this would be a fun project we could work on together during the long cold New England winter. Personally, I thought it was a waste of time and money, but the captain was grinning so broadly that I agreed it would be "fun."

The captain is a pretty cool, calm cucumber when it comes to sailing. So, when he immediately agreed to the drogue my stomach did a flip-flop, which didn't do it any good at this point. We dug out the drogue and got it ready to go but resisted deploying it as we were hoping against hope that the system would pass us by and conditions would improve. By nightfall, we were running with bare poles and with Simba still steering the boat and cruising at seven plus knots! At this point, we were taking breaking waves across the stern, it was time to deploy the drogue. I kept this thought to myself, but I desperately hoped that I had sewn the cones correctly and hadn't been daydreaming of distant shores.

We discussed how we were going to deploy the drogue, and how we were going to retrieve it once the storm subsided. This would become a pattern that I personally find very helpful. It gives everyone involved a game plan and an idea of what to expect. Sometimes this is in theory only, as it doesn't always work out as expected. In this case, the deployment went off without a hitch and once deployed the drogue created a slick that stopped the waves from breaking over the stern. This made not only the boat happy but also the crew as well.

Our poor old deaf Sonja decided at this moment that she could cross her legs no longer and after close to 72 hours it was time to go. It did not matter that it was nighttime and there was a storm raging. We donned foulies and harnesses, snapped Sonja into her harness and clipped her onto the jack lines. We gave her a gentle nudge down the side deck of the boat and even though she couldn't hear a bloody word, we cheered and clapped when she finally went.

The storm raged for close to 18 hours. We had no idea what the wind speed was as *Leaena* was not equipped with an anemometer. We found out much later when we met up with another boat that had made the same trip that the wind blew a sustained 50-60 knots for more than a few hours. The waves on the Georges Banks were the biggest I had ever seen.

During this time I thought it might be close to the end of us, the noise through the rigging was incredible. Every time we took a wave, water would find its way through impossible places in the boat, at one point our dorade box was ripped off and the water poured in like a fire hydrant, but the captain was able to save the box and secure it once again. As the boat surfed down the waves, everything would shake, rattle and roll around. You might hear a noise and be convinced that the rig was coming down, and it turned out to be a can of beans rolling around in one of the lockers! Every so often I would ask the captain, "Are you afraid we might not make it?" and he always answered, "The boat can take a lot more punishment than we can," and, "No, I'm not afraid that we won't make it." One of the plusses of getting to know your boat before you go means that you are apt to feel more confidence in yourself and your boat when undergoing adverse conditions. Deep down inside I was glad the captain insisted on going through all of the systems and rigging before leaving.

I must confess at this point that I totally slept through one of my watches, not that we would or could actually sit in the cockpit. One of us was always up, and every 15 to 20 minutes we would slide the hatch open and stick our heads out and take a glance around, we never really saw anything through the darkness, but it did give us a sense of security and kept us busy with a "job" to do.

When the storm finally blew itself out we were left with pretty confused seas, but they were no longer breaking so we were able to pull the drogue back in. We experienced several casualties, we lost our flag staff, a jug of fresh water, and everything inside the boat was saturated in salt water.

The next day the sun finally came out, giving us a chance to take a hot shower, which not only felt decadent but was also very necessary at this point. Showers were done and we were sitting in the cockpit exhausted but feeling clean and finally having a hot meal (the best can of beef stew ever!) when we heard a strange noise. It turned out the water pump was still running and had completely pumped out our main fresh water tank... thank goodness we had

Judi Drake – *Leaena/Echo*

decided earlier to close off the forward tank in case something happened.

During the next five to seven days we were in a pattern of one nice day and then we would get our butts kicked by another gale, never as bad as the first one, but miserable nonetheless. During one of these systems, we once again let Simba steer the boat. While huddled down below we heard a huge CRACK and a thud. I thought for sure, even though I had just looked, that we had hit something. It turned out our boom had cracked. After we got the reefed mainsail down and the boom secured, there was nothing more we could do, as at that moment the wind was as strong as I have ever seen. It was raining so hard that the rain had actually flattened out the seas, creating a pink hue on the water. It was one of the most beautiful things I have ever seen, and when I looked back at my husband, we were actually smiling and laughing at each other!

During yet another low the dog started to whine while we were resting. I kept stroking her, but she wouldn't stop, finally she started barking and when I unglued my eyes and put my hand down on the floorboards I was shocked when I found the water was up to my wrist. Shouts to the captain and frantic searching unearthed the culprit; we were siphoning water in through the bilge pump as the boat was heeling so much. The problem was easily solved and of course, smelly or not, Sonja got the bunk that night!

One day we practiced a man overboard drill when we lost our dish bucket. Oddly, as we did our maneuvers we sailed into about 100 dolphins surrounded by strange-looking buoys. We could only assume that they were weather buoys but we didn't dally.

We celebrated the 4th of July on the 5th because on the 4th it was foul weather once again and we wouldn't have been able to cook the hotdogs and beans!

During a weather forecast, we heard from a boat that was headed in our general direction. They were close enough to us that we could "use" their forecast. We could never quite make the name out; it was something like "Tampa Bay," "Panda Bay" or "Moomba Bay." When we heard their forecast for storm conditions if they didn't get south (we were actually north of them), we looked at each other and came to the same conclusion, it was time to head south. We were tired of bad weather and above all else, we did not want to go through any more storm conditions any time soon! We were actually close enough to them that we thought we might see their running lights sometime throughout the night, though we never did.

It was tough going to get south. We had to cut across the Gulf Stream, which at this point was trying to push us north, and of course, it was windy. Simba steered the boat like he was steering Mr. Toad on his wild ride, we videotaped the GPS speed log at 10k! It was a long night! When it was once again "Herb," *South Bound II* time (this is a free weather router guru service for long-distance cruisers – boats regularly check in with "Herb," his call name, via SSB when they are making a long passage) the other boat was now north of us; if I thought my upcoming watch was going to be long, I can only imagine what theirs was going to be like.

Once we sailed far enough south, we finally got ourselves out of the stormy pattern, but we also lost the wind! When we were only a couple of days out of Flores in the Azores, we decided that we would splurge and spend a night in a marina. The guidebook we had for this area said that the marina was not completed yet, but our book was a couple of years old, so surely it was done by now. We envisioned hot showers for all, a calm peaceful evening without the endless roll, a real sit-down meal topped off with a toast from our chilled bottle of champagne. We had a moment of fright when we realized that we were completely black and blue and that it might be construed as something other than constantly bracing ourselves against the impact of the motion of the boat.

As we came around the corner into the anchorage, we could see all the masts swaying – rolling from side to side. We said to each other that while that might be us tomorrow night, tonight we would be snug as a bug in the marina… but by the third trip around the anchorage reality was beginning to sink in. However, it took coming alongside another boat and asking where the marina was before we believed that it was not only not complete but never really started. We made our way over to the customs dock so we could clear in and practice our Portuguese. Once cleared in we made our way back out to the anchorage where we dropped the hook in about 30 feet of the clearest blue water I have ever seen!

As we sat in the cockpit, showered and changed and about to sip a cold glass of champagne, we realized that we were in the most incredible anchorage either one of us had ever seen. It didn't even matter when the boat rolled one way and the bottle the other, spilling our chilled champagne all over the cockpit. Not one to be deterred, the first mate went below and retrieved a spare non-chilled bottle. We then proceeded to toast each other and our first Atlantic Ocean crossing.

A couple of days later a boat pulled into the anchorage looking for the "marina" with three tired-looking people in full foul-weather gear and harnesses. We looked at each other and smiled. As the boat passed us by, we saw the name on the back was "Gander Bay" and we laughed, when they asked if we had any cold beer, we knew a friendship would be born!

From this first humbling trip, we learned a great deal about ourselves.

When I first set out, I didn't know what to expect. No one really does. My first trip was not one that everyone would do. It was pretty aggressive. I would never have attempted it had I not been totally confident in my husband's ability and his confidence in me. We spent time getting to know the boat and learning from our mistakes. We looked upon moving aboard as a challenge and a chance to experience an alternative lifestyle.

Cruising is a way of life, not a vacation. It is filled with a lot of hard work. Our friends and family often think it consists of frozen pina coladas and white sandy beaches. While we often indulge in a frozen drink or two on the beach, it is more often filled with long days of locating grocery stores, spare parts, laundry, keeping an eye to the weather, and when needed, long nights awake "babysitting" the anchor.

We often find ourselves out of touch with what is going on with the rest of the world. Amongst the cruising set everyone discusses the best anchor technique, what stores have the freshest fruits and vegetables, the latest chart-plotting technology, weather windows and Grib files (weather data). The "real" world and her problems seemed far away.

Before we left on our first trip, I was afraid that I would not meet anyone else that I felt I could relate to. Boy was I wrong. One thing I have learned is that I am not alone. If you pull into an anchorage with at least one other boat, chances are by the time the anchor is down an invite will be forthcoming. I have met people from all levels of the professional world that I would never have had the opportunity to meet had I not met them cruising. The friendships that are forged on the sea tend to be friendships for life, no matter if you continue to cruise or decide at some point to "swallow" the anchor. I would not trade one of my friends met while cruising for one day snug in a house.

My first trip at sea was my worst. Many people may say the same thing. It is a learning curve and you never know what is going to happen. I was so scared at times that I found if I didn't focus on the job at hand, I might just find my bunk and not get up until we arrived at our destination. I credit Dave for recognizing this fact. He not only gave me small jobs to keep me busy but trusted in me to see them through. Even the simplest task of checking our position on the GPS and recording it in our log was enough to keep me from thinking of the unknown. I now find myself, to this day, keeping a log at sea with updated positions.

Fortunately, we all have short memories and the thought of catching up with friends in distant shores is enough to make you want to weigh anchor and venture out once again. We learn from previous mistakes of what works at sea and what doesn't. For example, I don't try to make four-star meals at sea when conditions are not great, I know by the time I actually go down below and fight with the galley, I will only end up ticked off, upset, and seasick to boot. On those days, it is better to just have a sandwich and iced tea instead.

Going with the flow is probably one of the hardest concepts to accept. If you come from a world of deadlines, commitments and having to follow a plan without deviation, cruising will be a big adjustment. Things never go as planned, and if they do, look out! One of the hardest things for us to accept is when we are all set to go, the boat is provisioned, the dinghy is stowed and the first couple of suppers are cooked, but the weather is not cooperating and we have to sit and wait. By the time the weather is right, we have the dinghy back in the water, the precooked meals are gone, and we find ourselves back in the grocery store shopping for more provisions!

Cruising is really a comedy of errors. We found that even on the smallest of islands you can usually find some semblance of a grocery store. Some improvising may be required when trying to follow a traditional recipe, but it usually means new meals are born! We have learned that if you eat what the locals eat, you will always find what you need.

Laundry on the other hand can be a challenge. We often found many cruisers elected to have the local women wash their clothing, usually for a fraction of what it costs stateside. We usually do it the old-fashioned way with a bucket and a plunger. As long as you have the water and don't mind giving up half of a day, this works quite well. Otherwise, in most harbors a quick call on the VHF and "Voilà" your laundry is ready for pickup!

With the inception of the Internet, it truly has become a "small world." We find many cruisers, ourselves included, spending much of our time trying to choose a perfect spot to anchor based not on the sandiest spot but on Internet availability. Let's face it, we all want to video Skype our family back home and share our great anchorage with those sitting around the fireplace. This keeps many a grandma happy, just the chance to see the grandkids smiling faces on birthdays and holidays.

Leaving family and friends can be traumatic. We all make choices that we dissect over and over once underway. For me leaving my dad when he was terminally ill was not a decision I could have made on my own. My dad, as I said earlier, encouraged me to leave and not wait. I knew before I left there was a good chance I might not be able to be there when he passed away. We were able to keep in touch via e-mails and phone calls and when it looked like the end was near, I was able to fly home from the Balearic Islands and spend some quality time with him. He would not have wanted it any other way. This may not be true for everyone, so we must all make difficult decisions and sacrifices when necessary.

Another hard decision for me was the family pet. We talked about leaving her with a good home to finish out her days; she would have none of it. We took her with us and found ourselves having mixed feelings and wondering if it was the wisest of decisions. Every time we hit port, the first thing we had to do was put the dinghy in and take her ashore. She was good about relieving herself while at sea, but if she could smell land, she would insist on going ashore to do her business.

We choose not to cruise with guns – we are not gun people. We have lots of cruising friends who are, and while they cannot agree on what type of guns to carry, they can agree that if you carry a gun and pull it out to use it, you had better not hesitate. We would hesitate. That might be all it takes to make a bad situation worse. By having a dog aboard, we were left alone for the most part. No one knew, short of close friends, that she couldn't hear or that when she met you she might lick you to death. Just her presence on board was enough to deter even the most curious.

The decision to put her down in a foreign country when she could no longer walk, control her bodily functions, or recognize either one of us was incredibly hard. We swore no more pets, but one year later, we ended up with

Judi Drake – *Leaena/Echo*

a kitten when we landed in Trinidad! Currently we have a Shitzu affectionately known by a plethora of different aliases. The one piece of advice I have on this subject is to start with a puppy, or kitten, if possible. It makes life a whole lot easier down the line. In addition, do some research, not all countries welcome pets, as we found out on a recent trip to Jamaica. We were informed that if the "Admiral" (the dog in this case) was caught off the boat, she would be shot on sight and her crew imposed with large fees... needless to say after three weeks confined on board, Jamaica was not one of her favorite stops!

To sum up:

1. Go cruising for you, not for anyone else.

2. Try to be open to change, I know how hard it is to adjust to changing plans at the last minute, but often it is for the best.

3. Go with someone you respect and who respects you.

4. Take a moment before doing maneuvers and discuss with your partner how they will be done – this alleviates many shouting matches on the bow!

5. Don't be afraid to go alone if you are confident in your ability, we have met some astonishing women who single-hand.

6. Know your boat and your limitations on the boat.

7. Count to ten before swearing at your neighbor who you think anchored too close – chances are they will realize this all on their own and you might be risking a great opportunity for a new friendship.

8. Don't be afraid to laugh at yourself, we all make mistakes and these make great stories later on!

9. Don't hesitate to offer to host the sundowners on your boat, tomorrow night they are on my boat!

David and I have sailed over 40,000 miles and been to 30 different countries. After 11 years, we are still living aboard. We still often feel like novices and are continually learning. We were both in our thirties when we left on our first trip.

We are not retired, we often stop and work to replenish the cruising kitty. Our first cruising boat was a 35-foot wooden Cheoy Lee Lion. We outgrew her and decided to buy a bigger boat. Once again, I had a long list of must-haves and once again as soon as we stepped aboard *Echo*, they all went out the window. Sometimes we never learn!

Happy Cruising… Don't forget to stop by if you see us in port!

Judi Drake, age 46, graduated Boca Raton High School 1981. Has been married to her wonderful captain, David, since 1982. Judi has sailed from New England to the Azores, the Mediterranean, Africa, the Canaries, the Cape Verdes, the Caribbean (Eastern and Western), the Bahamas, Jamaica and the U.S. East Coast.

She is currently in Florida and will be returning to her job at Defender Marine where she will continue outfitting *Echo*. In the past she has also spent time working for West Marine.

Linda Thomas

Vessel: M/V *Freedom's Turn* – 39-foot Mainship Trawler
Residence: Okemos, Michigan
Homeport: Duncan Bay Boat Club – Cheboygan, Michigan
Blog: freedomsturn.blogspot.com

"Linda, do you have a ten-year plan of your own?" my husband Charlie asked me one day just about ten years ago while we were taking a walk.

Raising my eyebrows, I said, "None at the moment." Busy with the task of raising children, working and social activities, I suddenly realized I had not taken time to dream for quite some time. "Do you have one?" I asked Charlie, turning my head as we continued to walk and getting a good look at his face.

After a moment, Charlie responded thoughtfully, "I'd like to be retired in ten years and spend some of our time living on or near the water somehow. Who knows, maybe we'll buy a boat." With such a unique idea presented to me, I had a lot to think about.

When I was young, I liked to read adventure books like *Tom Sawyer* by Mark Twain, where I could imagine myself on adventurous trips. I also enjoyed books about wilderness survival like *The Call of the Wild* by Jack London. During my teen years, I had many pen pals from different countries, which gave me a glimpse into foreign places. I also had real vacations with my family that took me to special places.

Our family's trips were not worldwide travel but summer tenting and camping trips. For five consecutive years, beginning when I was 11, I was instrumental in helping my mom and dad get ready to go more than my siblings; I was the eldest of four children. My parents valued family time together and worked hard to get our family on these camping trips. There was a lot of love on those trips; I got to share time with the most important people in my life. There was also a new feeling of security each time we would come home from a trip. After exploring new vistas, I would feel the comfort and safety being tucked into my own bed and coming back to a more familiar routine. To this day, I still remember the thrill of planning and preparing for those adventures. I think I will always love to plan what special things I will be taking for the special places I will be visiting.

One year, when I was a junior in high school, I remember my mother standing for hours in our dining room ironing the clothes we were going to take on our next trip. Working together, I would fold and carefully place the ironed clothing for six into special suitcases that would fit into the trunk of our 1967 Chevrolet Biscayne. Suitcases for six meant that each had a specific place to go in order to fit into the trunk of our car. My father even built a car top carrier out of nice-looking wood and he painted it the exact shade of green to match the car. Our tent, stove, lantern, sleeping bags and deflated air mattresses went up there. From my child's eye, I saw the effort it took to make preparations for a good trip. That year's vacation was the ultimate trip for us as a family: we were going on a one-month-long camping trip from our home in Michigan all the way to California. We were going to see the Pacific Ocean and to visit Disneyland!

After Charlie and I had our two girls, we made an effort to take our children on summer vacations and visits to relatives far away as often as we could. We were also able to travel on some of his business trips, which took us to several states and to Cancun, Mexico. I also went abroad to England and the Cayman Islands with Charlie for vacations. A few years ago, I had the opportunity to go to Italy with a good friend. I consider myself very fortunate to have traveled to this extent.

Shortly after the day when we took our walk and first talked about living near the water or maybe buying a boat someday, the cold Michigan winter nights were upon us, giving way to good reading nights at our home in Okemos, Michigan. Curled up in his easy chair, Charlie began to read everything he could find about different cabin cruiser types of powerboats which would be suitable for long cruising vacations. He gave me a book named *Honey, Let's Get a Boat...* written by Ron and Eva Stob, the founders of America's Great Loop Cruisers' Association (AGLCA). In the book, they reveal how they came to a decision to go on a one-year trip around the eastern half of the United States by boat. It was just a passing comment of his when he gave me the book and said, "Here is a book you might like to read. It's about buying a boat and planning a trip. It'll just give you a feel for what a long-distance cruising lifestyle would be like." He also added, "Wouldn't it be fun to someday go on a trip lasting longer than two weeks?"

Charlie and I went to our first boat show in Detroit, Michigan a few years later. We took off our winter coats to sit on boats and imagined we were basking in the sun in warmer climates. But I have to admit I remember at the time being more interested in cooking classes being offered to boaters that day and the ladies clothing boutique that was on display than inspecting or learning about boats. I bought a smart-looking outfit that day to wear on a boat. I wanted to cook well and look good if I was going to be a "boater woman."

Initially, I found myself trying to just be respectful of Charlie and his dream. At this point, it was three years after he first asked me about my ten-year plan. I had gone along with the buying of a boat idea, wanting his dream to become mine. I recall now staring at this "Honey" book on our coffee table waiting for me to finish reading it. I also recall not wanting to even consider, not for one minute, the possibility of leaving behind our home, family and friends and to go live on a boat for a whole year or longer, as the book proposed we do. If we moved forward with this plan, it would be our first time as boat owners; if you don't count the small boat Charlie's parents used for their fishing vacations when he was growing up. "Let's do it." I said, "but let's not plan anything big for right now."

As time passed, I found that his impending desire to get a boat led me to dig deeper and finally dare to dream big as well. I discovered that if it became possible for us to put this together when we both retired, maybe I would have an opportunity to replicate that marvelous thrill of adventure I experienced as a child. Yes, owning a boat might just be the way to go.

Charlie and I committed ourselves to becoming a cruising couple with the purchase of a new 39-foot Mainship 390 trawler. We promised ourselves that we would spend our available summer days cruising the waters in close proximity to us, Michigan's Great Lakes and the Canadian waters of the North Channel in Lake Huron. We named our boat *Freedom's Turn* (it is our turn to have freedom!), and we were feeling patriotic after 9-11. Since we purchased her, *Freedom's Turn* has given Charlie and me six wonderful summers exploring the Great Lakes from our homeport of Duncan Bay Boat Club in Cheboygan, Michigan. We enriched our lives with the new joys of our very special boating adventures. We both agreed we would consider the Great Loop trip someday if the circumstances became right. It was a leap of faith for both of us to even say this statement out loud – especially for me.

Growing up, my husband had been told many times by his parents how he first came to Canada as a baby on a pillow. Charlie, his brother Bud, along with his mother and father drove all the way from West Virginia, taking their yearly fishing vacation in the small fishing village of Little Current, on Manitoulin Island in Ontario, Canada. Many other relatives usually joined Charlie's family each year as well, forming a family caravan heading north; automobiles packed with suitcases and people with all their small boats being pulled behind them.

As a young boy, Charlie remembers one of his favorite things to do in Little Current was to get an ice cream cone and walk down to the city dock wall with his family to see the big recreational boats tied up there. He was fascinated by the fact that boats were so big that people could live in them! He always hoped to one day have a boat of his own like these pretty boats, and someday he would bring it to Little Current and tie it up to this same dock wall. Fifty years later, when he entered the waters in Little Current as captain on his very own boat, Charlie realized one of his life's goals had been fulfilled. I know because I was there as his first mate standing by his side, and I saw happy tears fill his eyes.

I did eventually read the rest of the "Honey" book. I let myself dream of a long boating journey safely from my easy chair. In the meantime, I had retired and was happily spending more time with family and developing my hobbies. I felt happy and comfortable when we shoved away from the dock during our summer vacations to places like Mackinac Island, Beaver Island and the North Channel. I noticed that I felt more alive and free on our boat during these trips.

Charlie started talking more and more about his retiring in two years and doing the Loop. I admit I first felt fearful and could not let go of a dark cloud that started to hang over my head. The good things, I would say to myself, were that our children were grown, our health was good, and I had a partner who I considered was becoming one terrific captain. I always felt secure when we cruised, feeling confident that he would keep us both safe. We both loved our cruising times together on our boat.

On the other hand, this lifestyle change would put me way, I mean WAY, out of my comfort zone. He was only asking me to go away for a year. "Can I do this for a year?" I asked myself. "Do you think we could be happy for a whole year living THAT close together?" Through 38 years of marriage, Charlie and I have always encouraged each other to try new things by saying: "Go ahead, roll your window down and feel the fresh air." This time he was asking me to consider going off in a convertible and I feared the fresh air was going to completely engulf me!

Charlie got into the position to retire and proposed we plan on going on the Loop. Then, wouldn't you know it, our daughter Carrie announced her engagement to a wonderful young man named Jody, and we postponed Charlie's retirement and the trip for another year. It worked out for the best, especially for me because secretly I was glad the delay bought me more time to prepare, mentally, for the trip. Of course, the more important reason was that I got a wonderful new son-in-law and saw our daughter as a beautiful bride.

In preparation, I felt the need to find women-to-women information regarding how to cope with long-distance cruising issues. In my research, I learned that there is much more information printed about how to buy, run, and maintain a boat than there is about how to co-exist peacefully and productively with another person on a boat, especially while doing any long-term cruising.

About this time a whole sky full of black clouds kept coming into my thoughts. My concerns were valid to me. They included managing fear of the ocean, the weather and safety issues. When I give up my land life to sail off with my partner, I thought, "I will be putting my life in his hands and his in mine. We will have to trust each other completely." I felt I could trust Charlie, I had a lot of respect for his new captaining skills, but would I measure up to his in turn? The clouds started asking me many more questions. Could I be consistent enough day to day to get my boating skills right, especially in a tense situation? One black cloud was asking me if we would just get tired of each other. Another cloud asked how could I ever leave our family for so long?

"I can do this," I kept telling myself. I can do this for a year. I owe this to myself and to Charlie. I knew it was OUR TIME. *Freedom's Turn* was calling us to go and have some wild and crazy times with her. "Are you ready to be thrilled?" she said in my head. My mother was very supportive and said, "If not now, when? Go now because time waits for no one."

Sometimes you can just see the handwriting on the wall when you invite the risks of change to come in. It's like buying a great new swimsuit to falsely dare yourself into taking swim lessons when you know the pool isn't open yet. Any advice you can get before you have to jump in is crucial. Consequently, when our mutual friend Lisa contacted me a few months ago to ask if I would consider contributing a chapter for her upcoming book project about women on board and their long-range cruising experiences, I accepted with pleasure. It was because I thought here was a chance to share my experiences with others who are a bit nervous, like I was in the beginning, but I have to say that in my case, well, the pool finally opened, so to speak, and I signed up – for an amazing adventure.

Charlie and I have just recently completed our Loop. It took us 342 days and 6,069 miles. I committed myself to not only buying the swimsuit and taking the lessons, I also jumped in, eyes partly closed, feet first. My big leap of faith. Now I feel exhilarated with life each day as a result of this trip. I only hope I might add something here to help prepare women as they plan an extended boat trip. I claim not to be an authority on long-range cruising by any means.

We anchored out only 36 nights, choosing the familiarity of being tied up safely most nights. The rest was spent mostly in marinas with some free docks and mooring balls along the way. We would study the weather religiously so we would feel safe when leaving the dock. By renting a car seven times, Charlie and I got to see much more of the sights on land as well as restocking our supplies. Many marinas offered free courtesy cars to help with our provisioning, and laundry facilities were plentiful. Ending the day before dark was good for us and helped us relax from the rigors and excitement of the day. Getting up with the sun and going to bed when it got dark felt natural and the right thing to do. We felt very healthy living this way.

We made it a priority to make two trips home during the nearly 12 months we were away to see family and friends. We gained a lot from traveling with others, not only using their knowledge base but for the camaraderie. This was a saving grace for me for it was three months into the trip when I grew very homesick for my family, especially my mother. I started out on the trip with a saddened heart because I had just lost my dad three months earlier. This was a very difficult time for me. However, my boating friends soon became my chosen family and it was wonderful. Our social life was one of very select and very desirable company; fellow boaters who were a total joy to be with. We were all out to live the moment and share so many new experiences. I guess you could say we lived our best lives during those times we were together.

We kept our house, which was placed in the responsible hands of a wonderful house sitter who took in our mail as well. We also hired a terrific yard maintenance company to take care of the yard work. We arranged to have most of our personal business done online, and to keep further in touch we maintained a blog. I kept it up each week as well as took the photographs for it. The blog gave us a sense of staying connected, which was very important for me. In addition, I kept a daily log of places traveled and money spent, the amount of fuel used, etc. Charlie kept a log of the maintenance issues.

I had spent several months getting our boat ready to be a cozy home for us. It was very pleasurable to pack and plan! From a woman's perspective that also means surrounding myself with things to make me happy and feel balanced, whatever that may be. I packed my watercolor paints and paper, long-awaited good books to read, outfits and jewelry to make me feel pretty in case I felt drab and weathered (I did!) and a well-stocked galley as I love to cook. In addition to the blog, I relied on e-mail to help me feel connected to what was happening with my land life. Charlie got us two new cell phones; mine was a pretty purple. We had an Internet air card, which worked out very well for the most part. We had previously added a webcam to our laptop computer so when we were out of cell phone range in places like the Bahamas and Canada, we enjoyed using the Skype program to see and hear our family when we could get a Wi-Fi signal.

Life on the water became an almost joyous daily event. What were the many enticing factors? The thrill of the adventure comes first to mind. Going up the one-mile-high Lookout Mountain in Chattanooga, Tennessee in a tramcar to see a famous Civil War site was one of those thrilling times, or going through the locks where we had drops in the water levels sometimes exceeding 90 feet. Crossing the Gulf of Mexico to go to Key West, the Atlantic Ocean to the Bahamas, and then having sharks under our dinghy as we motored across the Sea of Abaco over to Marsh Harbor in the Abacos Islands were all thrilling moments. Other times that stand out include cruising the New York City Harbor, where we had our picture taken by a "buddy boat" as we cruised past the Statue of Liberty, and going under the Brooklyn Bridge.

We had lots of fun also. Happy hours took on a whole new level with our dear boating friends as we gathered together after a day of cruising and sharing stories with our drink of the day. At Halloween time, we had a pumpkin-carving contest after one of our friends was the "pumpkin lady" and delivered pumpkins secretly during the night. Someone (I know who) placed a fake butterfly on my bike, and I first thought it was real and had been there for a whole cruising day. There were impromptu cheers on the docks and T-shirts worn by our boater friends in support of our Michigan State University Spartans on game days. We were invited to fellow boaters' homes for meals and overnight stays. In the Bahamas, we felt like kids on spring break when we took the Hope Town Ferry on Elbow Key to Great Guana Cay, where we attended the annual "Barefoot Man" concert at the Nippers Beach Bar.

Another enticing factor in doing this type of trip was the opportunity to see our country by water as our forefathers had. A sense of history was always present each cruising day.

There were other unique experiences, like being on a floating marina (yes the whole marina was floating several feet higher than normal) during a flood on the Illinois River after Hurricane Ike. "There's a WHAT on our boat?" Charlie hollered when I heard a loud thud when we were on the Mississippi River and I screamed up to him, "An Asian carp has jumped out of the water and onto our boat, what a bloody mess!"

There was a tornado we had to dodge in North Carolina, and a fire near the Intracoastal Waterway (ICW) in Myrtle Beach (we had to wait for it to be put out the day before we went through there). We froze in our seats when the cresting waves at a passage in the Sea of Abaco (Bahamas), named "Don't Rock" (appropriately named by the way) reached a soaring ten feet high. I was so proud of the way Charlie handled the situation with supreme calmness and delivered us safely to shore. Our previous boating experiences all came in handy this day. We know how important it is to anticipate outcomes ahead of time. Traveling with a buddy boat that day was reassuring as well and always a good idea when the going got a little challenging.

There were also many moments of tranquility on the water that were especially inviting to me. The spirits of nature, which I felt and saw every day, moved me in a way that became bigger than life itself to me. Besides the outward "journey," I was experiencing an inward one as well. I viewed the trip as an opportunity for some respite and renewal. Gazing out at nature each day, those first few weeks and feeling the oneness with it and myself, I realized I was experiencing a deeper spiritual level of my faith. In the calmness of my mind, I knew that wherever God sent us, he would guard our lives as we traveled. This concept carried me through times like the above-mentioned unique experiences such as the cresting ten-foot waves in the Sea of Abaco.

Besides having more time for reflection, I loved the fewer external demands compared to my land life and relished in creating schedules that were now self-imposed. Life was simple in that we both lived more slowly and deliberately. There was even room for learning how to do absolutely nothing and loving it.

Women On Board Cruising

This inner journey gave me the opportunity to focus on my marriage and become a good cruising buddy. This effort in turn became the most rewarding aspect of my personal growth for the year after all we learned and did. I believe Charlie will say the same. We worked very hard to adapt to our living conditions, working to make them feel as comfortable as could be for both of us. We respected each other's differences of opinion while living in these confined quarters. This was not easy. Sometimes the captain is right no matter what! Good communication along with complete trust in each other is essential. Make things right between each other before you go to sea. Don't think you can work on your marriage after you leave the stress of land life behind. You will be in for a disaster – not from nature but from yourselves. We had plenty of conflicts, but at the same time worked very hard to preserve and protect the sacredness of our marriage.

The most difficult thing for me in regards to being happy on the boat was not to take it personally when my captain would use that "TONE" in his voice. This would happen when I would somehow not measure up to being the first mate that he said he needed! Admittedly, there are things on a boat that have to be done the "RIGHT WAY." I thought I was just being a bit more creative in my approach, that's all. Sometimes it is good though to just admit we made a mistake. We both had time to learn to understand where the other person was coming from on many occasions. Besides, we could not stay angry at each other for long living in less than 500 square feet of space! Most of our stress came at us unaware; from the fatigue that comes from being on the go, sometimes for several days on end. Fatigue zaps one's willingness to cope with EVERYTHING. I discovered this fact while on this trip.

To be totally honest, equally as significant as our shared thrill of our trip is what Charlie and I have learned about ourselves individually and as a couple together: with a stronger commitment to our marriage in this one year than we ever accomplished in the 38 years before. Cohabiting in a small space for long periods of time gave us the glorious opportunity to learn more than ever about the other person and our own selves on a deeper level and at the same time reaping the rewards of a newfound closeness with each other.

Our "Rules of Engagement" (this is an understanding and agreement between crew members as to what conditions they would cruise under, including, for example, weather, anchoring, docking and home visits) were made and could be changed with mutual consent. Charlie handled the finer points needed in the navigation and mechanical aspects, and I in the management of cleaning the inside and outside of the boat. I did the provisioning, the laundry and line handling for docking. During those first five years, prior to the Loop, we became familiar with most of the parts of our boat and how they functioned. This is crucial before you begin any trip, but it becomes especially important when you are a long way from home.

A final note about two important words: Patience and Respect. First, strive to be patient with yourself when making your small steps toward change and respect yourself always. This focus will help give you a positive outlook most of the time. This goes for anything you try to learn, but it is especially crucial when going on a long-range cruising trip. Your attitude most certainly will have an immediate impact on your partner's entire day because you are living so closely with one another. Second, respecting each other's differences will actually give you something in common.

Honoring these two words, patience and respect, will go a long way towards making your trip pleasurable for both of you. As I mentioned before, Charlie and I trusted one another with day-to-day decisions we ultimately made for the betterment of the situation at hand. Trust in each other is absolutely vital.

Life leads us to our own rewards by experiences we gather along the way. I think of these things each time I read my kitchen wall plaque that is inscribed with the words, "Enjoy life one step at a time." The choices we make once we place ourselves in the face of change can help prepare us to meet our challenges, both good and bad.

By saying yes to the Great Loop adventure, I said yes to living outside my comfort zone and away from family and friends for an extended period of time. I did not know how well Charlie and I would get along. I did not know if I could measure up to being a good first mate. All I knew was that he was thrilled that I was buying into the whole plan, and I would try hard to be the best cruising partner I could be. Our friends and family were thrilled for us, which definitely helped motivate me. I took the risk of long-range cruising, as so many other women have done before me. Along the way, I enhanced my boating skills and learned some valuable life lessons. I am proud of myself for doing it.

Now that I am home to my land life again, I see a change in myself that I will work hard to keep. I am patient with myself as I slowly adjust to being home again. While I am happy to embrace the security and comfort of my home again, I am also enjoying the daily reunions of my closest friends and family. I shall try to live a life truer to my new and changed self, someone who wants to live more simply and with more spontaneity. I want to dream again of another trip for Charlie and me in the future. This is my personal "Aha" moment. I suddenly feel enlightened with the feeling that I COULD do it again.

I recently read a quote that helped me see the truth. It is from Joan Baez, a contemporary singer and songwriter. She said, "You don't get to choose how you are going to die. Or when. You can only decide how you are going to live. Now!"

Making the decision with your partner to go cruising for an extended amount of time requires a major lifestyle change. As boaters, however, we consider our boating adventures priceless. For Charlie and me, our minds and bodies were freed from the clutter left behind. Our senses were filled and rewarded because we dared to dream. We dared to act and then we dared to "roll our windows completely down" to feel free. We felt the sun, the wind and the love of the water as never before. And oh, what a ride!

Women On Board Cruising

Linda Thomas lives in Okemos, Michigan with her husband of 38 years, Charlie. She graduated from Michigan State University with honors and a Bachelor of Arts degree in Interior Design. She worked for several years both as a commercial and residential designer until she became the mother of two daughters. After that, she worked as a director of a senior center where she loved creating recreational and educational activities for the elderly until she retired.

For her creative moments this past year, Linda enjoyed writing her online travelogue. The blog entries and this article for *Women On Board Cruising* were her first real attempts at writing. She looks forward to re-visiting her hobby of watercolor painting now that she is home for a while. She would like to use the photos she took to somehow document the many memories she made while on her trip. She and Charlie are looking forward to more long-range cruising in their future.

Pat Ehrman

Vessel: M/V *Sea Gator* – 38-foot Marine Trader Sundeck Trawler
Residence: Wyoming
Homeport: Fort Myers, Florida
Website: boathooked.com

The Question

It was a blustery March day on the Intracoastal Waterway (ICW). We cruised up the Manatee River and made *Sea Gator* fast in a "transient" slip at Bradenton's Twin Dolphin Marina, just hours in advance of the heavy winds and rough seas forecast. That afternoon I strolled the dock, content after indulging in shore-side luxuries. Lather, rinse, REPEAT! My clean hair whipped in the freshening breeze. I felt snug, secure and well groomed. Near the end of the pier, I encountered a pretty, dark-haired woman wearing a tenuous smile and a deer-in-the-headlights stare.

A lock of wet hair slapped my eye, and I brushed it away as we smiled at each other. "What a beautiful boat," I said, nodding at the pretty trawler behind her.

"Thanks," she breathed. "I don't know. We've never owned a boat before."

Aha! A kindred spirit! I myself was the brand-new co-owner of the trawler *Sea Gator*, our first big boat and a large step up from our previous vessel, a 16-foot un-christened canoe.

My new friend confessed, "I don't know what to expect." She explained that she and her husband had recently sold their home with the intention of living aboard, yet neither had any previous boating experience.

The spirit of sisterhood overcame me. "I didn't know what to expect either," I confided eagerly, "and we've only been aboard for a few months now. But one thing I found out is, I worry a lot."

Suddenly I exploded with babble, erupting like a can of warm Pepsi that's been rolling around on the deck all afternoon. "It's like a constant hum of low-level anxiety. I didn't know I was a worrier, are you a worrier? We have a cat on board. Her name is Goldie. I worry about her all the time and I mean ALL the time..."

"I worry about anchoring out when it's stormy. I worry about leaving the boat at anchor when we've dinghied to shore. And what if we drag anchor? What happens then? What if we plow into another boat in a marina? And what if one of us gets sick or if Goldie gets sick?"

"And what if, what if, what if? You see my trouble."

She did see my trouble. She paused for a long moment, eying me thoughtfully. Then she asked the million-dollar question:

"Is it worth it?"

A Dream, A Goal, A Plan

When 9/11 shattered our complacency, my husband Rick and I realized that postponing our dreams in favor of professional advancement was no longer tenable. We decided, with humble gratitude, that we would pursue our adventure NOW, and that we would simply take our work with us wherever we went.

We set a goal: we would try our luck on a boat before the decade was out.

Why a boat? Although Rick had grown up in New England and loved the water, he had never done much boating. He was intrigued. He longed to explore new horizons and a boat would provide housing, transportation and the challenges of new skills to master and new systems to tinker with, all in one big, happy, expensive package.

I knew nothing of the sea. I am an outdoorswoman of the Intermountain West, and I have every confidence in my ability to survive in the desert or mountain wilderness. As far as "open water" was concerned, I was happy enough with a good trout stream and a campsite beside a clear mountain lake. But I too felt the pull of adventure, and I sensed that I needed to push myself beyond my comfort zone.

May as well either go to sea or go to the moon, I thought. Both seemed equally remote to me.

Getting Ready

Space travel was quickly vetoed for many reasons, not the least being the lack of discrete toilet facilities aboard the space capsule.

The sea it is.

For several years, we discussed and studied, scrimped and saved. A sailboat seemed to require considerable skills, which we lacked, so we set our sights on a trawler. We read every back issue of *PassageMaker* Magazine; we bought and read *Chapman Piloting* and Don Wallace's *Seven Miles An Hour: Retiring on a Trawler with Cats*. We browsed boats on Yachtworld.com, and in his spare time Rick studied hull designs and living accommodations. At last, he set his sights on a "sundeck" model because, with two of us aboard full-time for the winter, we would appreciate the elbowroom.

Meanwhile, Rick, tech-guy extraordinaire, estimated that by 2005 wireless technology would be available, so we could transport our two self-owned businesses (his is a software company, mine is a landscape architecture design firm) to any place with access to wireless Internet and cell phone service. During our planning years, we opted for electronic transactions for our regular financial obligations, and we devoted ourselves to creating "paperless" work environments.

At home on the range, our house is remote and difficult for neighbors to monitor. So to protect the plumbing from freeze damage we equipped it with isolation valves and drains so we could empty all the pipes. Rick devised a clever system of electronic temperature sensors and webcams which would monitor the house and e-mail the results to him several times each day. If the temperature inside the house suddenly plummets, we will know something blew or broke open, and then we will contact a trusted neighbor to ski in to the place, wrestle sheets of plywood out of the shed, shoo curious coyotes from the living room and patch the broken window if needed.

Leaving Family and Friends Ashore

Our ducks were lining up. As departure neared, I realized I didn't mind the going, but I hated to leave.

Our families are scattered across the country from coast to coast. We would continue to communicate with them by phone and e-mail, so they did not anticipate missing us. Our friends' responses were a different story when, several months before our planned departure, I confided our intentions. Several friends were tearfully shocked and they cried, and then I cried, and then we all cried. Mopping unexpected tears I began to regret the whole idea.

However, it was too late to turn back – we had already arranged with the UPS Store to collect and forward the snail mail delivered to our storefront box, and you don't mess with the United States Postal Service. So that autumn we signed all the necessary papers, we packed and shipped way too much stuff, and we went to sea.

In one giant leap Rick, Goldie and I graduated from glacial lakes and a canoe to a 38-foot 135-HP diesel trawler plying the shallow waters off the southwest coast of Florida.

Learning the Ropes

So, there we were, on a real boat. What were we thinking!? Right away, we acknowledged that we had a lot to learn before we took our new-to-us boat even inches away from the dock.

We scheduled hands-on instruction with a licensed captain who we found through our broker (an Internet search for "on-board boater training" would also suffice). Captain Gary G. took us through three days of on-board training, teaching us the rudiments of diesel engines and electrical and plumbing systems (all review for Rick but new for me), navigation and communication, and how to pivot the boat within its own length (invaluable when backing into a slip).

The hands-on training proved to be both enormously valuable and highly entertaining. While backing in to a slip, Rick took advantage of the "rub rail" on the boat's sides. I used the rub rail on the way out. Between the two of us, we polished it up nicely. This brought home the fact that you steer the BACK of a boat. Unlike the steering wheel of a car, which rotates the front tires, turning a boat's wheel pivots the rudder at the stern, which is then hit with water from the prop, thus directing the stern to port or starboard. This no-brainer was cause for amazement.

At the end of the third day, we both sat for – and passed – the ABC, America's Boating Course exam (americasboatingcourse.com).

Hands-on training for landlubbers may sound like an obvious necessity, but while I was soliciting and comparing boat insurance coverage, an agent confided that, to his dismay, many new boat owners simply grab the keys and go. They set off from shore as though they are behind the wheel of a modest minivan, not a hundred-thousand-dollar battering ram. While marveling at this horror, Rick and I quickly agreed that we would be humble, ask as many questions as possible, and learn as much as we could. And keep a sharp lookout for the other guy.

Beware the Creeping Anxiety

So far, so good. Our first week as new boat owners was occupied with the on-board training, cleaning and repairing, and getting to know *Sea Gator*. We installed a holding tank and made other necessary modifications for living aboard. Rick conditioned the moving engine parts, and together he and his father buffed and waxed the fiberglass. I dusted, buffed and polished the cabin. And we shopped for and stowed non-perishable provisions, as recommended by Skipper Bob in the seminal *Cruising Comfortably On A Budget*.

Everything was going along swimmingly. Except for me, and I was sinking fast. To my surprise I objected endlessly to elements of the boat's décor, to storage problems, to the quality of DC lighting and the inconvenience of it all. I buzzed like a mosquito, annoying and relentless. Soon I was heartily sick of my own self, yet I felt powerless to stop. I was a train wreck in slow motion. How long could this go on?

Slowly I began to comprehend just how vast our change in lifestyle really was. I had never really experienced anything like the situation we were in. Despite all the planning and dreaming, I couldn't really know what it would be like until we were in it, and at that early time, I still didn't know. The symptoms of stress were emerging long before I realized how very far I had moved outside my comfort zone.

After lengthy reflection I came to realize that I was complaining about inconsequentials in an effort to exert some control of a situation over which I felt I had no control. I was in over my head both figuratively and literally, and because death by drowning is too fearsome to face, I diverted myself by obsessing over who tracked sand into the galley. We DO sweat the small stuff because sometimes the big stuff is unthinkable.

Since then I have witnessed the same subtle stress coming from others in many different situations, and I have learned to recognize little twitches in my own demeanor that indicate when I am on edge. Then the challenge is to face the situation and determine what, if anything, I can really do about it.

The biggest challenge I have had to face is evaluating the realities of fear.

Fear: The Unexpectedly Bad
We were mere days away from the dock with our new boat, and I was still trying to understand her systems and our new lifestyle, and at that point still wondering why I felt so out of sorts. *Sea Gator* was floating alone in the anchorage when, on the second day, the thunderstorm of the year tore across the peninsula. For the next three days lightning cracked, the wind screamed, the anchor line groaned, and I stared out the portlight wide-eyed and mute with terror, twitching each time we swung more than 20 degrees.

I had no idea it would be this scary. Was our line going to snap like a thread? Would our anchor drag along the bottom, would we fetch up against the rocks downwind in a wave-battered heap of unrecognizable fiberglass? I began to reconsider the whole sea vs. moon debate and to wonder how I might look in a space suit.

As a landlubber, I had devoured glossy cruising magazines and sailing calendars. They all featured balmy days, glassy waters and blue skies; evidently photographers find it inconvenient to photograph boats while buffeted in a storm. With no ocean experience I didn't stop to think that, obviously, the reality would be less balmy and perfect. I had not anticipated such ferocious weather, nor could I have known how it would feel to be marooned on a piece of flotsam attached to earth via a ridiculously thin line in a howling thunderstorm. I felt physically powerless, and it was terrifying. And no one we had met so far had mentioned similar experiences or fears. Was it because it was really no big deal to most cruisers? To me, it became the biggest hurdle to overcome.

Since that first storm, I have questioned other women boaters: "How do you deal with fear?" Those who take only day trips face it calmly because they will be safe ashore by nightfall. So I asked Michelle, who had followed her boyfriend aboard their first sailboat and immediately set out for South America. She admitted that eventually she "left the boat and never went back." Sue, on the other hand, snapped, "What's there to be afraid of?" Hmm, none of those responses were very helpful in my circumstances. Maybe there isn't a single magic bullet, but most cruising women have tried to find theirs.

Some women confidently defer to their husband as the more experienced sailor of the crew, and they are able to trust blindly that all will be well. That does not work for me because (A) Rick and I began as rookies together, and (B)

I have control issues, obviously. At the other extreme, one woman cruiser scorns passivity; she obtained her own master's license and assumes full responsibility for decisions made while she is at the helm. I tend to veer between these extremes depending on circumstances.

Responding to circumstances IS my magic bullet. I learned that I would have to consciously differentiate between "fear" and "discomfort." Fear is the anticipation of death, injury, or serious property damage, and it is not unreasonable since water and weather are powerful forces that deserve respect. Seen in a good light, fear becomes a tool with which to shape the next right action.

Discomfort includes anxiety, worry and the expectation of embarrassment. I admit that running aground, hitting a piling or dragging anchor must all fall somewhere in the confusion of discomfort. Seriously, is it more humiliating to drown or to be rescued? I am just asking. After I wrestle these variables into perspective I can proclaim aloud "OK, this is just really uncomfortable" or "This sucks and I want to go home before we're all killed." Then Rick and I can discuss the situation as it really is and for me an honest discussion lessens the dark loneliness that exacerbates fear.

The important fact that I sometimes forget is: we ARE still afloat. We DO have the power to choose our anchorages and our cruising days and our protection. Therefore, reason dictates that my worries are groundless. Logic is a negligible factor when I am overwrought, but it does help me in those dark moments to review our track record.

Back to our very first thunderstorm. At last, it wore itself out. In the ensuing peace we dinghied to shore in search of groceries and solid ground, and when we returned to the anchorage we found that another trawler floated serenely nearby. A friendly man waved from her bow, and we rowed across to meet our neighbors, who became the first of our dear new friends in our boating life. So, the week that began with fear and isolation ended with warmth and friendship... as it always does.

Picking our Weather and Running for Cover

Rick and I soon quantified our tolerance for lightning and wind and waves, and we established guidelines for handling the type of weather we would ride out.

As coastal cruisers, we do have choices about where we will go and when, and so we began to note our responses to various conditions. For example, we found that winds at 15 knots or greater made our daily cruise uncomfortable, and so we would stay put during those conditions if we could.

After that first big storm, whenever winter cold fronts approached we discussed our anchorage's protection and holding conditions. We decided together that if the winds are forecast at 20+ knots for any sustained period, and in the absence of excellent holding and faultless protection, we would set a course for the nearest marina and tie in for the storm.

We make the decision together. Although Rick has a higher tolerance for "excitement," he doesn't want to experience my anxiety any more than I do. Because the alternative is leaving the sea for good (in which case he will have to deal with "Honey, does this spacesuit make my butt look fat?"). He has been very understanding.

So, we ride out the occasional major front at a marina or mooring field where we keep very busy with work and boating chores such as fetching water, pumping out *Sea Gator's* holding tank, shopping for perishable provisions, and getting some exercise.

Safe anchorages, mooring fields and marinas all have tremendous potential for adventure and discovery. We began to anticipate the fun of exploring new towns and little islands, and we began to meet fellow boaters. That's when this new life aboard began to feel like "home."

Taking Nothing for Granted

Speaking of making decisions, and faced with so many unknowns in the early days, Rick and I realized that humility would be our saving grace. We would be unassuming, we assured each other; we would be sponges and absorb as much information and knowledge as possible. We would be cautious and never make assumptions.

So, we learned to obtain weather reports from multiple sources (NOAA weather via VHF radio and online at weather.gov and wunderground.com). We double-check each other's GPS points when plotting a route, and we consult guidebooks when entering a tricky passage. We decided to err on the side of caution and to just take it easy.

Because we know that best-laid plans sometimes go awry, we developed our very own "Anchor Policy": After setting the anchor, we stay aboard until tide or winds change at least once to be sure that our anchor is set. We have heard stories of folks returning to find that their boat has mysteriously gone missing downwind while they were ashore. We hope to avoid that possibility. Whenever either of us becomes anxious to go ashore too soon, the other intones with either smugness or regret: "That's not our policy."

Among all our new experiences, we have gladly learned everything we can about the fragile marine environment. We recognize that we are interlopers, and we try to practice reverence for the environment and its creatures. So, we store up our recyclables until we come to an enlightened town with a recycling program, and we don't dump our holding tank, galley scraps or trash overboard. It is the small stuff that adds up for either good or bad.

Asking Questions

Our on-board training was only the beginning. For many months I simply did the single next right thing and hoped for the best. Most important, over time I learned to practice humility by asking questions. I ask lots and lots of questions.

Curiosity is another trait Rick and I share, and we have found that asking good questions is a real pleasure. If someone is doing something that we don't understand, then we are all over it. Simple and sincere questions have opened doors wherever we go because – face it – nearly everyone enjoys talking about themselves and what they know.

My favorite all-purpose conversation starter is this: "Hi there, whatcha doing?" I recommend it to everyone. Occasionally I substitute the back-up query: "Excuse me, what's that?" Almost without fail, the questionee (if you will) happily shares his or her knowledge.

With time and experience, I have become less ignorant but still ready to learn and grow. I hope I maintain that desire because without it I would have a hard time getting up in the morning. Besides, complacency is dangerous, especially in a potentially hazardous environment. Finally, it is also quite boring.

During our time on the water – and ashore – we have encountered folks who appear impervious to either curiosity or humility. When subjected to a droning monologue by one of these I become frosty and bored. I would rather share time with someone who can laugh at themselves and talk about what went wrong or why it went right and what they learned from that experience. No person is perfect, but only the lucky ones admit it. These are the folks I admire and want to befriend. I adopt an insight from Billy Joel: "The sinners are much more fun."

Meeting New Friends

So, here we are on the water and learning stuff and still afloat and that's all great. But still, leaving my posse behind was a tremendous blow. I value my women friends' humor, wisdom, beauty and grace. And I was trapped in a 38-foot hull with a man! An excellent man, but still a man.

Since living aboard I realized that a good heart-to-heart, preferably with a "sinner" like myself, every week or so is critical to my well-being. An unforeseen benefit to being a transient is that I am forced to overcome my shyness in order to make new friends. Now I will talk to anyone about anything, anywhere, anytime. Please.

To Rick's great credit he enables my friendships. Sometimes he only waves goodbye as I dinghy away with my folding-bike crammed in the bottom of the Avon. Occasionally he ferries me to shore and amuses himself while he waits for my return. Even less often, he accompanies me on a social outing, and those are treasured events.

In search of fellowship, I have joined common-interest groups with chapters throughout the country. Other women cruisers find companionship through their religious affiliation. For pleasant and superficial feminine conversation a drop-in session at Curves, Pilates or yoga, Jazzercise or Zumba never fails. And there is always the reliable standby – the marina Laundromat.

One cannot overstate the importance of the marina Laundromat. It is truly the most common ground where all fine washables are created equal. When I'm not meeting new friends there I am learning great tips, such as Bounty's "Color Catcher," which allows you to combine colors and therefore run fewer loads. I will bet a woman cruiser invented it.

Rick and I have met new friends while dinghying past their boat; when sharing an anchorage; while walking on a deserted beach; and as transient members of a congregation. The only requirement is that all parties are open to a friendship with someone new. Experience has proved that it is worth the risk of making the first move.

Often new acquaintances lead to a visit aboard our boat or their boat. At these times, invariably, Rick and the other man leap into the engine room to compare pistons (or whatever it is they do down there). Left to our own devices we women often skip the small talk and get straight into the realities of our lives. "Tell me the story of your life and I'll tell you mine." I'm grateful for the companionship of every woman cruiser I have met.

Keeping in Touch

Still, severing all ties with our mountain friends is unthinkable. To reassure family and friends that we are still hull-side down we regularly update our website (boathooked.com) with news of our travels. I include activities, trivia, local history, people we meet, rants and raves, and lots of photos. That way folks can keep up to date with our travels if they so choose.

Consequently phone conversations with family and friends are more succinct: they already know what we are up to. What many people don't realize is that they still have to tell us what they are doing! "But we're not doing anything interesting," they moan. I say, "Just tell me what you had for breakfast – Wheaties? Granola? These are not hard questions, and I'll feel like I'm a part of your life."

One advantage to working full-time aboard is that we must always anchor within Internet and cell service areas. It somewhat restricts our choice of cruising grounds, but it ensures that we are able to keep in touch regularly via e-mail and phone calls and we don't feel as though we have dropped off the edge of the earth.

Keeping up Appearances

Speaking again of imperfection, one of the first questions I asked a boating woman was, "How do you keep your hair styled?"

She looked at me like I was nuts then said, "Well, I don't."

I was speechless.

However, it didn't take me long to decide that she was right. Being perfectly coiffed at sea is not a priority, and what a relief that turned out to be! Now I too am less concerned with superficialities such as my hair. I have learned to wear headbands as my haircut grows out, and to wear a hat at all times (hat-head is better than none). I have learned to wear sunscreen every day, which precludes precise eye and face makeup anyway. My nails grow better at sea level, but I keep them short. I have never met anyone who has an ironing board on their boat, so relaxed clothes are the norm. Adopting this practice has made life at sea a lot easier, and now I carry that easy attitude home with me too.

Finally, and most important: I have learned through bitter experience to never, ever get my eyebrows waxed in the state of Florida. Heed my words.

Taking Care of our Health

One year our worst fears were realized when I became ill as we were hunkered down in Russell Pass anchorage during a winter cold front. We debated the merits of weather, distance and time, and finally arrived at a doctor in the Keys seven days later. Had it been an emergency, we would have had to make very different plans.

The situation was an eye-opener. We are as cautious as it is possible to be, but no one ever sets out to get hurt. That's why they call them "accidents." We maintain our first aid kits.

Rick installed a water filter on our galley faucet so we can stay hydrated. The filter is valuable far beyond its cost when you consider the effort involved in ferrying bottled water to the boat and then recycling the containers. I refrigerate the water in a Britta pitcher so it is always ready.

The first few years aboard the boat brought an ominous shrinking of all my clothes, which later proved to be a gradual five, ten, 15-plus-pound weight gain. Holy cow! Even though we walked and rode our bikes when ashore, it simply wasn't enough – the confined space plus creeping hormones (and a new favorite: sweet potato fries) took their toll. We consulted a registered dietician and now we monitor our diets, seeking out fresh produce whenever possible. I have established a stretching and crunches routine, which is effective although tricky in the confines of the cabin with Goldie on my lap and Rick lurking nearby. Some women cruisers purchase a Curves membership, which many franchises honor. I search out Jazzercise or Zumba classes when ashore to enjoy the great workout and social benefits.

One ongoing surprise is how tired I feel sometimes. It seems the constant movement of the boat creates some fatigue, even when the weather is still and calm. This is especially true when we first come aboard after a period ashore. I have learned not to fight it and to accept that naps are a good thing. Now there is a benefit I had not foreseen!

Finally, on the topic of health and following that of sociability, I will mention booze. We do have alcohol aboard, and Rick serves it to guests, but it is treated as a beverage not a lifestyle. According to the U.S. Coast Guard, the effects of being on a boat, including continual motion and vibration, sun, and engine noise, all collaborate to increase impairment more so than when a person is on land. And if one falls overboard, he or she may experience increased disorientation resulting from inner ear disturbances.

While stone cold sober, I have managed to tumble down our swim platform ladder, down our saloon and stateroom stairs, and bash my head on the aft hatch (I thought it was open, it was not). Imagine if I had a buzz on! I have tried it both ways and my preference is to experience all of our new joys and terrors with a clear head.

Taking Care of Goldie

This is secretly my priority. Goldie is a tortoise-shell cat wearing white tights on her feet and belly. She is approximately ten years old at this writing and has the playfulness of a youngster combined with the circumspection of a mature girl. Everyone loves Goldie.

Much of my anxiety centers on Goldie's safety and happiness, so I strive to keep her secure. While we are underway, she snoozes in one of the PFD lockers at the upper helm station. There she is close enough to be under observation, but she benefits from privacy and a safe distance from the noise of the engine. She likes her cruising station and whenever the locker is open, she scrambles inside.

Cat safety rules are non-negotiable. When it is dark or windy or rough, Goldie must stay inside the cabin. She is permitted on deck only when we are all aboard and the weather is calm and the water is smooth. Some sailors teach their cats to swim to the stern of the boat by lowering them in the water and showing them the way, but *Sea Gator's* swim platform is above the reach of any swimming cat. So, Rick fastened some rigid boards to the platform and covered them with carpet for claws. I pray that Goldie will never have to use it.

Needless to say, I also worry while we are at a dock that Goldie will wander ashore and get lost. So, she wears a harness with her rabies tag and a tag bearing *Sea Gator's* name and my cell phone number. She is also "micro-chipped" (Goldie's vet uses Avid FriendChip at avidid.com) and at each checkup, I ask her vet to scan her to verify that the chip is still readable. Finally, I constructed a mesh screen which loosely blocks access to the side decks from the sundeck. Goldie could surely evade it if she chooses, so I believe she trusts it to keep other animals from coming aboard her boat. It makes her feel secure.

Goldie is the light of our little ship. Rick, proud holder of a Boy Scout Life Saving Merit Badge, has sworn an oath that if – heaven forbid – we go down he is to rescue Goldie before he rescues me.

Marital Bliss: The Unexpectedly Good

Who knew? Who knew that after nearly 20 years of marriage our lives on land would be so well organized that we could literally go for days with little more than "Hi, how are ya?" when we passed each other in the hall. When things got real dicey, we would add "Please remember to get bread when you go into town today." We gradually began to function independently.

Happily, our relationship is completely different aboard. Instead of getting on each other's nerves (much) in tight quarters, we communicate better aboard

Sea Gator. We have to because we agreed to make every decision as a team. That pretty much takes up the entire day.

For example, purely for safety's sake and even though I wear an ID bracelet, I won't just hop into the dinghy and motor away without conveying a detailed itinerary. And neither of us makes the sole decision on routes or anchorages, so all of our doings are discussed and resolved. The discussions have brought us closer together and more aware of one another's preferences and feelings.

We still disagree but our arguments are short-lived. The silent treatment has no place on board a boat. There is no dignity in marching away in a huff when three paces bring you to open water. And the stateroom is too narrow to work up any momentum in slamming a door – it just kind of taps shut, pufff-t, and then you have to hang around in there by yourself like an idiot. We get along more smoothly aboard because we have to.

I have re-discovered my life partner. Thank heavens Rick is still the good man I married, and he has even improved with age, as he has grown more patient. He is an interesting person with a good heart. Reviving our relationship and renewing our commitment to each other for the long haul has made the journey worthwhile. Even without the scenery and adventures, that would be reward enough.

The Answer

Amid the pencil-thin eyebrows, the fear and discomfort, the loving and squabbling, I often think of that dark-haired woman at the Twin Dolphin Marina with her brand-new trawler and her million-dollar question:

"Is it worth it?"

The answer I gave her then, in all my ignorance, is the same answer I would give her today: "Yes!"

I would assure her that, despite scary storms and goofy haircuts, there is tremendous personal satisfaction in learning each new cruising skill. That there is peace to be found in a secluded anchorage so silent you can hear dolphins exhale before you can see them, and that there is quiet joy in walking with my honey on a sandy beach. That even among a crowded anchorage there is the fun of weaving among boats in the dinghy to visit friends, and that the setting sun is beautiful when blazing through a bristling forest of masts. That there is nothing to compare with the pleasure of an afternoon nap with a cool breeze lifting the portlight curtains.

If you see her, tell her that I still get really scared and uncomfortable sometimes, no matter how hard I try to reason myself out of it. But that every time I push beyond what I think are my limits – however much I don't like doing it – I get stronger. And that the new confidence I have gained has helped me grow in my professional life and in my personal life at sea and at home.

I want her to know that I am still here – living on a boat. A BOAT! And that is just the coolest adventure there is.

Tell her, I'll see her on the water.

Pat Ehrman – Coming of age in the western deserts and mountains, Pat learned that she could go OUT there on her own two feet and get sand in her teeth and ice in her hair and still come back alive.

Pat was skiing in the Utah mountains when, on a perfectly beautiful day on a steep and powdery run, mutual friends introduced her to Rick, and the rest is history. They moved together to Jackson, Wyoming, where she became the first licensed woman landscape architect in the state. Her favorite mountain activities are working, hiking and biking with friends, drawing and gardening.

Rick brought her to New England to introduce her to his family and to romantic walks on the beach. But actually living ON the water has been a whole new kind of adventure.

"I didn't know what to expect. How could I? We didn't have tidal waters in the Great Basin."

Pleased and surprised that adapting physically to life on a moving boat has been fairly simple, she says, "The rest of my life is coming on line incrementally." Her shipboard duties include keeping her clients' projects up-to-date, cat wrangling, documenting the group's adventures on their website (boathooked.com), co-piloting *Sea Gator*, trip planning, navigation, and line and anchor handling.

Can a desert rat learn to love the sea? Yes, she can.

Carol Gordon

Vessel: M/V *Evelyn J.* – 47-foot Nordhavn Trawler
Residence/Homeport: Fairhope, Alabama

I am a list person. I will make a daily list of tasks to accomplish, list of phone calls to make and return, lists of items to complete in a long-term project, lists of things to purchase, list of life accomplishments to achieve, list of questions to ask the doctor, and so it goes, lots of lists. So, in typical fashion, I came new to boating with my lists in hand.

My husband Mike and I had planned our escape from life onshore for some time through the usual route. It began by Internet research, attending boat shows, participating in boating seminars, addressing retirement concerns, acquiring captain's licenses, flying to various ports to consider different vessels and finally ordering a new boat. We also had the usual conversation with family and friends about our planned boating adventure of completing America's Great Loop trip and beyond. Their reaction was in two typical categories – envy or lunacy (ours). All that, I now believe, is a normal experience for folks contemplating the boating lifestyle.

I also had my list of concerns, both minor and major, that are typical.

One of man's (and woman's) most basic needs is food. I was sure that acquiring fresh lettuce, other than the iceberg variety, would be difficult. Gone would be the opportunity to go to my local market and plunder the produce section for "whatever looked good" and bring it home to produce a fabulous masterpiece. Gone would be the chance for flipping through the cooking magazine, opening up a cookbook, turning on the food network channel and have something catch your eye. I worried that I would miss being able to run out and acquire the ingredients and produce that eye-catching dish. I would be relegated to marina store bounty, you know, what the early morning fishermen want; bologna, white bread, sardines, and peanut butter.

Our boat has an extra freezer aboard that I stocked with good bakery bread, quality cuts of beef, and premium ice cream. It was almost six months into our travels before I realized some, OK, I confess, it was really most, of my food loot was still in the freezer. Most fresh farmers' markets are within walking distance of marinas (the waterfront is where the locals want to be too), good grocery stores and local bakeries are actually plentiful and well stocked, your bicycle can take you to almost anything you need and cars miraculously become available when you need them for the big grocery hauls. So, take this concern off your list, it is no longer on mine.

I was also sure that I would not be able to exercise properly aboard and would subsequently blow up like a balloon, ultimately having to retire to a fat farm when I was so large I couldn't wedge my way down the walkways of our boat. I worried about not having the routine of exercise classes and my local walking trail, and I feared that this spelled a certain doom for my scales and me.

I envisioned doing laps around the boat while at anchor using my noodle; I looked into an adaptor for my bike to convert it into an exercise bike on the boat deck, and I stocked yoga and workout DVDs aboard. I actually did none of these things with the possible exception of laps around the boat on one occasion. I actually did not become a balloon. The movement between the various levels of our boat and walking around exploring each new locale kept us on the go. All this activity, in addition to biking (our new primary mode of land transportation) delivered plenty of healthy exercise while on the trip. So, I took this concern off my list.

I became concerned when friends said things like, "I just don't think I could spend that much time on the water. I would be bored!" Perhaps they were right. Exploring the world via water could become like one of our past vacations. We had chartered a large catamaran down in the islands complete with captain, chef, and lots of family. I distinctly remember declaring about day ten of our continuously ideal weather getaway, that if "I saw one mo,re beautiful island with a lovely harbor and crystal blue water I was going to puke."

So, I girded against this situation with lots of books (you know, the classics you promised yourself you would read), stashing golf clubs under the master berth, ordering *Edmund Scientific Star and Planet Locator* so I would finally learn the constellations, and purchasing a lovely watercolor kit and easel. Recently, I unloaded most of these items off the boat as they were just in the way.

You will not be bored. Every day is a new adventure, almost all of them very pleasant. You will marvel at your lack of time to read for pleasure, play sports, and learn a new hobby. You will be busy with the art of living aboard, learning and exploring the new territory that arrives at your boarding ladder every day. By the very nature of taking a prolonged trip or moving aboard a transient vessel, you have established that you are open to the possibilities that a new lifestyle offers and will take advantage of them. Please, take being bored off the list.

Leaving family and friends behind, not having your social safety net, not seeing a single familiar face when you walk into a restaurant, post office or grocery store didn't strike me as a good plan. Mike and I have lived our entire lives in the same state and between us only have about half a dozen cities and a dozen addresses we have called home. We love "our people." We have lots of them. Why would we leave our people behind? You don't really leave them. They are still there via your blogs, e-mails, phone calls and visits.

I was surprised that I didn't have the social isolation I feared in the beginning. Everyone talks about it, and it is true. Boaters are a community, in fact, an instant community that embraces all members with only the rare exception of a neighborhood grouch. There are lots of opportunities to meet and greet, break bread together, share a laugh, swap waterway information, exchange books and recipes, all the normal neighborly things you would do onshore. Often you "buddy boat" with someone you met along the way. Hopping and skipping in front or behind one another from port to harbor for months on end was a blast. We cherish the new "people" we gathered on our travels.

I also missed a number of concerns that I should have had on my list.

I hope this one is not so typical, but I totally underestimated the commissioning process of a new boat. Unlike building a house, building a boat is territory I was not familiar with and didn't have a lot of resources beyond the sales folks. Relying on the sales reps makes all purchases wonderful, easy to use, and essential to your health and well-being while boating. To become familiar with all these "essentials" took substantially longer than advertised and required a much steeper learning curve than anticipated. I recall many a day at the yard dealing with the commissioning staff making decisions throughout the vessel and as soon as they would leave, the evening crew of the electronics provisioner would come in for the next round. By the time our heads hit the pillow at the end of these long days, we were spent. It was an overload of new information.

Upon reflection, it was good for us. Discovering and absorbing new things is always healthy and is a life affirmation that will keep you sharp well into your days (actually on my list of "Life Rules"). I just didn't see this "learning moment" coming. My advice is to buy a used vessel, which requires smaller lists.

One other thing I didn't really "get" until we got out there was that there are two distinct ways to "live aboard," transient and stationary. We traveled with a few extended stops during our nine month trip and truly enjoyed it. In the process, we experienced new venues often with many festivals, markets, and historical and cultural events which were in lots of communities both large and small. However, we also decided to try having a "condo on the water" parked in a beautiful locale (winter in Key West) for several months. Having guests aboard was much easier due to the logistics. We went to the airport every week to drop off or pick up, and we really got to know the area and even established a routine. Both modes are desirable, so if you can, put both on your list.

I also did not anticipate that having all that fun traveling would require that you take some downtime from your fun. You need to have some time in your schedule to do nothing, go nowhere, and entertain no one. Not much, but some. Again, I just didn't anticipate being exhausted from having such a good time. It hit me one day when I was so grateful for a bad weather day that required cancellation of our plans. I spent the day relaxing, oblivious to the setting and not scrubbing or washing a thing. Put that on your list of concerns – downtime.

Troubleshooting, you know, identifying a problem, tracing it to its origin and solving it was also not on my list. This skill, which is taught and learned in numerous corporate classrooms, came in handy for me. On a boat, you listen. You listen for a change in an engine hum, new ticks, a thump on the hull, a drip you don't anticipate, a click that doesn't "sound right," or the screeching of a dreaded alarm. Then you use your problem-solving skills to figure it out. Most of the time it is simple, but sometimes it requires manuals, phone calls and even an outside expert.

But remember, usually, no one is going to die. Embrace the moment, breathe through the stress, enjoy the challenge and triumph in your solutions. Work as a team. Mike and I did what I consider an outstanding job of dividing and conquering. He took lead on the mechanical issues and I took the electronic. Everything else was random. A boat does take attention just like your house or car, so anticipate giving her time and attention, and don't forget to listen, resolve and celebrate your efforts.

Living aboard gave me a new list. It gave me more confidence, credentials, honed skills, stronger marriage, new friends, and fabulous memories. And as many before me have said, just get out there. There will always be a reason not to go, delay, postpone due to life getting in the way. Try to take whatever concerns you have off your list and just go.

Carol Gordon, college graduate, ordained minister, Sweet Potato Queen, graduate of Chapman's School of Seamanship Professional Mariners Training, holds a 50T Captain's License and retired at 47 from a commercial insurance career to escape to a water-centered lifestyle.

Carol Gordon – *Evelyn J*

She's been married a couple of decades to Mike, a policeman who retired in the same week. Carol has two sons and one grandchild with another on the way. After purchasing *Evelyn J*, she moved aboard and traveled full time for a little over a year. She currently lives on the water in Fairhope, Alabama and is trying to work on her golf game and sailing. Since selling *Evelyn J*. she is now looking for another boat.

Pam Harris

Vessel: S/V *Reunion* – 60-foot Sundeer
Current Vessel: 46-foot Zimmerman Down East Cruiser
Residence: Durham, North Carolina
Homeport: Morehead City, North Carolina

My college roommate told me that I was the least likely person she had ever met to sail around the world. I understand why she said that. I did not grow up around boats. I am not athletic. I became nauseated swinging on a swing set as a child. I have been sick in cars, planes, and even more so on any type of boat. I had never even owned a pair of boat shoes, not even cute ones. I love my roots and my ruts, but I also love the captain of my boat.

    Joe and I were high school sweethearts, dating from the ninth grade through most of the eleventh grade. He loved boats and had his own boat long before he was old enough to drive a car. We went our separate ways for years until we met again at our 20th high school reunion; hence the name of our boat, *Reunion*, that we took around the world in six and a half years. In the 23 years that we have been married, I have been part owner of seven boats, one lake boat, two Albemarle fishing boats, two sailboats and now two powerboats. When we were engaged, Joe suggested that we take sailing lessons because he'd had a nice sail on a friend's boat. I said, "Of course, dear." I had no idea this one simple statement would change my life.

    The decision to embark on a circumnavigation is not made lightly or in haste. Joe and I had sailed a Pacific Seacraft 37 for many years. We had traveled to the Chesapeake Bay, south on the Intracoastal Waterway to Key West, to Bimini and the Bahamas and back, taking three to four weeks for each trip. Our comfort level with sailing was about average. We were as competent sailors as anyone we knew, not world-class but competent. A window of opportunity in our lives began to open for more extended cruising – Joe's oldest son was taking more responsibility in the family business. All of our children were grown and on their own. My elderly parents were in fairly good health, and Joe and I were in good health. Gradually we began to think about a larger boat with more creature comforts and a longer trip. The magazines *Ocean Navigator* and *Cruising World* had been sacred texts at our house for years, so we had read about other sailors' trips. We avidly followed the circumnavigation of Tania Aebi, the first American woman and the youngest person to circumnavigate the globe alone when she made the journey in 1985.

We met Tania at a boat show and bought her first book *Maiden Voyage*. We decided that if she could make the trip alone, we could do it together. Tania's book was an important part of our aboard library. We sold the Pacific Seacraft and committed to build the Sundeer. For about a year and a half we didn't have a boat, but we were researching, planning and overseeing the building of *Reunion*. We began to stockpile spare parts, foul-weather gear, more spare parts, charts and cruising guides, more spare parts and finally really cute boat shoes. I told Joe that he had multiple spares for everything on the boat except me. When the UPS man brought the 75-pound storm anchor the reality of what we were going to do sunk in. I think it sunk in pretty well for the UPS man too.

Joe and I are old enough to have a traditional marriage with traditional roles. We carried those roles over to our boating lifestyle. He didn't cook, I didn't change the oil in the engine. We felt that we were each more efficient if we could work with the strengths that we already had. Our circumnavigation was spent aboard *Reunion*, a 60-foot Sundeer, designed by Steve and Linda Dashew to be sailed by a short-handed crew, typically a husband and wife, usually one stronger partner and one less strong partner.

Reunion had two staterooms, two heads, a spacious main saloon and a great galley with large refrigerator capacity and a spacious freezer. The refrigerator and freezer made it possible to stock up adequately for long passages. Having two heads is the greatest luxury possible and also the greatest necessity. Two heads made it easier to share the small space. We could each have some privacy – the greatest luxury of all on a boat. The layout included a "big" forward berth with a queen-size bed and an en suite head. The smaller guest berth was aft on the port side with the aft head on the starboard side. The galley, main saloon and navigation station were in between. Sleeping forward was great at anchor or in port, but too unsettled on a passage so when making ocean passages we only used the aft head and aft berth and the galley because any farther forward on the boat could be very uncomfortable. Since we shared half of the total space of the boat when we were at sea, we came up with some ideas to make that space easier to share. We both slept in the same almost double berth, but not at the same time. The other person's pillow had to be carefully set aside and not used. A pillow seems like a small issue, but when we were hot and sweaty and somewhat smelly, having our own fresh pillow became important. The aft cabin had one small shelf, half for each of us, which was enough space for a book or a water bottle.

Neatness is essential. We kept our personal things in a small basket; therefore we each had a small bit of the space that was ours and ours alone. The togetherness is intense on long passages; there is nowhere to go if you get mad or just need to be alone so each member of the crew really needs to respect the privacy of every other member of the crew. Because this is an extremely difficult situation, many crews that we knew parted ways by the time we arrived in New Zealand, about the halfway point around the world.

I thought it was important to take something from home to my life on the boat, something that would make the boat feel more like home. It is easier to feel comfortable on the boat if you feel at home on the boat. I took a set of china dishes in addition to the plastic dishes that most cruisers use. We used the plastic ones at sea, but eating on real dishes at anchor and in port felt like home. We took a few of the books that we loved, movies, and music CDs. One boat that we sailed with kept fine crystal wine glasses for use in port, carefully packing them away for each passage. I added some great decorative baskets from Tonga and molas, the fabric art of the Kuna Indians in Panama. *Reunion* became even more cozy and homelike as we traveled.

Moving aboard a boat to begin a long-term cruising lifestyle can be intimidating at best and really scary at worst, but there are some ways to mitigate those fears. Being able to communicate with those at home helped us feel that they were still part of our lives and we were part of theirs. Just being able to pick up a cell phone or send an e-mail makes the distances seem less.

The adjustment to the routine of life on board a boat happens quicker than one can imagine. For *Reunion* 48 hours was the magical time frame. I stopped thinking about land, about home or anything else not to do with the boat. Even seasickness ends after 48 hours. Routines for life aboard should be thought out ahead of time, but it is important to remain flexible.

We found that rallies made many of the intimidating passages less scary for us by being able to go with an organized group. Rallies rely on the expertise of many. We went with the Bermuda Rally and the Caribbean 1500 on our first two ocean passages. Most sailing magazines have ads for rallies with contact information. A rally is not a race, but is a group of boats all headed for the same destination at the same time. *Reunion* was the first boat to arrive back in port on the return leg of the Bermuda Rally, but who says a rally is not a race? Radio chats among the rally boats are scheduled twice a day. Weather conditions are updated by the rally organizers on a daily basis. Reservations at marinas are also handled by the rally organizers. Each crew only has to worry about the sail itself; all the details are taken care of.

Women On Board Cruising

There is comfort in numbers when traveling in a rally, and great parties at the completion of the passage. About 12 boats participated with us in the Bermuda Rally and close to 40 in the Caribbean 1500. The captains and crews come from many places and many lifestyles. At a pre-departure get-to-know-you party each captain introduced him or herself and told something about their land life, their jobs and interests. The two captains who got the biggest round of applause were the diesel mechanic and the gynecologist.

Many cruisers like to travel with other boats. Buddy boating can be a very helpful way to feel comfortable with cruising. However, there are some negative points to buddy boating as well. It is hard to find two boats that travel at the same speed, that have the same schedules and the same plans. We didn't travel with other boats after the initial rallies until we prepared to sail across the Gulf of Aden and up the Red Sea. The romantic images of pirates portrayed in the movie *Pirates of the Caribbean* is not the real view of today's pirates. Pirate attacks in the Indian Ocean have made headlines recently. At the time we would be crossing the North Indian Ocean and the Gulf of Aden the pirates were less sophisticated and less mobile, without the benefit of current day "mother ships." The sailing wisdom at the time suggested that cruisers stay at least 100 miles offshore because the pirates' vessels were limited to about 100-mile roundtrips from Yemen or Somalia due to the fuel reserves they could carry.

We knew that we could be vulnerable off those coasts and even more vulnerable when we were close to the mouth of the Red Sea because the sea-lane narrowed to a total of 50 miles, reachable from either coast. These realities helped us decide to make that passage in the company of two other boats so we could look out for each other. The boating community is a very friendly group of people. Traveling in groups is very helpful emotionally as well as having the benefit of extra hands with repairs or information.

I missed the company of other women but was able, from time to time, to find great companionship with women whom I could walk with and also share opportunities for conversation about things other than boats and boating issues. There is always something to be shared and learned with other boaters.

There are weather routers who will help determine the best times, weather wise, to make long passages, and we used a weather router for about a year until we were comfortable with our own ability to make good choices for weather safe passages. Weather routers are normally land-based and have access to much more information than a typical boater might have. We signed up for a year for a fee and the weather reports came by satellite e-mail. The router we used is no longer in business, but information about weather routing can be found on the Internet.

I think storms are every cruiser's worst fear. I am sure that everyone I have ever told that I sailed around the world has asked, "Did you have any bad weather?" Yes. If all the days at sea were beautiful and calm, then everyone would set sail and the accomplishment wouldn't be so special or challenging. We often said, "If it were easy, everyone would do it."

We were on the way from New Zealand to Fiji when a storm hit us. We were 500 miles from both New Zealand and Fiji in the middle of nowhere when we were hit by lightning. Joe was on watch when the strike hit at about 11:00 p.m. He saw only a blinding white light, and he rushed below to get me up. The biggest danger from a lightning strike is to receive a hole in the boat. We determined that the hull was intact and that we had no apparent damage. Then we saw that all of our electronics were fried. We had no instruments, no VHF radio and most importantly no autopilot.

Because of the direction of the storm and the winds present, we decided that it made more sense to continue to Fiji. For about 24 hours we were able to stay on course with the sails balanced. Finally, we knew that we couldn't sail to Fiji without changing course. We could sail, but not in the direction that we wanted to go. We could go to Fiji, but not with the sail plan that we had previously set in place. Then Joe said, "I've got it, I know how we can do this." Thank goodness! I had signed on with the right captain! He knew how to get us out of this fix! He said, "I want you to go below and put on all your foul-weather gear, including your boots, stand here at the helm and steer this boat for two hours." I thought what the heck kind of solution is that? But he was right; it was the solution. A sailboat left unattended will head up into the wind. When the direction of the wind changes, so will the heading of the boat. This heading into the wind is what makes an anchorage so pleasant; the boat is always facing the breeze. This same factor is why the boat must be steered, either by the autopilot or by a crew member. When the autopilot is engaged, a few tweaks from time to time are all that are needed. With no autopilot the only way to keep the boat on course is to hand steer.

For 500 miles and three and a half days we steered the course, two hours on and two hours off 24 hours a day. We knew where we were and we knew where we were going, and we knew the compass course to get us there. You cannot do anything else while you hand steer a compass course. If you stop to look around, you'll get off course. You can't go to the bathroom, get anything to eat or let your attention wander.

On the last morning of this passage I could see a small smudge on the horizon that I knew to be land. We still had use of the single sideband radio and had been in touch with a few other boats. One of those boats was able to reach friends on a boat called *Wind Runner* who were already in Suva Harbor and were looking out for our arrival. We got close enough to contact *Wind Runner* using the VHF we had in our abandon-ship bag. We came into the harbor after dark to the spotlight held by our friends. They continued to talk us in to a spot where we could anchor, giving us the water depths and lots of encouragement. We dropped anchor that night with such gratitude and relief. I had never been so tired in my life and I had never been so proud of an accomplishment in my life. I was halfway around the world, and I was a real sailor at last. I had done what needed to be done. I had endured and triumphed. I had such a sense of self-awareness that I think can only be gained when weakness is overcome and challenges are met. I was stretched way beyond my old comfort zone, and the result was a slightly enlarged comfort zone.

Many boating magazine articles have been written on the watch schedule. We had read many of them again and again but had not come up with what we thought would work for us. On our first night at sea on the Bermuda Rally Joe said, "If you can stay awake until 2:00 a.m. I'll take the rest of the night's watch." That seemed like a good idea except that I was seasick and could do nothing but take Phenergan and go to bed. He woke me at 3:00 a.m. saying that he'd done all he could do. By that time I felt better and so took the watch.

After lots of reading and even more discussion, our regular watch schedule came about by accident and it served us well for the next six and a half years. Joe stood watch from 9:00 p.m. to 3:00 a.m. and I stood watch from 3:00 a.m. to 9:00 a.m. One of the reasons that this schedule worked so well for us was that only half of my watch was in total darkness. By 6:00 in the morning the sky begins to lighten, then the sun comes up and being on watch in daylight is not a bad deal. At 9:00 a.m. Joe would get up, we'd have breakfast, and then I'd have a nap. Later in the day we had lunch and then Joe would have a nap. We had dinner together and then began the process again.

We had our cat, Snappy, on board with us, and she very quickly understood that when Joe got up, meal preparation happened. If he ever overslept, she would get up on the berth and bite his toes to let him know that it was time to get going. Six hours is a long time to be on watch, but it is not such a long time to be off watch getting rested. Rest is crucial and hard to come by on a short-handed boat but so essential, especially for the stronger member of the crew. Since emergencies are always lurking around every corner, it is important to be alert and well rested. We had no formal watch schedule in place during the day.

Deciding whether or not to take a weapon was part of our planning. We knew we would be in areas that might not be safe. The bad guys have bigger and better firepower than most cruisers, so bringing out a weapon will usually make a dangerous situation worse. Also, when you check into a foreign country you must declare a weapon if you have one. Customs will then confiscate that weapon for the duration of your stay in their country. Therefore, a weapon would do you little good while in foreign countries during most of your trip.

To retrieve the weapon when you leave you have to return to the port of entry, often an upwind sail that backtracks all the progress that has been made. If the weapon is not declared and the boat is searched, customs can take your boat as well as your weapon. We didn't travel with a weapon.

More time is spent thinking about food, acquiring food and preparing food than almost any other topic aboard a boat. Again, many articles have been written on this subject. I don't think I read enough of them. I forgot that people all around the world eat. They might not all eat what I'd like to eat, but food can be found everywhere. Somehow I thought I had to put six years worth of EVERYTHING on board.

Fishing is easy. We had lots of fresh tuna, dolphin (the fish, not Flipper). We had a large freezer which made saving individual portions easy. The open-air markets could make your mouth water, and you could bring home all you could carry for a minimal amount of money. Sometimes haggling over price was expected, but the produce was so fresh, so plentiful and so cheap and the sellers so poor that paying what the vendors asked was fine with me.

I did have to get accustomed to the challenge of this kind of shopping. I was overwhelmed at the first market we went to. The sellers spoke a foreign language and the currency was a mystery as well. I think once I came back to the boat with just a cucumber. I got much better at shopping as we traveled. By the time we got to Dominica I could easily pick out the best produce and knew what would last longer and what we had to eat first. Being a creative cook on a boat and using the local fare can be a bit of a task. In the Galapagos Islands we were given an entire stalk of bananas. I like bananas, but the entire stalk tends to ripen at once. By the way, a stalk of bananas is a LOT of bananas. We had banana muffins, banana pancakes, banana bread, banana sandwiches, but the most creative use of those bananas was mashing the last few into a pulp and freezing them. When rum was added we had a nice, if unconventional, banana daiquiri.

For most food preparations simple is better. One-pot meals let the cook spend the least amount of time and energy putting a meal together. When you are preparing dinner while standing on a heeled-over sailboat, simple one-pot meals become increasingly meaningful. I also tried to prepare two days worth of meals before leaving port on a passage. Back to that magical 48-hour period of adjustment. Spending too much time below during those first 48 hours might be doable, but I was happy to pull out a casserole and heat it up rather than spend time below. We had two essential foods on board *Reunion*, peanut butter and hard-boiled eggs. Both have good protein, both are easy on the tummy, and both can be eaten without fanfare.

If there were a special food that the crew enjoyed, I would take lots of it and not depend on finding it worldwide. One boat we sailed with had a passion for one particular brand of orange juice, so it was always available. Having familiar foods or other provisions goes a long way to making the boat feel like home and therefore raising the comfort level. We were in a supermarket in Singapore and I turned the corner into the paper goods aisle and saw Bounty paper towels. I literally got tears in my eyes. Home is only a paper towel away.

Nothing says home to me more than a cat. Home is where the cat is, especially on our boat. I can't imagine life without a cat. The only thing better than a cat is lots of cats. As I mentioned earlier, we sailed with a beautiful tricolor named Snappy. She gave new meaning to the term "companion animal." Snappy took night watches with us, snuggled up close and made the night a friendly place. To take an animal on a circumnavigation we had to jump through hoop after hoop, but we decided in the beginning that we would do what it took to take Snappy with us. She spent a month in quarantine in both New Zealand and Australia.

There are pet relocator services that do all the paperwork, which is extensive. They will pick up the pet and make the plane reservations. This service is a good idea because there are so many regulations about transporting animals. Their business is to take good care of the animals, and we found that they did a great job. I am not sure how Snappy would describe the service, but she always arrived back to us on time and in good health. Her quarantine time was spent in good, clean, healthy facilities. We were able to visit her at any time in New Zealand and on Tuesdays in Australia. In both countries we used those 30 days to travel internally. We saw parts of each country that we could not have if we didn't have the "babysitter."

A microchip is a must for globetrotting pets since the rabies vaccine can be tied to the microchip number and therefore to the specific animal. Rabies doesn't exist across the Pacific, and they don't want it to take hold. Snappy flew across the Pacific Ocean and the Atlantic Ocean several times. We no longer have Snappy or the sailboat, but we now have four cats who share travels on our Zimmerman 46. They are not as enthusiastic about boating as Snappy was, but we tell them that if she could do it, they can too.

Each year, on the 1st of December, our circumnavigation trip came to a halt. My one need and request when we were planning this trip and I was deciding whether or not I could make such a commitment was that I be home for the month of December for Christmas. I had elderly parents and young grandchildren and needed to be home to be with them.

In November we began looking at our cruising schedule and would find a good place and time to leave the boat that would include easy access to an airport. Leaving the boat for a month was always a concern, but we never had a serious problem. Being able to be home for Christmas made the trip easier for me. I also went home at least one other time during the year on a "whenever it works" schedule, but we never announced it ahead of time.

We met many people while traveling around the world for whom circumnavigation is a way of life. For us the trip was a journey with a beginning and an end. Every external journey is also an internal exploration. You cannot sail around the world meeting different people and experiencing foreign cultures and return the same person you were when you left. We learned that the United States is not necessarily the center of the world. We received a world news bulletin daily by way of satellite. Most days the two-page report contained nothing about the U.S.

Pam Harris – *Reunion*

We met people who were passionate to learn about us and about our country. We also met people who had an extremely adverse opinion about the U.S. We felt compelled to put a real personal and positive face on Americans. Many people in the more remote parts of the world wouldn't meet another American in their lifetime. Being a good representative of our country was important to us.

We weren't day sailors before we made the circumnavigation, and it didn't make sense to us to try to be day sailors when we got back. A boat can be a maintenance overload when you are living on it, but a real maintenance nightmare when you are not, so we thought the only sensible thing to do was to sell *Reunion*. When the yacht broker from Fort Lauderdale came to sail her away, we watched from the dock as she sailed without us for the first time. We watched from the bridge as she got smaller and smaller. I was the one in tears; they surprised me. I thought I'd only feel relief that I had no more night watches, no more meal preparation in a slanted galley. I realized that I was at the end of a journey, the end of a lifestyle, the end of a period of great personal growth.

I still miss a quiet anchorage, the serenity of a night passage, sunsets, (NOT sunrises), time alone with Joe, time alone with my thoughts. I miss many of the friends we sailed with – not all of them. We still see many of them and communicate with more. I am grateful for the time "out there," for those I met, for all I learned, for how much stronger I became. In the beginning I set sail reluctantly, but in the end I returned an enthusiast. It was a life-changing and life-enhancing period in my life.

Pam Harris grew up in Charlotte, North Carolina. She attended Agnes Scott College in Decatur, Georgia and graduated from the University of North Carolina with a degree in English literature. She has taught 12th grade English and English as a Second Language. She worked in banking before retiring to set sail.

Pam moved to Durham, North Carolina in 1985, married her long lost love, Joe Harris, in 1986. She and Joe sill live in Durham with four reluctant feline crew members – Millie, Buddy, Max and Lizzie. They have a blended family of eight children and 15 grandchildren who range in age from newborn to 16.

Pam now enjoys life aboard the Zimmerman 46, being at the beach, and when living on land, vegetable and flower gardening.

Liz Stagg

Vessel: M/V *Second Wind* – 34-foot PDQ Catamaran
Residence: Huntsville, Alabama
Homeport: Joe Wheeler State Park, Rogersville, Alabama
Blog: secondwind-greatloop.blogspot.com

I was a hard sell. When husband, Bob, first uttered the words, "What would you think about spending a year cruising on our own boat?" my response was swift and certain, "Not gonna happen!" Being cooped up on a boat for 12 months sounded like a miserable experience. "Besides, I don't know enough." Then he received the Christmas gift that opened my mind and my world. It was a copy of *Honey Let's Get a Boat...* by Ron and Eva Stob. Every night in bed, Bob read and hooted; he laughed so hard he would start to choke. Not wanting to miss a good read, I picked up the book myself. That's exactly how our Great Loop adventure started. I hope it never has to end.

During our preparation stage, we0 joined the all-important America's Great Loop Cruisers' Association (AGLCA). We poured over every word and link on their website. I especially enjoyed meeting the "Loopers," as they are called. What a friendly, fun-loving group! We read many of the Loopers' blogs or websites, soaked up cruising articles, visited boat dealers, attended Trawler Fests and several AGLCA Rendezvous. In doing so, my mind opened wider, and my confidence grew. A major turning point was the moment I realized that long-distance cruisers were just regular, friendly people, not boating jocks who spent every minute discussing the intricacies of inverters and the pitch of props. Veteran Loopers regaled us with tales of adventure and the bonus of newly forged but lasting friendships. Their energy and excitement were contagious. I could do this! I would!

Bob and I eventually figured out our "must-have" features in a boat. Being something of a klutz, I needed to feel secure while moving around the boat and handling lines. I wanted wide side decks with good handholds all the way around so the boat would be easily accessible for getting on and off the docks, and a flybridge ladder with sloped rather than vertical steps. Bob wanted diesel engines with a capacity for greater-than-typical-trawler speed, shallow draft, efficient fuel consumption, and good visibility from both upper and lower helm stations. We both wanted an attractive, open saloon with enough seating space to entertain several people for cocktails and dinner, as well as comfortable cabins for both our guests and ourselves.

The perfect Looper boat for us turned out to be a 34-foot PDQ Power Catamaran. Although the boat looked a bit unconventional, it was nearly new and had all the features we wanted. Bob, the engineer, could tell you many technical details that he was excited about, but I loved the ease with which I could move around and the openness of the interior. We are both tall, but neither of us felt cramped in any area of the boat. Our Loop now completed, I'm still happy that we chose *Second Wind* as our home on the water for a year. She has served us well.

Starting the Journey and Conquering Fears
Though excited about the adventure ahead, I still had white knuckles as we cast off lines from the sanctuary of Joe Wheeler State Park, near Rogersville, Alabama. I wasn't a bit concerned about Bob's skills as captain, but did I know enough to do this trip? The first test would be transiting a whole series of locks as we made our way south to the Gulf of Mexico. We would get there by going south on the Tennessee River and Tennessee-Tombigbee Waterway. The locks along the route are major structures designed to handle huge commercial tows, and the prospects of negotiating so many locks along with the tows seemed daunting. How easy it was to imagine missing the bollard and banging into lock walls – or worse – other boats. Even though Bob and I had passed through a few of these locks before, I was pretty sure that luck, not my line-handling skills, had gotten us through without mishap.

Bob deserves the credit for changing my attitude toward locks. First, he bought a set of fairly inexpensive hands-free headsets by Cruising Solutions so we could communicate in calm tones instead of yelling. Second, he fabricated a "bollard grabber," a piece of line with a big semi-rigid plastic loop, which made it easier for me to capture the bollard. Third, Bob had mastered the skill of going s-l-o-w-l-y and c-l-o-s-e-l-y to the lock wall. By the third lock, something clicked. I was no longer intimidated. Working together, we would be just fine. And we were!

I confess to having had some concern about boredom, especially thoughts of cruising long days in unpleasant weather. How would it feel to be cold and wet as we slogged along? Would we become bored and irritable? That test came quickly as we cruised down the Tennessee-Tombigbee Waterway. Many refer to this section of the Loop as "The Ditch," and it was surely one of the coolest, wettest October days we could remember. Steady rain, brisk wind, and 55-degree temperatures plagued us as we covered 56 miles on one particular day. We encountered several big towboats on narrow passes, and we locked through three more dams in cold, drizzling rain. In addition to all that, our electronic chart plotter developed a glitch.

We were chilly and our jeans were damp, but boredom simply wasn't possible while we watched intently for tows, concentrated on charts, spotted markers, caught the bollards in locks, studied guidebooks – and planned dinner with fellow Loopers. I distinctly remember smiling in anticipation of the chili dinner we would be sharing that evening with our new Looper friends Paul and Jane. After dinner, planning our next day's destination proved to be a new source of entertainment.

So by the end of this particular day of miserable weather, we had learned that boredom was impossible. In fact, I was filled with an amazing sense of well-being. We were seeing new sights, learning how we would share responsibilities, and gaining confidence with each challenge conquered. But especially – most especially – we were embracing the easy camaraderie of fellow Loopers. I thought of the number of times we had crossed bridges in our car, looking down at cruising boats on cold, rainy days like this and wondered, "What are they doing on the water on a day like this?" This day gave me the answer to that question: They were quite possibly having the time of their lives. No, boredom was not likely to be a problem on this adventure.

As with many prospective long-distance cruisers, my third concern was that of homesickness. Heading out on a several-week vacation was one thing, but being gone for a year without seeing those much-loved faces from home was another. In our early discussions about doing the Great Loop, Bob agreed that if I ever got seriously homesick – no matter where we were – we would drive or fly home for "a little visit." Simply having that option made all the difference. We did arrange three trips home during our Loop journey, and each one was wonderful.

The thing that surprised me though, was that as soon as I became satisfied that everyone was fine, that we had not been forgotten, and that our house was still standing, our thoughts turned back to our new life on the water. Every night our dreams were boat-centered, and we realized that we were actually experiencing adventure withdrawal. We still loved our home folks, but the call of the water and our new Looper friends were magnets pulling us back to where we had left the boat. I had become addicted to the cruising life. With the fun of meeting new friends, ready access to cell phones and e-mail, plus the happy prospect that friends and family would join us for stretches of the trip, homesickness was simply never a problem. Another fear was dispelled.

After we finished the first 450-mile leg of our journey, I asked Bob to rate his experience so far. I prefaced the question with my own score, a solid "ten."

To my astonishment, Bob said "seven."

What was going on here? I had been the reluctant one; Bob had been gung-ho to do the trip from the beginning. I was shocked and felt a bit guilty when he explained why his rating wasn't stellar. I will never forget his words, "I've been so concerned that you wouldn't enjoy the trip that I haven't been able to relax and enjoy it. I want you to be happy." I assured him that I was fully engaged and having the time of my life, so he could put that concern to rest. We were a team of equals. Following the dream that had begun as Bob's was now mine too, and I was in it for the long haul. I wanted to make him experience "ten" too.

Most people prepare for quite a while before casting off their lines for a long cruise. We planned for more than a year. Now having completed this marvelous journey, I would like to offer a few observations and lessons learned that would have been nice to know before we started.

Fly the Burgee
The close, familial nature of the cruising community is legendary. We quickly learned the importance of flying the AGLCA burgee. At home when we pass cars on the highway or pull into a parking lot, it is hard to imagine a single bumper sticker or car tag that causes perfect strangers to feel free to approach us and offer a sincere invitation of friendship. Yet I can't count the number of times we heard a knock on our boat, followed by a friendly greeting. "Hi, we are Loopers too. Why don't you join us for happy hour?" Cocktails usually would lead to dinner, and plans soon followed to travel the next leg of the journey together. After a few days, we had shared life stories, and a new friendship was formed. Today when we pull into a marina, we always scan the boats at dock for that distinctive burgee, and we are thrilled when we spot one. Of course, we knock on their boats, and say, "Hi, we are Loopers too!"

The cruising group is large and diverse, but a bond is implicit, and the code of reaching out to others is followed. Loopers catch each other's lines when they prepare to dock, and they help each other out when there is engine trouble. They love the water, and they thrive on adventure. They laugh a lot and quickly feel like members of your family. You can depend on them. It doesn't matter what your career path was before your journey began or the size of your boat, the cruising community is generally open, accepting, and caring. Flying the burgee was the key to the greatest reward of our Loop trip: the friendships we made.

Mother Nature Is in Charge
Veteran cruisers know that you can't follow a schedule when you are boating. Mother Nature doesn't give a whit about airline schedules or carefully laid plans to meet your daughter or son, your cousin, or your best friend. After several stressful battles between storms and best-laid plans, we finally learned how to work with Mother Nature: just give in and relish the delay. We experienced more

long bouts of lusty 40 to 60 mph winds than we could have ever imagined. We were "weathered in" for days at a time in some of the least-likely places: Welaka, Florida; Belhaven, North Carolina; and Deltaville, Virginia. Honestly, many of our most memorable times came as a result. With Mother Nature in charge, we intimately got to know places we would otherwise have stopped at only for the night, and we had an opportunity to really get to know the other weathered-in boaters experiencing the same delay due to weather.

Even now, we discover fine, black grit in boat crevices from the topsoil that blew from North Carolina farms while we hunkered down for four days in the small town of Belhaven. Without such a delay, I don't believe we would ever have seen the unique Belhaven Memorial Museum, which featured two fleas dressed in wedding attire (to be viewed with a magnifying glass, of course), a preserved eight-footed pig, a door wreath made of human hair, plus a large, eclectic assortment of dusty clothing, oddities, and artifacts. It was like exploring the attic of an eccentric grandmother. Just another memorable exploration in paradise, providing many chuckles over dinner! Our five weather days in Deltaville yielded even more satisfaction. While we endured day after day of super-strong winds, we also enjoyed parties, dinners, laughter, and excursions. The bottom line is that Bob and I came away with a group of lifelong friends and boating companions. Mother Nature knows best after all.

When the weather experts agree that bad weather is inevitable, we learned the necessity of deliberately cutting short a stay in one good place to move to a better hidey-hole. Once as we made our way down the east coast of Lake Michigan, we heard that yet another big front was coming through, and it was going to be a doozey. Michigan has numerous noteworthy stops, each one highly recommended. Even though we wanted to stop at each of them, our friend Paul suggested that we make a short run to the next harbor, Petoskey, Michigan, and hunker down there. As opposed to staying in a smaller town, Paul realized that Petoskey was large and diverse enough to keep us thoroughly entertained for several days straight. He was right. After Bob added chafe guards and rubber snubbers to our storm configuration of lines and fenders, we spent a delightful five days visiting with other Loopers and exploring this remarkable town as 50 mph winds blasted us day after day.

Bring Food to Share
We laugh about eating our way around the Loop, but if you have read the blogs of long-distance cruisers, you have doubtless noted that food is a central theme. One of the first lessons I learned was the importance of having a stock of ingredients and recipes on hand for regular impromptu "pitch-ins" or "covered-dish" events. You can count on some kind of shared food gathering every time a few cruising boats find one another in the same spot. Sometimes a picnic table at a marina is designated, or one boat invites everyone aboard. Regardless of the party spot, you will want to bring food to share. There are no requirements that

your offering be fancy, just tasty. It may be a dip or a casserole, a dessert, deviled eggs, or simply good cheese and crackers. Fortunately, locating grocery stores is rarely a problem. Coming up with a variety of food ideas and simple recipes is one of the best preparations you can make before you cast off your lines. If you can come up with a special signature dish, your fame will precede you.

Lines and Fenders
While most women take shifts driving the boat, it is typically the male as captain who does the docking, while the female first mate (aka "the admiral") handles lines and fenders. I can think of a dozen exceptions, but women handling lines is the norm. For some reason, my dear rational, usually generous husband believed that we had "more lines and fenders than we could possibly use" as we started our trip. Easy for him to say; I was the one scrambling at the last minute to adapt to the unique conditions of each stop. He simply couldn't relate to the frustration of having set up the starboard side of the boat only to hear, "The harbormaster now wants us on the port side" with a matter of only seconds to make it happen. This became our one point of contention. Considering the thousands of dollars we'd invested in electronics and other tools, what was a few hundred dollars more? I nagged, and Bob resisted. I fussed, and he still couldn't see the need. I'm not sure which argument finally got to him, but I am happy to say that by the time we were halfway around the Loop, the man finally came to his senses. It really is the little things that make you happy.

Here is what I learned:

What Worked on Your Last Boat May not Work on the Current One
The diameter, length, and number of lines and fenders you need are determined by the design of your boat. Whoever does the line-handling job is in the best position to know what tools are needed. The configuration you need for a floating dock may be entirely different from a slip defined by pilings. Sometimes in a tight lock chamber, other boats may need to raft to the other side of your boat without much notice. To protect your boat from vicious docks and pilings or the railings of other boats, you need a full complement of lines and fenders for each side. They need to be easy to identify and convenient to grab. In a few conditions when there is no margin for error, you will want to set up both sides just to be prepared. If you are the primary line handler, don't let the captain shortchange you in the lines and fenders department. Life is more harmonious when each of you has the tools to do your job.

Bring the Clothes You Like
Almost everyone started out with too many clothes, and many of them weren't the right kinds of clothes. If you have been mostly weekend boaters before, you may be used to throwing in a few T-shirts and some old shorts, then heading out for a

fun time on the water. One of the soundest pieces of advice my dear friend Jane gave me was, "Don't pack your slummy 'boat clothes.' Pack the things you enjoy wearing at home." It was true. The very same items I rarely wore at home (color not quite right, size a little off, a bit dated, etc.) soon got shoved to the back of the locker and were finally mailed back home to be given to charity.

The most versatile clothes for me were Capri-length slacks and tops with three-quarter-length sleeves. Because we moved with the seasons, the average temperature was probably somewhere in the 70s. Of course, a sweater or fleece jacket and long pants felt mighty good on cool mornings in Florida, and there were several days in Canada where shorts and sleeveless shirts were definitely in order. It was also good to have one or two "nicer" outfits saved for special occasions. The good news is that getaways with the girls for "retail therapy" is fun and allows you to fill in any wardrobe gaps while you are traveling.

Don't Fret About Getting a Decent Haircut

It was not the availability of grocery stores or finding quality medical care that concerned me most before we started our trip. Cruising veterans had assured us that these two essentials would not be a problem. It was the challenge of getting good haircuts that made me apprehensive. A fashion maven I am not, but memories of butchered haircuts on earlier vacations had me worried. Several women confirmed that I was not alone in this concern. How would we be able to locate decent hair salons from the water? How would we get to them? Would the hairdresser understand the intricacies of dealing with my naturally curly short hair? Most important, could he or she match my existing color?

Before we left, my home hairdresser wrote down the color formula she used on my hair. She suggested looking for hair salons that carried my particular brand of hair product. Although that sounded like a great idea, the hair salons convenient to the marina didn't necessarily carry the line I was looking for, but they did have comparable products and could use the formula as a guide. The best bet was to look for shopkeepers, restaurant hostesses, marina employees, or other local women with nice hairstyles for recommendations. Some of the best (and the worst haircuts) I've ever had in my life occurred while we were cruising the Loop. The good news is that we were having so much fun that having the ideal haircut and color on board didn't matter nearly as much as I thought it would.

Traveling with the Pack, with Guests, or Solo

Because of the seasonal nature of boating, we traveled with other Loopers at least half the time, possibly more. Sometimes we cruised with only one buddy boat; at other times several boaters banded together to travel the same itinerary at the same general speed in a flotilla of sorts.

Each boat has a preferred cruising speed, so the slower buddy boats often left earlier in the day than we did or arrived later in the afternoon. Even if we weren't always in touch visually, we stayed in contact via the radio. These boaters became our family as we bantered on the radio about weather conditions, marveled at the scenery, planned the next day's adventure, laughed a lot, and told tales. It was especially comforting to have the security of a buddy boat if a problem cropped up. We discovered that it was rare, however, to travel with the exact same group for the entire journey. As each boat veered off in different directions to follow individual itineraries and schedules, we often bade fond farewells to our friends, knowing – and sincerely hoping – that our wakes would cross again. Traveling with like-minded boaters offers a special brand of joy.

At other times, we were fortunate to have family members and close friends join us for significant legs of the journey: the Everglades and the Florida Keys, the leg from Savannah to Charleston, Chesapeake Bay, and the Rideau Canal. These were people who have been and still are a vital part of our lives, so it was a joy to add this exciting chapter to our history together. Having cautioned them to bring aboard a minimum amount of "stuff," they shared our excitement as we rounded bends, searched for markers, watched for pesky crab pots, spotted wildlife, and snapped thousands of shots of picturesque countryside. While it is hard to explain to non-boaters why the cruising lifestyle can be addictive, our guests "get it." They fully understand the challenges and joys of cruising because they experienced it day-to-day with us. We still relive incredible moments with them, such as the late afternoon when we sat with our family members in our dinghy, watching with bated breaths as two dolphins corralled a large school of fish against the shore, dark water churning into a melee under the mangrove swamp. We were so close to the action that we could hear the dolphins breathe! As we made our way back to *Second Wind*, laying at anchor, a splendid sunset appeared. To this day, I can mentally jump back to that moment: the still, coffee-colored water, the musky salty/fishy smell, and the awe I felt as we shared the mysterious Everglades with our dear family members.

Bob and I also traveled solo for long stretches, especially in sections of Florida. During the winter, it seems that Loopers are widely scattered along the Sunshine State's 2,276 statute miles of tidal shoreline. Yet, during these stretches, even in remote areas, we never once felt lonely or fearful. In fact, we enjoyed the closeness provided by our insular water world, and we relished the life of carefree adventurers. A nine-day side-trip down the St. Johns River became one of many favorite passages. The names of places along the 285-mile river were exotic: Palatka, Welaka, Hontoon Island. Because we traveled many of these miles during the cool days of late February, most fisherman and recreational boaters were still at home. The river was ours.

The lower portion of the St. Johns River is narrow and twisty. The water is dark with tannin, and the shores are edged with water hyacinths against a backdrop of cypress trees, pines, and palms. Anchoring in remote coves, Bob and I communed with Mother Nature as never before. Our neighbors included an eagle, egrets, osprey, ibis, and anhinga, those incredible black birds with snake-like necks. When we finally spotted some alligators, and a big manatee greeted us with his snout so close to our dinghy that we could have touched him, I distinctly remember being giddy. Our senses in overload, Bob and I were reminded that we were sharing a unique adventure. As our friend Carol said at an AGLCA Rendezvous, "I've never felt so alive!"

Boat Noises

When you are on a boat, you fully expect to hear the sounds of engines, generators, fans, etc. Their rhythm becomes background music to your on-board life. After several weeks, though, Bob and I were kept awake one night by a strange popping/clicking sound, "tcht, tcht, tcht, tcht, tcht." What in the world was that? Bob got up, checked all the gauges, walked around the boat, and poked inside and out. Everything looked OK. The next day, a veteran cruiser explained that what we heard was a type of shrimp that nibbles algae off the bottom of your hull. Whew!

On another morning as we prepared to leave a dock, we heard water trickling somewhere inside the boat. Where was the sound coming from? It appeared to be coming equally from every single location – fore, aft, port, starboard. Had a water line broken? Not wanting to head out until the mystery was solved, Bob finally called the PDQ technical support staff. They assured him that he had done all the necessary troubleshooting and suggested that the sound might not even be coming from within our boat. Who knew that hulls could pick up sounds from other boats! They told us not to worry, so we headed out. Amazingly, the "mysterious trickling sound" disappeared. Apparently, the technicians were right. The sound of running water had been transferred to our hull via salt water from another boat or from a leaking waterline onshore.

I think I could write an entire chapter on boat sounds. When winds were particularly high and the hull mashes into fenders, which in turn rub against pilings or docks, the sound effects are stunning. One night I wrote down all the notes of our evening lullaby: "eaaakkk, rrraarfff, screeeek, plunnck, eerrch, croarck, eeeeak." Eventually all of these sounds were as familiar and unobtrusive as the sound of our ceiling fan at home.

Document Your Trip

In addition to keeping a boat log, I highly recommend keeping a narrative journal, posting it to an online blog if possible. When I first started our blog, I had no idea that I would alternate cursing it and loving it. Blog-keeping ate up hours during times when I was eager to do something else, like going to bed. Posting photos required even more effort. However, the investment of time and energy of maintaining a blog and taking the photos was well worth it. Family and friends liked knowing where we were and seemed to enjoy sharing our adventure vicariously. They actually fussed when I skipped a day or two. But, honestly, Bob and I have reaped the greatest reward. We can go back to that blog at any time and re-immerse ourselves in sweet memories of a year well spent.

On to New Adventures

In the midst of our active, sometimes hectic, lives at home in Huntsville, Alabama, we often reflect on the simpler, carefree life of long-distance cruising. We stay in touch with Looper friends, continually planning our next rendezvous. "Winter in the Florida Keys sounds just fine! Yes, we would love to join you in January."

For me, if there is a single lesson to be learned, it is this. My life is ever so much richer because I ventured far beyond my comfort zone. I smile when I recall how adamant I was that living on a boat for a year would be miserable.

What a thrilling adventure we had navigating through large, open waterways like the Gulf of Mexico, the Chesapeake Bay, and Lake Michigan; traveling down winding rivers, large and small; and negotiating a varied system of locks and historic canals! We experienced the quiet solitude of anchorages, miles from civilization. We swam with manatees, and we watched loons, egrets, eagles, and alligators with awe. We learned much about our country and ourselves, and in doing so, our friendships multiplied. Every single day revealed fresh, glorious sights and new adventures. We now see the Tennessee River in a new light – it is more than a lovely place to swim and water-ski, it is the pathway to grand adventure. From here we can cruise anywhere in the world. The next time adventure calls, I'll think long and hard before turning down a new opportunity.

Liz Stagg has always been drawn to water, whether it is the familiar waters of the Tennessee River, the Atlantic Ocean, or even the neighborhood creek. Before an early retirement allowed Liz and Bob to embark on their Great Loop adventure, she enjoyed a long career in the training field, designing and delivering courses for clients in government and industry. She often wrote articles for training journals and presented papers at national conferences.

Liz and Bob are proud to have instilled love and respect for water sports in their grown children, Scott and Susan. The whole family enjoys gathering at their beach house in Emerald Isle, North Carolina whenever they can all break away from their busy lives. At home Liz and Bob stay heavily involved in volunteer civic activities, serving on a variety of boards. However, they jump at every opportunity to travel to fun places, cruise under power on *Second Wind*, or sail on their sailboat.

Lisa Targal Favors

Vessel: M/V Kismet – Fathom 40 Fast Trawler
Residence: Traverse City, Michigan
Homeport: Charlevoix, Michigan
Blog: favorsgreatloopblog.com • Website: favorsweb.com

Do you remember what it was like as a child to wake up in the morning on a hot summer's day? School was out and three months off from the rigors of formal education seemed more like an eternity spread out before you. As you laid in your bed after a long night spent dreaming, with your small eyes still closed tight, the gentle tickle of sunlight on your skin produced the urge for you to move. You were anxious for the day to begin. People to see, things to do, places to explore, neighborhood news to exchange, plans to meet up with a friend down the street.

My early childhood was spent in a busy neighborhood on the northwest side of Detroit, Michigan. During warm weather, kids often played outside on the street. Time stretched out from sunrise to sunset more like a season than a short eight to nine hours of playtime.

We'd ride our bikes all around the neighborhood, mostly to see what was new, daring to expand our horizons as we'd quickly get bored with the now familiar territory. We taught each other stupid bike tricks and helped one another beef up the accessories on our bikes or gave assistance when a repair job was needed. Many impromptu football games were assembled right on the street outside our home. A group of us used to lay on little Johnny's front yard at night and stare up at the stars with a mighty awe while pondering and questioning what all that beauty and spaciousness meant in the bigger scheme of things. We had many opportunities in those days to just be kids.

The Targal family summers were spent at our beach house in East Tawas, Michigan, on Lake Huron, a three-hour drive from home. Our family, of five kids (four brothers and myself), was lucky to have the Breznau family as neighbors, since they had seven kids. My brothers and I soon found one or two in the bunch to become our summer friends. One of my fondest memories of my childhood was that between the 12 of us we built a big tree house.

On the edge of our property sat the perfect tree for a good size "fort." Building this amazing structure was a joint effort with most of the real work done by the older male members of our motley crew. We salvaged discarded two-by-fours and old plywood from junk piles behind neighboring cottages or scavenged logs that washed up on shore. We scrounged our cottages to furnish our small space and make it homey. Of course, the main builders of this tree house got first dibs on which nights they'd sleep there, but in the end we all took turns, mostly age and gender related, bringing food, games and several flashlights while staying up late to tell scary stories in the dark.

Later, as I got a little older, I built my own dwelling up in a stand of trees, more of a platform due to my limited carpentry skills, where I could take a bowl of newly gathered huckleberries to eat in peace and quiet, far away from the "pack," while communing with nature.

We treasured the time spent with each of our friends, questioning life and contemplating our futures within these very confined spaces, which by design lacked the comforts and amenities of home. This was an excellent perch from which to see the world, contemplate the secrets of nature, and wonder where our young lives would lead us.

When I became an adult, I suddenly found myself labeled "responsible." Like my parents before me, my playtime now became mostly relegated to vacation "events" with family. These short-term holidays gave little time for me to fully relax from the daily pressures of my busy, working and family life, let alone provide time to reintroduce myself to the freedoms I remembered as a child.

As the natural progression of life continues for all of us, a time will come when the children have grown, the dog has passed on, and "retirement" looms ahead. Life changes! How do we avoid the complacency and decline some older adults fall prey to when family and work responsibilities change?

I think today many more retirees are seeking to reintroduce themselves to their inner child as they contemplate a major lifestyle change, one different from the norm. Whether you're already retired or are still working but have some mobility, there are many different avenues you can take for the rediscovery of your lost youth. World travel, RVing, returning to education for a more inward journey and a long sought after degree, or maybe moving to a retirement community where the daily activities would exhaust a twenty-year-old, just to name a few.

On a side note, my husband, Jim, and I have met several young families during our travels. The parents believe this is absolutely the best lifestyle for their children. We are in awe of their creativity in defining a unique lifestyle that best suits their family. We wished we'd thought of this ourselves when our family was growing.

I can only share insight into what has become my vehicle of choice to explore the world and reintroduce adventure into my life after my responsibilities have waned. Jim and I chose early retirement in place of more work years and time spent accruing additional financial security – it just made sense to us. What I'm talking about here is lifestyle, not vacation, and becoming a long-distance cruiser has helped me achieve most of my goals for a satisfying transition from working to a freer continuation of life. (The word "retirement" just does not fit what I'm talking about here.)

I've been the child, and later the responsible adult, now, I'm seeking to rediscover my inner child as a long-distance cruiser. Jim and I have chosen boating as a means to get back in touch with our un-tethered youth. My perch is now the pilothouse of our 40-foot Fathom trawler, *Kismet*, and the scenery and wildlife I do so crave slowly floats by me or constantly changes as we stop at different places to appreciate it. I often sit on my new perch and wonder... What will my future hold and how can I shape it to suit my needs? Where will all of this traveling take me, and will I tire of moving so far away from home? How will I feel when my cruising days come to an end? How do I fit into Mother Nature's bigger scheme of things? Have I taken enough risks to maximize my potential to make my life richer and more meaningful?

After we disposed of a lot of "stuff," and put the rest in storage, sold our house and moved full time onto our boat, a tremendous feeling of freedom materialized all of a sudden. Wow! What a revelation! This new way of living was freeing in ways we never could have imagined. All of a sudden we found ourselves houseless, floating around on a boat. "Now what?"

We'd kind of put ourselves into an irreversible position; we had to ask ourselves that question repeatedly while at the same time discovering together what the answer would be. We found ourselves in uncharted waters almost unprepared for what we'd find. Naively, we planned a course without knowing what the outcome would be. Ultimately, we realized it really was OK because we were unraveling the mystery together.

After taking the plunge, we discovered that we were looking forward and upward a lot more. We became creative in planning our lives around new adventures. If one of us had a good idea, we both jumped on it like eager children who had no worries or cares. After taking this initial big step, we developed a trust in each other to commit to new ideas together, and this helped us immensely as we began charting our new course in life. If we weren't a team in our previous lives, now we definitely knew we shared the same jersey, and we both felt good in it.

Women On Board Cruising

Jim and I, while so different in most things, are almost always on the same page when it comes to making life-changing decisions, especially when the word adventure is involved. I guess it's easier when both partners' hearts are in the same place, but I think it doesn't have to be impossible to overcome if they're not. The most important thing is for both partners to learn about the other's level and tolerance for comfort and find a way to support those feelings and concerns. If your partner doesn't respect your basic needs and desires, spending long periods together in the confines of a boat is a major disaster waiting to happen.

I feel fortunate to be able to share this lifestyle with the man I love. We didn't always live our lives together with the outlook of children. We were each busy with careers and raising a family. Boating started out as a hobby for us, a way to relax on weekends and vacations. I never knew Jim's inner child prior to our first long-distance trip (and to tell the truth had completely forgotten my own), but I was happy to meet them both over the last five years that we've been cruising together.

What I've tried to do here is to paint a picture for you, one that could help you to imagine how you might enrich your own life by choosing long-distance cruising as a means of finding adventure. It's a way of life that's full of fun, movement and learning opportunities. Let's face it, when was the last time you woke up early on a warm Saturday morning excited to meet up with a group of friends to make a "Loop" of the neighborhood to check out what was new – to meet new, like-minded souls and play hard... for eight to nine hours, nonstop? Long-distance cruising is not just about boating; it's so much more about adventure, educational opportunities, teamwork, fun, socialization and simplification of lifestyle. Looking for an adventure? Here's an idea for you to come alive inside – kind of like sitting in a tree fort and feeling like you're on top of the world, or riding your bike around your neighborhood with your friends in search of new frontiers and adventures.

After cruising over 12,000 miles, Jim and I are sometimes asked for advice or help by a friend or an acquaintance in convincing a partner who's usually, but not always, the woman in the couple. They'd like us to help her overcome some of her apprehensions about long-distance cruising. These men are almost desperate in their desire to get their wives "on board." We always try to share with the hesitant partner some experiences and solutions to problems we've personally encountered, or we try to answer questions so there is light where there was only darkness before. If that isn't enough, we always hope that our enthusiasm for this lifestyle shows through enough to open a door or two.

I'd have to say though that it really doesn't matter so much what we might say to a guy's partner, what matters the most is whether the guy tries or not to address his partner's concerns himself.

I hope the following thoughts, observations, and little personal stories are helpful in this regard.

Lisa Targal Favors – *Kismet*

Being Aware

Sometimes when I wake in the morning, before my eyes are even open, I try to remember the circumstances of our dockage the day before. Same sheets, bed and stateroom – different locale. For a few moments, before I am fully awake, I feel a little disoriented because I can't remember if I'm tied up to a dock or anchored in a remote location, let alone what city we may be in or near. I may have just been dreaming of a time spent in the Bahamas or in our homeport in Charlevoix, Michigan and part of me may still be there as I'm slowly waking up. This scenario sure keeps me thinking, getting the parts of my brain actively working to figure it out so I can feel connected again.

In essence, we're taking our home everywhere we go in our quest to move and remain actively aware. A day here, a week there, a summer in the Chesapeake Bay, a winter in Florida. We ordered our current boat in the Pacific Northwest and found ourselves spending a few months cruising Puget Sound and the San Juan Islands before we shipped the boat back to the Great Lakes. Every time we move there is a different view out our windows and a new area to become familiar with. I heard someone comment the other day that doing the Great Loop, or other long-distance cruising, has got to be a surefire treatment to stave off Alzheimer's as the health experts say it helps to do things differently and change your routines and habits often. Well, when cruising, you have to reassess your situation constantly. The only real consistency is that every day the routine will faithfully change yet again.

We wake up early in the morning full of anticipation (odd for me, who used to love to sleep in) of what awaits us in our newest harbor. Who will we meet today? Where will they come from and where are they going? Will we be reacquainted with another cruiser we met previously? Will the guy on the dock next to us help us solve an engine problem after breakfast, or will the dockhand or fellow boater, who has a car in the marina, give us a ride to the grocery store? Will we get to talk to a local who might share some tips about what to see while visiting their hometown? What time is happy hour, and what do we need to bring? Will I learn something new this week? Will my captain share his fears and his joys with me today?

Learning Opportunities

I'm always wondering what I'll learn next. Jim is a big history buff but, left to my own devices, I probably wouldn't delve into that vast educational bin, but because of his interest I can't help but absorb some historical education along the way. I appreciate this opportunity to share another's passion, as I know he does when he accompanies me to art museums. Long-distance cruising readily lends itself to educational opportunities, as you travel through many historical spots on the waterways.

Just like the tree houses of my youth, our boat has become that haven from which to learn about many of nature's wonders along the waterways. You get a completely different perspective from seeing the country from the waterway rather than from a highway.

We learned first hand about how people used to see the country. Towns were built along the shoreline, and people used to travel from town to town by boat or ship. It's still this way for boaters, and it truly is a different travel experience. Sure, the historic towns have either disappeared or expanded. More industry lines the waterways now, more vessels of all makes and sizes traverse the water routes today than yesterday, but you can readily access what you need as you travel around the United States by water. Moreover, if you're in areas that are more rural, you just learn to become more resourceful, and becoming more resourceful in turn builds confidence in your abilities.

I've learned a lot about boating over the last 20 years, most of which during the last ten years. You know that you have gone over to the other side when you've learned what 5200 is (marine adhesive sealant) and are often the one to suggest that it be used somewhere on the boat. This is my life now. Ropes are called lines, living rooms are saloons, kitchens are galleys, bedrooms are now staterooms, and bathrooms are called heads. Never in my previous life would I have even heard of: inverters (a device for transforming direct current into alternating current); zincs (sacrificial anodes); windlasses (a device that allows the raising and lowering of the anchor); impellers (a rubber rotor blade that impels, as a rotating device used to force a fluid in a desired direction under pressure.); or Glendinnings (an electric device that winds a power cord into a cabinet). I've learned a lot.

Acting and Living Simply

Each day we ask each other and ourselves just a few questions. "Where are we going and what do we need to exist today?" If we're moving, we need to agree on arranging the accommodations for the night if necessary ahead of time. "Can we make a meal of what we have on the boat?" "Do we need to secure transportation of one kind or another to reach a distant grocery store or can we just walk?" "Do we need a pump out or to take on fuel?" "Will our proposed accommodations be a quiet spot where I can read and collect my thoughts, or will there be a chance for social interaction and making new acquaintances?" Our activities seem to revolve around the simple necessities of life – eating, sleeping, personal comfort, companionship or alone time, boat chores and staying safe.

Accommodations on live-aboard boats vary. In our level of cruising, with a 40-foot trawler we have all the necessities of a comfortable environment to meet our tastes. I have to say though that I really miss having a dishwasher. This thought quickly disappears though when I think of all the excellent and changing scenery I have out our big saloon windows. If we bought a house and gave up our current lifestyle, I'd have that dishwasher, but I'd always have the same scenery out of my picture window. Everything would be certain and the same. The lack of changing scenery is a scary thought for me at this time. Right now, I can't give that up, not full time anyways.

Mother Nature Reigns
At our lake cottage, I spent a lot of time learning about nature's rhythms and diversity. Living by the water, we also learned how dramatic and fickle nature could be. Our family would sit in our cottage on a stormy night with all the lights off watching a lightning storm move across the horizon on Lake Huron. Now, as a boater I've learned to respect Mother Nature's great power and try to take time to savor her incredible beauty.

Jim and I keep an ongoing eye on the current weather conditions. We pore over the stats daily, especially when we travel or are contemplating travel in the near future. Our safety and comfort depends on our vigilantly monitoring the current and forward weather conditions.

Whether you're out in big open water or traveling down a tapering river or canal, nature will at one time or another display her horror or hold out her sparkling jewels. She'll offer up opportunities for the brave and adventuresome to commune with her directly as they gear up to take stock or deal with what she decides to put forth at any given time. Trust me, the good times far outweigh the bad in number and satisfaction.

Time to Play
We feel like we spend more time playing now. We strive not to be so serious as we try to take advantage of the freedoms we now experience in our new lifestyle.

Here are just a couple of examples of boater's finding time to "play."

One afternoon when we were on Elbow Cay in the Abaco Islands, I enjoyed watching Jim and our friend Charlie as they prepared to go fishing in their dinghies. They were excited even the day before while they double-checked with each other on what gear to take and what refreshments to pack. Charlie's wife Linda and I waved to them as they headed out, and I commented that they looked so much like excited kids going off to play. They were so hopeful that they'd secure their first ever live catch in the Abaco Islands.

Of course, when they returned, the fish stories of the day ensued – over a fishless dinner. Neither one of these guys are fishermen. Neither was familiar with the catch available in the islands. The only fish they caught that day, or the whole time we were there, was big, flat and colorful. They debated over whether this was possibly something fit to eat and finally decided that since it was so colorful it couldn't be edible and threw it back into the water.

A few weeks later, while grocery shopping, Jim and I came across a photo of a young girl holding the above said fish, and Jim asked the shopkeeper, "What kind of fish is that?" She said, "Why, that's called a trigger fish, it's my favorite fish to eat, and it's the hardest to catch." Well, it all made for a good fish story anyways. However, the point of the story is that the guys had fun, came home smiling and were all played out. The laughs that began during the day continued as Linda and I listened to the "boys" tell us about their excursion over dinner.

A group of our boating friends have been meeting in Marathon, Florida, where they've all succumbed to a malady known as "Keys Disease." They've met each other while on their various boating adventures and formed a group opinion that the Florida Keys is where it's happening. Some have cruised south from the Carolinas, a few have come from the interior river system, and one or two from New York, Florida and Canada. They meet up as a group to slow down their lives and experience a more lazy routine. By the time we caught up with them recently, on our way south to Key West, they'd already taken over the dock behind their boats with items scavenged from curbside garbage pickup – tables, umbrella, chairs, gas grill, wicker couch with ottoman and a large old TV set which they keep on 24/7 so that moisture wouldn't collect inside and destroy it. It even has an address, 1 Palm Tree Court. This is their big social center. They have a big cookout (sometimes 30 or more people – boaters from all over Marathon) every Tuesday night and many happy hours in between. These people know how to play hard, and if anyone knows about reverting to childhood, it's the 1 Palm Tree Court group.

Buddy Boating VS. Soloing

There are boaters who almost exclusively "Buddy Boat" and some that never do. Jim and I fall in the middle somewhere. It really is a personal preference. Some boaters like to be social 24/7. We enjoy the company of cruising with another boat, sharing trip planning chores and weather watches. It's comforting to have a close friend in front or behind you while traveling – especially in unknown territory or hazardous cruising situations. When you stop for the day, you have a ready-made social opportunity and dinner plans with familiar people.

Jim and I also enjoy each other's company immensely and enjoy time to just be alone together. Solo boating also kind of forces you to work a little harder at meeting folks when arriving at a marina, you aren't distracted by social plans already underway before you even tie up to the dock. So, we try to split our time by hooking up with friends for defined cruises and then taking off on our own for a while.

Anchoring VS. Marinas

To anchor out or tie up at a marina? Again, personal preference reigns here. Some boaters exclusively anchor out, and some will only tie up at a marina. We fit somewhere in the middle of this debate once more. However, anchoring out overnight is a love we've had to acquire.

Our first attempts were scary and unnerving and probably a little humorous to the observer. We didn't sleep well because the first time out our anchor lost its hold in the middle of the night, and we found ourselves careening toward another sailboat anchored nearby. That happened too many times in our early attempts for us to feel comfortable about this type of overnight boating. However, over the years we've learned a lot about how to set the anchor and what type of equipment is needed to ensure a good night's sleep.

Using chain instead of line is imperative for windy weather situations or strong currents. If you want to try anchoring out, make sure your boat has the appropriate length of chain for its size. Buy the best darn anchor you can find. Last year we bought a Buegle anchor and have weathered very windy nights in all areas of the Eastern United States many times with rapid currents, all different bottom conditions and never lost a hold, even with another boat tied up to us. We also have an anchor alarm, and knowing that it will sound off if we move past the set parameter provides a greater feeling of security. If you're a novice at this, get some instruction from a fellow boater. A little education can go a long way.

While traveling in the North Channel, Canada (one of our first trips out of our normal cruising grounds), we got a lesson from a sailor who at first laughed his head off along with his buddies while watching us attempt to set our anchor near their boat. Pretty soon they were launching their dinghy and rowing over to our bow to give us a lesson we've never forgotten. Drop and pull back, drop and pull back, let the anchor settle, then pull back hard to feel it grab hold.

After learning the proper technique, we've come to love both anchoring and docking for different reasons. The peace and solitude at anchor can be addictive while the socialization found at a marina can warm your heart and fill up your boat card book. We try to do both. We anchor out when weather looks good and there are no other pressing reasons to go ashore or if we're in an area where it would be a shame to sit in a marina when Mother Nature is calling with her astounding beauty. Eventually we do need to just get off the boat to move around, and the lure of a marina, dinner at a restaurant and a chance to exercise our limbs in a nearby town sounds very appealing.

Inside VS. Outside
After talking to several future women boaters over the last few years, a question has often presented itself and I realized that many non-boating women think that most cruising is done in big open water. While it can be that way, I have to say that there are many boating trips that can be taken in fairly well protected rivers, channels, cuts and of course the lengthy ICW. Some people like to cruise outside in the ocean to make time in getting to their destination. This is a popular route for sailors, as they have deeper keels and need deeper water not always available in the ICW. After many years boating the big open waters of the Great Lakes, it was a revelation to me to enter the river system from Chicago, Illinois to Mobile, Alabama and discover the benefits of slowing down to enjoy the scenery on the protected waters of the rivers. Fast boating is no longer in our vocabulary. I now prefer this form of travel, especially on the East Coast's ICW, for the same reasons. Traveling along these routes not only provides scenic distraction but mostly calm waters and historical venues. Of course, if you do any major long-

distance cruising, there will always be big bodies of water that you'll have to cross to continue on your way. I just brace up for the trip, take a few Dramamine (yes, unfortunately I'm prone to seasickness), but we'll always try to pick a good weather day with fairly low wind and waves.

Vital Communications
Transmission of information between captain and crew is a necessary routine and one most legendary for its negative effects on crewmates. Many women boaters will complain about their captain's "tone." After much trial and too many errors in the beginning, now, before Jim and I leave a dock or anchorage, we have a quick briefing to go over the particulars of our current situation (which changes every day when we move and encounter different docks, anchorages, currents, winds, etc.).

It's important for both of us to be on the same page as to how we're going to leave the dock. I ask Jim where he wants me and what we need to do to shove off. It's far easier to make this part of our routine rather than suffer the consequences of inadequate prior discussions. Since we came to this conclusion after much trial and error, our routines have become insanely easy and almost effortless as we follow our established procedure.

On another level of communication (the less vital side) I have a funny story that relates to this subject, one we still laugh over to this day.

After a long day's ride in very rough water, we pulled into an anchorage in Oxford, Maryland. We were beat and glad to be out of the wind and waves in the bay. The Town Creek in Oxford provided us with a comfortable anchorage for the night. The next morning we had coffee, took showers and while Jim thought we were getting ready to depart for Rock Hall (our next destination), I thought he was busy taking the dinghy down so we could go into town for a walking tour of the quaint town of Oxford. This is a port we'd never been to before and had often talked about visiting. Unbeknownst to Jim, as he was busy preparing the boat to leave, I'd changed into nice clothes and prepared for a town visit. I thought I'd heard him getting the dinghy down, but when I came up from the stateroom all dressed up (not my typical travel attire) with camera and purse in hand, Jim turned from the bow of the boat to see that I had this puzzled look on my face as he was in the process of lifting the anchor.

"Are you resetting the anchor?" I asked. It took him a minute to take in the unusually well put together outfit, and more importantly, the look of excitement I sometimes display when I'm on the cusp of a shopping trip. He suddenly got this very uncomfortable feeling that he'd missed something really important. One of those guy moments when, it appears, they don't pay close enough attention to their mates. Communications! Well, we had a good laugh and agreed to compromise. He explained that there was a weather window closing in on us, so we both agreed that we shouldn't linger and risk having to fight bad weather in an effort to reach our destination. We did get to tour Oxford on a return visit, so not all was lost.

Lisa Targal Favors – *Kismet*

Division of Labor and Chores

Our roles are pretty traditional. Jim and I have divided the chores so that we don't get in each other's way. He cleans the outside the way he wants it done, and I do the same inside. Simple! No consulting, no clashes.

By the way, have any of you women out there wondered why the cleaning gene appears at the ready whenever a guy gets close to a boat? I don't get it. Some men will scrub and polish their boats all day long but never pick up a cleaning tool at home. I say let them go for it; I love to see guys cleaning boats. Jim is pretty particular about that shine on the fiberglass, and it seems to me that he takes a strange pleasure in how it looks and feels. Not me! We joke a lot when talking about the inside jobs and the outside ones; some call it the pink and blue jobs. We're happy with our division of labor and that's all that matters.

We're as different as night and day, but we feel that our strengths and weaknesses actually compliment each other. We've heard that some boating couples like to replicate chores on their boat. Jim and I have another philosophy. Our roles are pretty traditional, and we try to utilize each of our strengths at full capacity and fill in with help from the other when needed. Each of our strengths seems to compliment the others without much overlap. We feel that our chosen set-up maximizes what we accomplish because we're not duplicating tasks or needing to be proficient in everything.

I handle the lines and fenders (my choice), which I've gotten pretty good at, and operate the windlass when we're setting or retrieving the anchor. I've learned to lasso a pole and pick up a mooring ball with relative ease. I've gotten pretty good at throwing a line around a pole or onto the dock to grab a cleat. I'm still learning though. Sometimes I don't get it quite right and always vow to do better next time. Jim drives the boat and navigates. He's in his element doing this, and he's very good at it.

Jim is definitely the captain, and I defer to his expertise and ask for direction when underway. I'm in awe of his competence and comprehension of all things to do with moving and maintaining the boat. Some of my contributions and expertise focuses on other areas than the actual running of the boat, and we feel the division of labor is for the most part equal. When moving, I handle lines and he captains the boat. I fill in for naps etc., but I never dock the boat, just not an area I feel comfortable in, as I feel I lack greatly in spatial navigation and steady nerves. Jim is also a very accomplished navigator, and we feel he has a better grasp on that whole area, and I think the person in charge of driving should also be fully aware of where the boat is headed. At the same time, I feel it's important to know how to operate the boat etc., in case of emergencies. I try to ask questions when I don't fully understand how to do something. I feel that in an emergency and if something were to happen to Jim, I'd need to have a working knowledge on the steering of the boat, the VHF radio operation and setting the anchor. I've heard a lot of recommendations of the Sea Sense course offered to novice women boaters (they also train couples together). I wholeheartedly agree that this is the way to go for those who need a jumpstart in this area.

Quite often I'll work on computer projects, non-boat related, while underway unless we're in a new or scenic area. So, this arrangement works in that both of our skills are being put to good use at the same time without tripping over each other on the same tasks, and since we're so different, we'd handle things much differently than each other, which could make for some overstepping situations.

Deepening the Levels of Trust
One of the things we learned fairly quickly was that being a team meant learning to trust the other teammate when in a scary or uncomfortable situation.

Recently we were anchored off the Intracoastal Waterway (ICW) south of St. Augustine, Florida, across from Fort Matanzas on Rattlesnake Island. We'd anchored in this spot because we wanted to visit the 270-year-old fort on the island. After we dropped anchor and got settled, I started to notice how fast the current was running, about four knots. I told Jim I was concerned that since our dinghy motor was on the fritz it might be hard for us to row back to the boat going upstream against the current. Jim tried to reassure me and promised me that he'd get us back to the boat before dark. It was late in the day, and we only had a couple more hours until sunset. We were trying to make the second to last ferryboat ride over to the fort. Jim's plan was to row us over to a beach close to our anchorage instead of trying to go downstream to the dock where the ferryboat was located. (In this instance we couldn't just dinghy to the island where the fort was, due to the park's rules we had to catch the ferry boat on the other side.) He said this shorter distance would make it easier to row back to the boat by moving across the water instead of upstream. It sounded like a good plan, and even though I still had this foreboding that we were going to get stuck sleeping on parkland for the night (and it was unseasonably cold that day), I decided to trust in his plan.

All went well on the trip to shore, we visited the fort, met some engaging park staff, and as dusk was slowly closing in on us we headed back to the beach where our dinghy sat. The tide had gone down some, and we had to drag it back into the water and in the process we heard a loud hissing sound coming from the bottom of the dinghy. Yes, we'd managed to drag it over the edge of a partially submerged, razor-sharp shell. My earlier anxiety was not totally unfounded, just misplaced. I looked at Jim, then at *Kismet* sitting so pretty in the sunset just a short distance from where we stood on the beach. It took a moment for me to free myself from the uncomfortable fear and jump into the positive thoughts and action mode. I was NOT going to spend the night on that cold beach. We had to walk back to the park office, near the ferry dock, and with embarrassment admit to needing help getting back to our boat. Well, luckily the park employees hadn't yet gone home, and they immediately came to our rescue. It actually turned out to be a meaningful event for us because not only were we reminded about how helpful people are but how, after taking stock, Jim and I worked together to get out of a jam. My trust in our ability to work together to find a solution when faced with a problem went to another level. I was also pleased with myself – that I didn't freak out. At the end of the day, we both agreed that if this is the worst of our problems, then we've been pretty fortunate in our boating travels, and I felt a warm glow between us as we both thanked our lucky stars.

Sharing Space

I feel fortunate to have married a man who feels that it is more important to enjoy life than to move up the corporate ladder just to acquire more security. It was kind of scary to depart early from the security of our professional lives to embark on the unknown, but I trusted Jim's instinct to focus on the important things and make our lives more about exploration and adventure than the existing daily grind of working for someone else or eventually, when much older, retiring to a conventional situation. We thought it was important to take time to explore while we're still young enough to enjoy it. In our opinion, it can never be soon enough. Don't wait, do it now if you can.

We took off from Charlevoix, Michigan (our homeport) heading out across lake Michigan on a 6,000-mile voyage, and for the first couple of weeks we were euphoric. Then it hit us like a thunderous cloud. "How on earth are we going to share this 400sq.ft. space together and thrive?" There definitely is a big adjustment to living full time on a boat in close proximity to another person, even one I truly loved. The first few months were the most difficult as we defined our new roles as captain, crew, husband, wife, teammate and friend.

After ten years of married life together where we moved around in our land environment, as much independently as dependently, now we seemed to be joined at the hip. I found myself silently singing the song by Dan Hicks, *How Can I Miss You if You Won't Go Away*. We were doing EVERYTHING together or in close proximity to each other. The grocery shopping, the cleaning and boat chores, socializing, and the funny thing was Jim now became the authority (in his own mind) on grocery shopping, a realm that was in all our married years my responsibility. Being a branch manager of the Merrill Lynch office in Traverse City, of course he thought he could now focus on managing me. Boy, was he WRONG! I'll have to say one thing in his defense, he sure is a fast learner and usually eager to please. I can only hope he's able to say the same about me!

I was surprised to learn more about Jim while experiencing our new lifestyle but additionally surprised to learn more about myself. One of the things I found out about myself is that when we travel (whether on the boat, by car or airplane) and then return home, I find I need to collect myself before diving into projects head on. I need to readjust before I can perform. Jim, on the other hand, is completely the opposite. The minute he arrives, he's busy putting things away, straightening up and checking things off his list. It took me some time to understand that we just function differently and his way of coping is just different to mine, not good or bad, just different. This was a revelation for me.

Because of Jim's restlessness and his constant motion, we move to explore. Because of my need to "nest", we'll chill and relax. We found this benefited both of us by making our lives a more rounded experience as we respected and embraced each other's personalities.

In our "land" lives, our differences were harder to understand; it was easier to just toss the thought of them off to the side, and there was plenty of room and opportunities to do that – on land. I think being in the close confines of the boat actually brought about positive understanding and tolerance in this area for both of us. We had to work diligently to make this work because it soon became apparent that we had to get this right if we were to continue to live our mutual dream in harmony. I guess you could say we were somewhat motivated.

Communication is a necessity in any relationship. To Jim this communication stuff is tantamount to being forced to jump into a pot of molten metal, but over the years, he's learned that it's a necessary task for a healthy marriage. It felt like we were starting from square one. We had to find ways to be independent of each other whenever an opportunity presented itself. For example, Jim began to spend time going over charts or mechanical issues with other captains, and I'd walk or talk with other women. After the major adjustment period passed – approximately two to three months – I began to savor and appreciate what a wonderful opportunity this was to get to know my husband more and experience a deeper, richer relationship. We've become stronger as a unit. I'm not really trying to say we're living in some kind of "La La Land" now – we really aren't. We still have to work at this daily.

On the positive side, an added benefit to the cruising lifestyle are the many opportunities for romance. With plenty of starry nights and beautiful sunsets over the water, not to mention the chilly nights anchored out without heat, and with only each other to cuddle with in our small boat bed.

Humor Reigns

Jim and I like to find the humor as quickly as possible after an event that, in the moment, is far from being funny. This has helped us keep an even keel as we plow forward in close proximity on the waterways. Whether we find ourselves in good or bad circumstances, we enjoy the many benefits of laughing; we also like to think it keeps us young at heart. It can be relatively easy to find humor in even the worst of circumstances, we know because we've been there – it's much better to laugh than cry.

Jim's fond of saying this about our newly chosen lifestyle, "It's like being kids again… but with benefits." Gotta love him!

Social Possibilities

Occasionally women have asked us this question: "Don't you feel isolated and lonely traveling by boat?" NO! Never! This is one of the biggest misconceptions many women have about the cruising lifestyle. They're afraid that they'll be stuck on the boat all the time with only their partner for company. A scary thought for some women apparently.

As young children on the loose, running in packs on the beach, we acquired skills on developing human social connections, learning to work together to build a fort or fix a bike. I cruised the neighborhood with a pack of my siblings and/or friends exploring our surroundings while pushing against the boundaries set for us by our parents. Now, we often choose to caravan with a pack of "buddy boats."

We use VHF radios to keep in touch as we travel, keeping each other on alert for dangers lurking in the water or outrageous sights of beauty. Sometimes it feels like bumper boats (hopefully without the bumping) as we navigate the waterways, locks and bridges. We'll jockey the boats to raft up to each other to either anchor together in a small cove or go one by one into a marina to rest for a night or two, week or month. We help each other fix electrical or mechanical problems on our boats using each person's expertise, resource or tools. You would not believe the amount of recipes exchanged and meals shared in the company of good people.

Some boaters constantly have friends and/or family come cruise with them so they never get bored or lonely.

You can definitely be as socially busy or laid back as you wish. I'd have to say that our life on the water is way busier than when we were land based. There is rarely a port we arrive in where we don't recognize one of the boats in the harbor or run into one of our cruising buddies. Boaters are some of the friendliest people you'll ever meet, and if you choose to put yourself out there, your efforts will be rewarded.

Exercise

Many long-distance boaters use bikes (folding bikes are popular and save space on board) as a preferred mode of transportation since you can't easily stow a car or hoist it aboard most boats. When getting into port, if it's not too late in the day, the first thing some boaters will do is unload their bikes, or in our case, we put on our walking shoes to go explore and head out into town in search of museums, hardware stores, post office, ice cream or food. We decided that when we're at dock that we should get off the boat most days for a walk and much-needed exercise.

I've met some women who religiously exercise with weights or routines on board. A friend of mine will regularly visit a particular exercise chain which is so popular she doesn't have too much trouble finding one in many of the towns she stops in. I've also witnessed women working out on their boat's flybridge or back deck with their own particular routine.

We don't think that the cruising lifestyle in any way, shape or form equates to inactivity, just the opposite. The changing scenery and towns make us curious to explore, and to do this you have to move. This is a good thing.

Leaving the Comfort Zone

It takes a brave woman to uproot herself from a comfortable lifestyle, to depart from her normal routine and course in life, to indulge a partner in a lifetime dream. I've met many women who started on this path hesitant to embrace it – just going along for the ride. These are brave souls who risked losing the safety of their known lives for the unknown; they've given up a year or more of their lives to try something different. It may not have been their choice or desire in the beginning, but they gave it a shot. They're extremely adventuresome because they traveled outside of their comfort zone in search of something new while trying to keep an open mind. They took a risk, and they reaped the rewards of personal growth.

Jim likes to say that he thinks I love boating more than he does (and he really loves it), so maybe I'm more the exception to the rule. Most women I talk to who are CONSIDERING this lifestyle have misgivings, probing questions and a general lack of information about cruising. On the flipside, most of the women I talk to who ALREADY are boaters, they own it. I can't tell you how many thoroughly competent women boaters I've met. Some put me to shame with their knowledge and the lengths they're willing to go to own their passion, but don't make the mistake of thinking that all of these women started out with complete confidence in their abilities and decision to leave their personal safe harbors behind. You really don't have to KNOW IT ALL before you start boating or leave on a trip. Take it one day at a time. With this philosophy, you really can do ANYTHING.

Fear is a funny thing. Don't let fear keep you home. Some fear is actually healthy to possess, but too much of it will hold you back from growing. Sure, I have a few fears, in fact one terror I have in particular seems kind of strange coming from a boater. I have a fear of big waves. I have nightmares about being caught and sinking in high seas, usually the night before crossing big open water. Let's see now, I get motion sickness and have a fear of big waves. I guess it's just short of a miracle that I'm so passionate about cruising.

Home Waters Tug at Our Hearts

I do have moments that are uncharacteristic of my newfound, free and easy, inner child, these are times when I've felt the tug of family ties – our parents, siblings and our three boys in particular. I also miss our long-time friends from our hometown. Jim and I ask ourselves this question: "In an effort to meet and see more of the world, were we shortchanging our family responsibilities and long-term relationships?"

Communications have become easier in the last few years for everyone, even people out on the open water, with the Internet, email, Skype and cell phones. However, the need for actual physical proximity with our loved ones is a strong pull and a major concern for many women, myself included. Many couples establish what we call "Rules of Engagement" to handle this particular situation along with a few other important issues that crop up.

Rules of Engagement

Communications between partners is vital to the success of any major lifestyle change. If a woman needs to get a grandchild fix, maybe she needs to schedule trips home every few months. Maybe the captain and crew are younger and not ready to leave their professions, we've known couples who, having flexible working situations, boat one or two months on, one or two months off while going back to work on their time off the boat. I was not quite ready to give up work altogether, I had so many areas of interests that I wanted to pursue, and with Jim's support we've made accommodations on board so that I can continue some of these activities while cruising.

Many boaters have established their own set of "rules." A popular one concerns traveling on bad weather days. This is where both captain and crew have a say on whether to go or not. If the captain is geared up to push ahead, but the crew has reservations and the circumstances are outside their established comfort level, the boat does not leave the dock on that day.

Some women have used the rules to insist on being in port every night so they can eat out at a restaurant and not have to cook on board. I've even heard about rules that define how long a couple can stay mad at the each other due to the close confines of the boat with nowhere to hide or escape.

Get the idea here? The established rules are really meant to establish comfortable limits and guidelines to enable captain and crew to feel safe and be happy living on board, and in some cases to ensure that the boat will actually leave the dock – AT ALL.

The Need to Stop

I have talked to several women boaters who have expressed that sometimes they just need to stop moving for a while. Women have a more innate need to connect with their surroundings. There have been many times I've had to ask Jim to consider staying a few days somewhere, just because I feel as if my head is spinning with the surroundings changing every day. This happens a lot when you're traveling to cover territory because of schedules. There are many good deals at marinas for weekly or monthly rates that make the daily rates look like highway robbery. Stay, relax for a while – enjoy.

Why Doesn't My Wife Want to Cruise with Me?

This is for the guys, now pay close attention. The answer to your question is really quite simple.

You must be willing to compromise. Make sure your partner feels part of the decision-making process. I'm talking about starting out with her involvement and input on choosing the boat she'll find herself spending huge amounts of time on, then making sure her other needs and desires of any sort are taken into consideration. This is key to helping a woman trust in her partner, which leads to a feeling of safety and comfort. She'll be more open to leaving her home, family and friends.

I've heard many statements from women who don't really want to join their husbands boating. "I'd like to get to a marina early enough so I can get off the boat and shop, but all we ever do is drive from one place to the next, and it's just plain boring." "His tolerance for bad weather is far different from mine, if he'd just listen to me, I might like boating better." "I'm not allowed to be part of the decision-making process that ultimately will affect me." These women will either never get on a boat or have already jumped ship – before they even got to experience it.

Guys, if your wife is saying these types of things and ultimately won't cruise with you, could this be why?

If the female partner in your relationship is prone to severe motion sickness, consider getting a boat with stabilizers or installing some on your current boat. Where the woman is concerned, it's mostly about being comfortable and safe. How can you relax and enjoy your surroundings when you're turning bright green or holding on to something for dear life?

Start small; if open water is a major concern, take your partner on some river or canal cruises. Break her in slowly and work up to the big stuff as she gains more confidence in her ability to deal with the boat and her fears. Patience is key.

Here are a couple of examples of Jim's concessions to me over the years. I was always complaining that when going through locks (remember I'm the line and fender handler) we never had enough fenders to cover both sides of the boat, only one side, which wasn't enough when needing to change sides in a lock at a moment's notice. We now have fenders mounted on both sides when transiting locks; therefore, we don't have to make hasty last-minute changes – making my life easier. Another example is that I wanted to have two or three pots of herbs on the back of our boat. Jim HATES to have dirt of any kind on his precious fiberglass, but he does understand that this is one of my needs, and he acknowledges that in the end he benefits by the added flavor to his meals. For many years when we lived on our first big boat, Jim always wanted to keep the water heater turned off and just turn it on a little before we needed it. I guess he was afraid the unit wouldn't last if we left it on. Invariably the water was never hot when I needed it to be. I found it very inconvenient and frustrating to not have hot water when I needed it.

These were ongoing sore spots for us. Somewhere along the way, Jim must have realized this and reconsidered his stance because on our next two-year trip, without me even begging, we always had the hot water on and more fenders in our locker – with just a few concessions, I am indeed a happy woman!

We are often approached by men who want us to talk with their partners – they want to see if we can convince their significant other to get "on board." The men so badly want their partners to take off with them on a boating adventure, but the women are just not sure. They don't want to leave their homes, children, grandkids, and aging parents. In some cases, the realities are too much to overcome, but I think there's a simple solution for most.

Establish an OPEN dialogue (this is one where you, the man, just listens). Ask your wife what her concerns are. One woman we talked to thought she'd be traveling in open water all the time, and when we assured her there are plenty of areas to cruise in protected waters she said, "Really? I had no idea, maybe I can do this." This is where we start to see the light bulb turning on in their eyes.

After establishing a list of concerns, try to get answers or solutions for her to mull over. Seek out other long-distance cruising women for her to talk to. Maybe she has thought of some solutions herself. Get creative and be willing to give in/up something here. If you establish your partner's needs and find solutions she'll be comfortable with, things could start to go your way.

The alternative is to cruise by yourself or with your buddies, but I think in the perfect world most men really want a HAPPY partner by their side.

We met a sailor just the other day, and he was talking about where he was going, and during the conversation he mentioned that he was getting ready to store his boat earlier than usual this year for the spring and summer. It was strongly suggested, by his wife, that his presence would be required at home for their big anniversary celebration. He said that his wife, although very accommodating of his love for sailing, wanted no part of it herself. "She pats me on the head and says 'go and be a good boy'." He sails for months at a time on his own. I don't know whom to feel more sorry for, the sailor for having to adventure on his own, or his wife who has missed amazing adventures, but that's just me.

> The test of an adventure is that when you're in the middle of it, you say to yourself, "Oh, now I've got myself into an awful mess; I wish I were sitting quietly at home." And the sign that something's wrong with you is when you sit quietly at home wishing you were out having lots of adventure.
> – THORNTON (NIVEN) WILDER (1897-1975)

So, women, those that can't make up your minds, don't end up wishing you'd taken a chance on adventure. Just do it. What do you have to lose? You may just find the happy little child hidden within you. Get her on board and let her breathe!

Lisa Targal Favors, a native Michigan artist, has studied fine arts and graphics arts. Former co-owner of Nelles Studios Bronze Foundry and part owner of Off Bridge Street Gallery in Charlevoix, Michigan, where she exhibited her dry point prints. She's exhibited in several galleries and exhibits throughout Michigan, including a one-man show at Tapawingo in Ellsworth, Michigan. For 15 years, she was an art director/graphic designer at Knorr Marketing in Traverse City, Michigan. She also served on the board of directors of Traverse Ad Club (TAC).

More recently, she has been on the Advisory Council of America's Great Loop Cruisers' Association (AGLCA). She's also writing articles for BoatU.S. Cruising Logs (boatus.com/cruising/kismet/log.asp) and sells stock photography to boating magazines. The Favors have edited and published *When the Water Calls... We Follow*, a book written by 27 different boaters of their experiences while doing the Great Loop. They also maintain a popular cruising blog (favorsgreatloopblog.com).

Wife to Jim and mother to one son and two stepsons, Lisa and Jim lived and worked in the Traverse City area for twenty years while raising their family. She has been houseless and cruising for the better part of the last five years with almost 20,000 miles and counting under her belt. Her passions include time spent with family, dancing, painting, traveling, gardening, cooking, photography, and boating – of course!

Ellen Langer

Vessel: M/V *Our Turn* – Med Yacht
Residence: Flagler Beach, Florida

I thought I knew everything about boats and boating until I began to cruise the inland waterways. Born and raised on Miami Beach, the daughter of an offshore powerboat racer, my love for the water was in my blood. I fished, swam, and scuba dived at every opportunity. Before college I learned to navigate by compass and the sun. My dad and I would often travel to Bimini, Bahamas for dinner. After college I left home and became a "Carolina Girl." I took as many opportunities as were offered to crew and relocate vessels for owners. I began to sail and hone my sailing skills, but I never discussed my love for sailing with my powerboat friends and family. I crewed on boat deliveries throughout the Caribbean, while maintaining a business in North Carolina. I longed to just sail away. After ten years in North Carolina I returned to Miami Beach to help my ailing father. I took over his small boat business, selling and repairing outboard motors. Again, I was on the water every chance I got.

Then I met Roy, and my life changed from a single and independent gal to part of a team with a dream: except Roy wanted to cruise inland on a powerboat and I wanted to cruise offshore. (Remember, it's in my blood.) We talked of a future together on the water, and everything clicked. I'd heard talk of the Great Loop boat trip and passed the idea on to Roy. He began to get excited over the thought of traveling by boat on the inland waterways, while I began to wonder what boating would be like on lakes and rivers. We would have to learn about river currents, barges, and most of all... LOCKS! We continued to work for four more years. In the meantime, I sold my 25-foot center console with twins, and my flats boat. Roy sold his 36-foot Sportfish, and we bought *Our Turn*, a 1988 Med Yacht, Taiwan built, with lots of headroom and a spacious rear deck.

I read as much as possible concerning the Loop trip. I read the America's Great Loop Cruisers' Association (AGLCA) newsletters, the book *Honey, Let's Get a Boat...* by Ron and Eva Stob (co-founders of AGLCA), more books on living aboard, and I looked at a few websites of those who had completed the Loop. I never chatted with other cruisers much prior to doing the Loop; embarrassed I might have to admit I didn't know it all. (Now I talk with everyone.) Then, I met the Stobs while at a Miami Boat Show and signed Roy up for a membership with AGLCA. I continued to sell Roy on the idea of doing the Great Loop. My independence and headstrong nature told me I could convince him, and we could do the trip together.

Roy worked on the boat and never got involved in the actual trip planning. I bought all the chart and guidebooks, and he bought a new GPS. I loaded over 200 units of canned goods and cases of wine and beer, as I planned like an offshore cruiser. I was set for a year! Every evening when I asked, "When are we leaving?" I got, "Blah, Blah, Blah. I'm working on this or that!" Everyone was talking taxes and mine were done, so I said, "That's it! April 15th will be our deadline. I'm leaving on the boat with or without you." What I hadn't realized was that he was nervous to leave his comfort zone and start a new life. He was worried about family, friends, doctors, mail, etc. Things like his car suddenly became so important. How could he live without his car? On the other hand, I was so ready! Needless to say, we left Fort Lauderdale, Florida on our own Great Loop adventure April 15th, a Tax Day to remember!

We didn't get far on the Loop our first year out. We had such great times in all the small towns up the Eastern Seaboard that we got as far as Rhode Island and then headed back south to the Florida Keys for the winter. We spent weeks in areas I never could have imagined would interest me. I loved Block Island, Rhode Island; Charleston, South Carolina; Beaufort, North Carolina and the rivers of the Chesapeake Bay. I so enjoyed the Chesapeake Bay area that we returned there the following summer and still didn't start the Loop. It took us over two years of living on board just to get to Canada from Fort Lauderdale, Florida, our original homeport.

Roy runs the boat. He fixes everything and does all maintenance. I shop, cook and plan our trips. I navigate by chart, and he navigates by GPS. My background has taught me never to rely on electronics. I pick all our stops and show him on the chart where I want to go each day. We are definitely a reverse roles couple. But who's to say what works?

Since we have wireless Internet I research the towns we plan to visit on the net. I find local farmers' markets, festivals, maps and listings of shops – I get off the boat every chance I get. I chat with everyone as I feel the more information I gather the better off I am. (This is a big change in my know-it-all attitude.)

I have learned many lessons from those I have met. Once a very elderly woman gave another woman and me a ride back to our boats at Portsmouth Marina from the grocery store. It was a bad neighborhood, and she thought we shouldn't be walking through it. I inquired why she herself was driving through, and she replied that she lived there. I asked if she worried about picking up strangers. She replied, "This is how I meet people." So now I follow her example and help out whenever I can. I'm not sure though that I'd pick up someone on the street. I'm from Miami, after all!

On part of our Loop trip Nat, my recently widowed friend, joined us. Roy loved having two cooks, and I enjoyed the company and the opportunity to share the cooking and cleaning. Roy would joke that when one cook was angry with him, he would just go to the other. But, in reality, it was wonderful to have someone to walk to town with, shop with, cook and clean up with, and to know when to give me some distance when I needed it. That's why I strongly recommend women introduce themselves to other women boaters whenever possible.

As for all the stuff I put on the boat; boy was I wrong, all I accomplished was to weigh down the boat, which in turn burned more fuel. I find great availability of staples everywhere we cruise, and if not, I prepare to live with what we have on hand for a few days until we get somewhere with more stores and selection! Part of my fun is walking to town to reprovision and explore.

We live so simply while on board it is unbelievable! I have found that a short haircut and natural color is a must. Once I colored my hair in a marina bathroom and sat there for 40 minutes while reading and sweating. I kept wiping my face with a paper towel, and then when I washed my hair, finished my shower, and went to look in the mirror, I found that I had brown streaks on my face. The hair color had stained my face as it dripped. It took days to wash off. I used every cream I could find and even a trick someone told me about: putting household ammonia on my skin. I was desperate! It didn't work and it left my skin chafed and red. Such humbling experiences!

The rewards of a shared life and shared experiences with my partner are what really excite me about this kind of lifestyle. I am envious of those cruisers I have met who have spent most of their lives together, but I often also hear them say that they are just now getting to really know each other. The hours on end I spend with Roy while underway are very special to me. We have conversations about everything! We are both newbies at the relationship thing, and yet it works.

I'm not taking control, nor am I the captain. I do love being in control though. One day while cruising the Chesapeake Bay I was at the helm and saw what looked like a short cut on the GPS. I began to cut across the channel when Roy came up and said, "Just what are you doing?" I replied, "I'm taking a shortcut!" Then he pointed out I was about to run us aground, and he quickly took control. (I have also pulled him out of a jam or two, but those will go unmentioned!) I have to remember to think "team", although I have also learned that "the captain is always right!" Things happen to me the same as anyone else. When starting our trip following inland routes, I found that I was just as green as a woman who has never been on a boat.

Pulling into Shelter Island, New York our first summer on the boat, I leaned over the rail with the boat hook to grab the mooring line. The line was stuck, lots of grass on it, so I gave it an extra oomph! Well, gravity took over, and over the bow I went, head first into some very cold water. We had company on board, one of them came to the bow, and I passed the line up with instructions about where to cleat it. I then swam to the stern, where Roy had the ladder down for me. I came up like a drenched rat, the rest of our company was still sitting on our back deck, and I said, "Anyone for a cocktail?" The best part was that they never knew I wasn't supposed to swim for the ball. It's still a great laugh!

I love to anchor, but my partner stays up all night worried. I have the best night's sleep if I can just get him to open the windows and turn off the air conditioner and generator. We just have to agree to disagree, so I try to get my way occasionally while anchoring only in nice weather and in beautiful locations. I have been known to take off on very long dinghy rides while exploring new territory, finding folks to meet and talk to, while Roy sits on the back deck with the dog smoking his cigar.

While we were in Charlevoix, Michigan, my girlfriend and I took off across Lake Charlevoix to have lunch. It turned into an all-day event. The return trip back to the boat across the lake was against three footers breaking onto the bow of the dinghy. We were drenched, we bailed the water out as we rode, but we put our hats on and pulled up to the rear of *Our Turn* like ladies, with our inflatable life vests covering the important spots on our wet bodies, just like nothing was out of the ordinary.

One night Roy was watching TV about a hurricane brewing in the south. We were at anchor by Block Island, New York. I thought I should go above to check our holding. When I opened the cabin door I felt a gust of wind close to 40 mph. The wind grabbed the door and you know who hollered, "Hey, be careful." I mentioned to Roy that the sailboat next door was out of view and must have broken loose. Roy got the engines started as I tried to get a better view of where we were. I noticed a lot of lights shining everywhere, and I wondered why all the boats were moving now. Instead it was us, underway, they were shinning their lights at us to warn us that WE were the ones actually moving. As the wind was now blowing hard, the 200 feet of anchor chain we had set earlier wasn't holding at all. I tried to lift the chain, and it jumped the windlass. Barefoot, I put my foot on it to stop it from free falling. With the strength that only comes under great anxiety, I lifted the chain back up on the windlass and began to slowly pull up the chain while Roy tried to hold the boat in place. We were being tossed around in the wind in an unfamiliar anchorage. I was afraid we might run over the chain with the props. Finally, we got the anchor to grab, and we stopped within 20 feet of two other boats. The storm cell passed soon after, but the Coast Guard was on the radio with a warning for boats in the area to get secure as another cell was coming. The harbormaster came on the radio and said grab any mooring NOW! We radioed the harbormaster back for assistance and stated we were 45 feet and couldn't just go on any mooring. He directed us to a suitable mooring where we sat scared while the next cell came through. We were terror-stricken while hoping the mooring was strong enough to hold us. We had our life jackets on and the engines running just in case we broke loose again. After it was all over a quiet moment followed, then a kiss, and a "We can make it together!" Ah, the rewards of traveling with one you care so much about.

LuSea, our 15-pound dog, was also grateful that terrifying moment was over. We found LuSea at the local animal shelter just before we began cruising. She is the life of our party. She has free run of the boat, mostly laps and beds. She is great company! She uses an indoor/outdoor doormat on the bow for her business. I try to never walk her more than once every few days so she won't break the habit of using her mat. Training her on the mat wasn't that difficult. A few days of not walking her, and another dog's scent on the mat, and she finally gave in and began to use it. I gave her a treat then, and I still give her treats every time she goes on her mat. I see others traveling with big dogs that must be walked, but that's not for us.

The folks we meet while cruising are just the best! I especially remember the lockmaster at Lock #5 on the Trent-Severn Waterway in Canada, who waited for us before closing the lock for the day. We were traveling with another boat when we entered the first lock (Lock #1), we weren't sure if we had enough time to complete the "flight" (this is a set of locks spaced close together), so we asked the friendly lockmaster if we had enough time to go through all five before they closed for the day. We also asked which lock was the best to tie up at overnight so we could go to a restaurant for dinner. I told him it was my birthday and I wasn't cooking. The lockmaster at Lock #1 called all the locks ahead of him to let them know our plans. So the lockmaster at Lock # 5 waited for us to finally get to his lock and arranged for a second vehicle. He dropped us all off at the local Chinese Buffet. It wasn't the Taj Majal, but we all had a great time, and I didn't have to cook on my birthday. All the lockmasters throughout our Loop were very helpful, and so friendly.

We enjoy hooking up with boats and traveling together for camaraderie. The radio conversations on those trips can be quite entertaining. One of the boats we traveled with was a jokester. As we were coming through a narrow channel where it would have been impossible to pass another boat, we had announced our "Securite" (a signal to warn other boaters of a boat in a narrow or dangerous channel where only one boat at a time should travel) when we were in the channel. Our buddy boat radios me and says, "Wait till you see this 50-footer and all the half-naked men on board." I say, "Yeah, yeah." I know he is kidding, but... just as we cleared the channel and rounded the corner, there was the boat. And there were five young men, all in Speedos.

LuSea gives us "WooWoo" when she has used her mat, and wants a biscuit. So one day we were traveling offshore with a fast power cat when all of a sudden they turned away from us, heading out about three miles offshore. When they returned and caught up with us again, he was on the radio going "WooWoo!" I guess they had a successful "poop" (code for pumpout). We laughed for hours as they kept "WooWooing" us on the radio. I couldn't resist giving him a treat of his very own "dog biscuit" at happy hour that night.

At the end of the day, as we approach an anchorage or marina, the first boat in gets secure then helps others tie up. Quickly following are the many memorable happy hour activities where everyone you have just traveled with all day miraculously appears at the designated spot with trays of good food. The more we cruise the more people we meet and the more friends we have in every port. It is a lifestyle I would not want to change!

We have also made long hauls just by ourselves. For example: when we were in Carrabelle, Florida (in the Panhandle) waiting a long eight days for a decent weather day to cross the Gulf, we noticed that the wind was finally beginning to calm down, so we seized the opportunity at 2 p.m. and took off all by ourselves for the 17-hour run to Clearwater, Florida. We each took turns at the wheel until we were tired. The one sleeping stayed next to the helm so the one driving could easily grab the other when they needed a break. We wore our inflatable life jackets all night, and even kept one on LuSea. Over 60 miles offshore, and I was at home, in my comfort zone, away from all radio and cell phone contact, moving along in total darkness, Roy asleep by my side.

We don't have an Epirb or SAT phone. The following morning I thought, *This is the time I wish I didn't know so much*, as it was a pretty stupid move to not have these life-saving devices on board, considering my knowledge of the hazards while traveling in open water. Sometimes I can be so darn stubborn, and I hope that "I can do it by myself," "prove it to the world" attitude doesn't get me in too much trouble one day.

I now slow down to pass others, calling ahead to advise the sailors or slower trawlers of a "slow pass." I am proficient on the radio and handle all radio conversations. I wonder, if I ever get back in a fast center console, will I run at high speeds again over a slow trawler's wake just for the thrill?

We had been on board for three years without a break from our home on the water, so this summer we put *Our Turn* up on the hard and took a car trip to Nova Scotia, Newfoundland, and Labrador. It was a wonderful change of pace for us, but we couldn't wait to get back on the boat and simplify our life again. It's all the people, and the happy times spent together we enjoy. Most boaters have a common goal to enjoy life, where the folks we met traveling on land didn't seem to have that sense of freedom and ability to relax. They are still trapped in day-to-day issues. Being on the water seems to help wash the stress away. Maybe the wind blows our problems away. Whatever the reason, I look forward to returning to the back deck of *Our Turn*, where we have had many impromptu get-togethers, with free and easy spirited folks. It may be a marina gathering for a potluck supper, or a dinghy ride with the folks at anchor beside us. I just love the boating lifestyle.

I definitely enjoy the road less traveled. I try to locate the off-the-beaten-path side trips, rivers and anchorages. These less traveled places are where we seem to just fit in. I never look back to the days of the independent woman I was, as now I realize I must be of benefit to the team. As for my partner, Roy, I couldn't ask for a better first mate, or captain as he sees it! The travels and the people we meet are what now shape us. The experiences we yearn for are those no one else will ever have. I love every moment of our life on board.

My one parting piece of advice to all you women boaters would be to strike up conversations with other women you see around the marina you are in. We all need that female companionship, just a nice walk and talk. After all, we are all in the same boat! Now… if I can just get Roy to go sailing…

Ellen Langer, born and raised Miami Beach, Florida, has always loved the water. She has spent her life traveling and looking for adventures; passing up circumstances that would ground her. She spends her time divided between her love for rehabbing real estate properties and cruising with her partner Roy. She strives to fulfill her motto, "No barnacles will grow on my bottom!"

Susan Armstrong

Vessel: M/V *Golf Cart* – 35-foot Nordhavn Trawler
Residence/Homeport: Naples, Florida

"You wanna do what? Are you friggin' nuts?"

Such was my reaction when my husband, Bruce, first broached the subject of spending our summers living on a boat and cruising the Intracoastal Waterway (ICW). I had no idea what such a voyage entailed, but I did have visions of us adrift in the Atlantic, miles from any shore, all alone – just us and the sharks. That's not the way it was at all.

We'd boated on Long Island Sound for many years in our 24-foot runabout. These had been primarily daytrips, but we did stay overnight several times on that boat. It was more like camping out. Although the peacefulness of anchoring out and the beauty of nature at night were undeniable pleasures, the sleeping bags, a Coleman cook stove, and a Port-a-Potty were not exactly my idea of amenities. Still, there were times when we talked of cruising farther in a more comfortable boat. Little did I realize how far that "talk" would take us.

This was the point where my husband, who is full of wanderlust, brought up the idea of long-range cruising on the ICW. I thought "going farther" meant that he just wanted to take weekend trips on the Sound. I resisted – he persisted.

After some discussion, I became convinced we would not be marooned on a desert island. I learned that the ICW is, in large part, a series of waterways that are relatively protected from high seas and bad weather. Canals, rivers, and lakes – "OK, so this may be doable," I thought. Actually, the thought of traveling through so many different areas, all the sights we would see and experiences we would have, was beginning to sound intriguing to me. At some point during these talks my would-be captain heard about the Great Loop, read *Honey, Let's Get a Boat...* by Ron and Eva Stob, and our fate was sealed – in his mind at least. I was still a bit skeptical, but I was gradually getting used to the idea.

This kind of voyage was obviously going to require a bigger boat. The search for just the right one began in earnest. We settled on a Nordhavn 35, a single-engine diesel trawler with a single stateroom. It had almost all the comforts of home – including a real bed, an electric stove, refrigerator, microwave, and a real flushing toilet! Next, we needed to name her. We'd recently moved to a golf course community on the Gulf Coast of Florida and our new neighbors asked if we were going to buy a golf cart. Aha! Our new floating apartment became *Gulf Cart*. Our friends thought we were crazy to think about spending several months together in a space that was only 35 feet long and 13 feet wide. They could possibly be right, but we would never have known unless we tried.

Although we'd both taken several Power Squadron boating courses years earlier, in preparation for live-aboard cruising Bruce got his captain's license and I took a Sea Sense Boating School course for women. These things didn't give us all the answers to potential boating problems, but they gave us a starting point to understanding cruising basics, and some feeling for what we might encounter along the way.

My seafaring hunk did most of the equipment planning such as electronics selection, chart purchasing and research on required documentation. I was largely responsible for provisioning the boat and, surprise to me, I was good at it! I was so good we ended up with enough food to feed a flotilla. I had no idea how often we would be able to get to a grocery store once we were underway, so I bought as much as I could ahead of time. I basically bought all the non-perishables and bulky items that we'd need for the summer – paper towels, toiletries, canned goods, cleaning supplies, coffee and shelf-stable milk. I had this fear that we might run out of food sometime, so as a precaution, I bought an emergency food supply. I bought it at Costco... in bulk. Imagine Bruce's reaction when he saw me stow aboard three huge jars of peanut butter. I don't know whether he was amazed or hysterical since he was laughing so hard. I still haven't lived that one down. Let me tell you right now, you don't have to worry about grocery stores while cruising in U.S. waters on the Loop – leave the bulk peanut butter at home!

D-day (departure day) arrived. We said goodbye to our landlubber friends and moved onto the boat. I was a little apprehensive, but I figured since other people had done this before us, then we could too. From the beginning, Bruce was the captain and I was the navigator/first mate, though we each took turns doing both things. It was a learning experience for captain and crew. Along the way, we found there were two important rules that helped keep us on an even keel.

Susan Armstrong – *Golf Cart*

Rule #1 – There will be no criticizing of captaining, line handling, or boating skills until after cocktails are served.

Rule #2 – Cocktails will not be served to captain or crew until the boat is secured for the night.

You'd be surprised how unimportant some details become if you have a little time to cool off before you talk about them.

We gradually developed a rhythm to our day-to-day activities. Most days, we would rise just after sunrise, do all our daily boat checks, and be on our way. We liked to travel until early afternoon and then stop for the day to enjoy our surroundings at dock or anchor.

While traveling, most of our time was spent together at the helm station – we found a second set of eyes was always useful, even in calm water. If there were no apparent hazards to watch for, it was pleasant just to watch for wildlife.

It wasn't very long before a really ugly monster raised its head – my own personal fear of running aground. Questions kept running around in my head... "How will we get off?" "Will everyone see us and laugh at us?" "Will we survive?" (I never claimed to be logical here.) I can't really put my finger on why this distressed me so much, but this fear stayed with me for a large part of our journey. It didn't matter whether we were in four or 44 feet of water; I was still always watching the depth finder. We could be in 25 feet of water, and if we suddenly dropped down to 16 feet, I'd warn my ever-forgiving captain that we were getting shallow. He is truly an angel for not throwing me overboard early in the voyage for my vocal displays of distress. This is where Rule #1 came in handy!

Then something magical happened. We were in a section of the journey where we had no electronic charts. So rather than watching the upcoming depth on the display, I watched the channel markers to be sure we stayed in the channel. Voilà! I didn't even think about the depth! After that, I made an effort not to focus on the electronic display so much. From this point on, I was so much more relaxed about the depth situation.

Besides, what's the worst that can happen? If you do run aground, you may have to wait for a tow to get you underway again. Alternately, you may get to sit on your boat for a couple of hours reading a good book and waiting for the incoming tide, waving to all those passing cruisers who seem to be staring at you. No, they're not laughing at you – that's sympathy in their eyes because there, but for the grace of God, go they.

During our trip, we spent about half our time anchored out. I found these to be great opportunities to watch for wildlife on shore or just to enjoy the scenery. The night skies were amazing when there were no city lights around to dim the stars. We learned to anchor out only when the weather was cooperating, but any long-range cruiser will probably be forced to spend the night on the hook at some point in bad weather. Anchoring out is not fun when you have to spend a stormy night awake making sure the boat stays in place.

We found marinas readily available in most areas we cruised, and we took full advantage of them. For one thing, they were a haven on weekends. We could stay in our snug, protected slip and leave the open water to the locals who were hell-bent on having a rollicking good time.

We found our stops at marinas to be rejuvenating. Captain and first mate, in our case, got along quite well, but after three or four days of being alone together exclusively on the hook, we both needed other opportunities for human contact. You could always tell the cruisers who'd been anchored out for a while – they were the ones that couldn't quit talking. Marinas also provided a chance to do laundry, re-provision, get mail and, more importantly, eat out. In addition, if we were lucky, we'd have cable TV and be able to find out what was happening in the world. Cruising isn't just about being on the water. It's also about stopping along the way to see the historical and cultural sights on land, meeting people, and sampling the local cuisine.

I truly loved the cruising life. Most cruisers will tell you that the people you meet make the experience worthwhile. That is unquestionably true. There seems to be a special camaraderie among boaters and would-be boaters. If we needed help, it was always there. I needed dental work done on short notice once, and a local dentist made time in his schedule for me just because he wanted to be a cruiser someday too. If we needed a ride, often a local resident would loan us his car, even if we'd never met before. The company of other cruisers was a pure joy, either talking on the radio or meeting them in person at marinas.

To be fair, not every day of cruising was idyllic. We suffered some injuries, we got in some nasty storms, and some days of travel were just way too long. However, none of those were reasons to stay home. The situations we encountered could happen to anyone, traveling or not. The pleasure of the journey far outweighed any problems we had.

I learned a lot cruising the Eastern United States. Geography becomes much clearer when you're only traveling at 7.5 knots – you have a chance to really absorb your surroundings. Towns you've been in before are sometimes completely different when seen from the water. The type of people you meet often changes during a long-distance trip, and this diversity in turn broadens your attitudes toward others and toward life in general. I think the most important thing I learned is that I can do it. I now know that I have the ability, the stamina, and the sense to complete any task I truly want to complete.

We've sold our boat now, and we're on our way to new adventures. However, I still find myself drawn to marinas to see if there are any cruisers around that might need help or a ride somewhere. I'm interested to hear where they've been and to listen to their stories of those places and experiences. As I write this we're driving to Alaska, and whenever we cross a river, I think what fun it would be to be cruising THAT waterway. In fact, we're still cruising, albeit in a different "vessel." We're still exploring and meeting new people – we're just on a different form of long-distance adventure by car instead of boat.

Susan Armstrong is a wife, a mother, and a grandmother, she is 60 years old chronologically but much younger mentally. That means she's gained some wisdom through the years but still likes to go out and play, especially after her arthritis pains ease up in the morning.

Susan's official residence is in Naples, Florida, but she's traveled enough that she's learned to call wherever she is at the moment… home. She and her captain have been married for over 40 years, they've spent the last six summers living aboard *Gulf Cart*, the last four of those cruising the Great Loop.

Jan Nelson

Vessel: M/V *Wanderin' Star* – 55-foot Hampton Pilothouse
Residence/Homeport: Punta Gorda, Florida
Website: TracyandJan.com

Although I currently live in Florida, I was born and raised in Minnesota, a state known as the "Land of 10,000 Lakes." I was hooked on being near the water from my earliest years when I learned to swim and went fishing with my parents and siblings. Later, I enjoyed getting out on the water on canoes and water-skiing. It wasn't until I was living on the western shore of Lake Superior that my husband, Tracy, and I decided to get a large boat.

Our business was located right on Lake Superior. Every day we watched that huge body of water. Some days our office view was a stormy one with enormous waves crashing onto shore. Many days we gazed at the tranquil blue waters, beautiful blue skies and watched the fishing boats, sailboats, and other vessels that seemed to play on the lake. And we thought, "Why not us?"

We purchased our first "big" boat on a snowy Thanksgiving weekend when my husband, two sons, and I decided to take a look at it on a whim. We climbed all over that boat, peeking into cupboards, closets and corners, our sons found and claimed their bedroom, a mid-cabin berth they nicknamed "the coffin," and Tracy checked out the engines and other mechanical systems. We were in love. However, when we sat in the pilothouse chairs and looked down the long bow of this first boat, a 24-footer, we looked at each other and said, "Oh my gosh! Could we learn to drive a boat this big?" The salesperson assured us that he would show us how to drive it when we picked it up in the spring, but we were still intimidated and decided we needed more knowledge.

Women On Board Cruising

That first winter, we signed up for the Coast Guard Auxiliary's Safe Boating Course. After Tracy and I completed that course, we realized how much we still didn't know, so we promptly signed up for the local Power Squadron's Safe Boating Course. We also signed up our two sons, then ages 13 and 11, for the course. The second course repeated many of the things we learned in the first course, but this second time something clicked, "Aha! Now we've got it!" We heard fun boating stories from the instructors, and our excitement increased as we waited for spring to arrive. We were ready to proceed – fearlessly.

Our family spent many fun years on our first boat as we explored Lake Superior, including the beautiful Apostle Islands and the primitive wilderness of Isle Royale. As our boys grew to six-feet tall and outgrew "the coffin," we moved up to a 32-foot boat. This larger boat had two propellers. I looked at all the complicated levers and dials at the helm of the boat and thought, "This was way too difficult. I'd better let Tracy drive from now on." Like most husbands, mine was most comfortable when he was in control, in this case, at the helm. In addition, I noticed that it was rare to see a woman at the helm. However, when we went for a sea trial, it was Tracy's misfortune that the boat broker's salesperson was a female. Curiously, I asked her, "Do you drive all of these big boats?" and she replied, "Sure. It's not hard." She drove the boat flawlessly. I was impressed and thought to myself, "If she can do it, I can do it!"

Ever since then, my husband and I have continued to share being captains on our boats. Our agreement was that whomever was at the helm was the captain and the one responsible for giving instructions to the other person or guests aboard. The other person was responsible for listening and following the captain's orders. If there's one thing I learned over the years, it's that anyone doing a lot of boating will eventually make a mistake. Those bloopers could turn into a dent or scratch! But hey, dents and scratches could be fixed. Big mistakes? That's why you have insurance. Fortunately, we haven't had an insurance claim. Yet! I put the first scratch on our 48-foot boat, as I miscalculated and turned too quickly when leaving the fuel dock at St. Bart's in the Caribbean. *Scrraaaatch!* It wasn't pretty. But that's how we learned.

That first big-water boat was a used 24-foot Sea Ray Sundancer, and it still feels like the largest boat we have owned. Ever! We thought we'd NEVER learn to drive that boat, and I think our marina neighbors at our dock wondered the same thing. There were several ugly docking and undocking moments as we tried to figure all this maneuvering stuff out. However, we both eventually learned to drive it, and in time we graduated to boats of larger sizes, 32, 42, 48 and a 55-footer. However, none of these later boats would ever seem as big as that first 24-footer.

Some people were amazed, when they saw a female docking and undocking our larger boats. Frankly, I thought that was the fun part. Tracy enjoyed knowing that on a lazy, sunny afternoon, he could take a nap on the bridge while I captained the boat. People often looked at him with surprise after hearing that I shared the captaining duties with him. Several times I heard him tell people that of the two of us, I was the only one who captained our 55-foot Hampton solo. This was when I brought the boat from the dock of our home to a marina about six miles away. It was a sleepy Sunday afternoon with few people on the marina docks to help me in. But I saw one person and shouted to him, asking if he'd help me with the lines, I got the lines ready for him before I got close and gently brought the boat into the dock without mishap.

When dividing boat duties, I tended to care for the inside of the boat cabin (cleaned, made meals, did laundry) and my husband took care of maintenance of all the mechanical aspects of the boat (engines, pumps, etc.). When we cruised in saltwater, washing the outside of the boat needed to be done after every trip. Sometimes we both washed it, or if I was fixing dinner, my husband would handle it alone. Waxing the boat? I don't suppose anyone felt they waxed their boat as often as they should, and we tended to put it off too. It's amazing, how many hours it can take to do a good job of washing and waxing a boat. Once we had a boat-cleaning business do this for us in Fort Lauderdale. They did such an outstanding job that almost every time we were in Fort Lauderdale we made an appointment with them to clean our 55-foot boat, *Wanderin' Star*. But get this; it took five men and one woman working hard and steady one and a half days. That's 72 people hours.

As I've mentioned, we started boating all around Lake Superior, which isn't a lake to sneer at. It can be calm, peaceful and breathtakingly beautiful... or it can be snarly and mean. If you're familiar with all the ships that have sunk on Lake Superior (remember Gordon Lightfoot's song, *The Wreck of the Edmund Fitzgerald*), you realize that this is a body of water to respect when cruising it. Superior, the largest of the Great Lakes, was our boating territory for many years. We eventually branched out, exploring all five of the Great Lakes.

We also cruised the Caribbean. We began in Puerto Rico as we headed east and then southward. We checked out each island – the Spanish, U.S. and British Virgin Islands, St. Martin, St. Bart's, St. Kitts, Saba, Montserrat, Guadeloupe, until we reached Dominica. We entered and cleared customs at each island. We then turned around and island-hopped back to Puerto Rico. Such incredible adventures to experience and beautiful areas where we did a lot of snorkeling. The cuisine we tried, especially at the French islands with their perfectly prepared meals and delicate sauces – delicious! Imagine being anchored in a protected harbor of turquoise waters, sandy beaches with palm trees surrounding you, having cocktails while sitting on your back deck watching the sun set. "Does life get any better than this?" we asked ourselves.

As wonderful as cruising could be, there were also challenges. One important thing these Caribbean countries taught us was to go with the flow. Need to get some boat work done? Don't get stressed out because you're now on Caribbean time. You had an appointment? Don't be surprised if the other person was late

– one or two hours late was considered prompt and actually arriving any time during that day was considered on time. The country may have the boat repair parts you need. Or not. You may need to have parts flown in, which could take several days. Overnight shipping? It won't happen, so relax, it will probably take two, maybe three days to get the needed part. Go with the flow!

For example, when we had one of our engines die, we cruised on one engine to an authorized Caterpillar dealer in Guadeloupe. We made an appointment for them to come fix our boat engine problem. The mechanic came aboard, he looked at the problem, asked a couple questions of my husband, and after 15 seconds started backing off the boat saying, "Too much work, BIG job, too much work, VERY BIG job," and then left. When the authorized Caterpillar dealer won't help you, what can you do? GO WITH THE FLOW! My husband worked for three days, testing this and trying that until he finally fixed our engine problem.

Foreign languages? We noticed that knowing just a few words in the local language (good morning sir or madam, good evening, please and thank you, etc.) went a looooong way toward pleasant conversations and improving your chances of getting things done. When you watched other Americans in grocery stores or custom offices who spoke only in English, the locals were polite but brisk. When I'd stumble and fumble, trying to say my words in their language, I'd notice their faces would soften. They'd smile at you. They'd try to help you finish your sentence. They were probably thinking, "This woman sounds so ridiculous! But at least she's trying." You'd be amazed at what you can accomplish by trying to meet someone halfway.

A few years later, after talking to two different couples that had done the Great Loop, and after spending a week aboard one of the couples' boats while experiencing part of their Loop adventure, we decided, "Let's do the Loop!" We were now retired and living in southwest Florida. We started the Loop from the dock of our home in Punta Gorda and took our time heading north while exploring the East Coast's Intracoastal Waterway (ICW). We snapped photos while gliding past the Statue of Liberty. We headed up the Hudson River into the Great Lakes for the summer, then in the fall journeyed southward through the river system beginning at Chicago, finally ending in the Gulf of Mexico and eventually back to our home in Florida.

What was a typical day when cruising on the Loop? It might have started with checking the weather first thing in the morning and then leaving the marina dock at an early hour. Tracy would take the helm while I made breakfast. Without a nine-to-five job to rush to, I found that I had lots of time to experiment in the galley. I frequently had a big batch of bran muffin mix in the refrigerator. I took out some batter, added some berries and threw the muffins into the oven while mixing up a breakfast egg casserole. When the muffins came out of the oven, in went the casserole. I headed up to the bridge with fresh fruit, warm muffins, a hot casserole and steaming cups of coffee. As we cruised and ate, Tracy and I would smile at each other and frequently one of us would say, "It just doesn't get any better than this!" Sometimes we'd pass a slower-moving boat and realize they were the folks we'd met the night before at the marina dock. My husband would call on the marine radio and ask them if they'd like some hot blueberry muffins. I'd wrap a couple up in a napkin, put them in a bag, then I looped the bag over the boathook, and extend the boathook out and over to our new friends on their boat.

After a leisurely breakfast, one of us pulled out the cruising books, found the area we were in, looked ahead 50, 75, maybe 100 miles and said, "Where shall we stop tonight?" We'd read about the areas, discuss the pros and cons, make a tentative plan, and then call the marinas ahead to see if they had room to make a reservation. We had a plan. When we hit our destination, the marinas would frequently have laundry facilities and loaner cars. Since we had a washer and dryer aboard, we'd sign out the loaner car and head into town or the big city. If they had one, we'd do a city tour. If there was nothing else that appealed to us, we'd only stay at that spot for a day. Other times, we'd stay there for a week or so.

I was surprised when I realized how poor my geography and American history was. I had gotten decent grades in those courses when in school; why had I missed so much? When you travel at speeds as slow as 8-15 miles per hour and make overnight stops along the way, you experience a more hands-on learning experience. I realized how very little I learned in school but felt I was somehow now filling in the gaps. We found this educational opportunity fascinating.

I especially enjoyed reading the little local town papers in the Southern States. There were often articles on the Civil War. Because of this, I started to learn more about this war that I was never taught while attending schools in the north. Like the fact that the Emancipation Proclamation didn't free the slaves in all the states, only the states that rebelled. It was a hoot to read about the War of 1812 while cruising around Lake Ontario. On the United States side, we read that in one battle during the War of 1812, the British forces were held off. Then when we crossed over to Canada and read their account of the same battle, they claimed the British successfully contained the Yanks. Two different perspectives on the exact same battle!

When people heard about our trip-planning method (leave the dock, eat breakfast, and make a plan) some people might have asked, "Wouldn't it have been better to make a longer plan? Maybe a month-long plan or at least a week-long plan?" I don't think that scenario works well for boaters. There are too many variables like weather, finding interesting things to see and do; or, sometimes just feeling lazy and wanting to do nothing, go nowhere! We felt it was important to remain flexible.

When we completed the Loop, we decided that we weren't done quite yet. We continued cruising, first to the Florida Keys for Christmas and New Year's. Next, we spent a winter exploring several of the 700 Bahamian Islands. We cruised on our *Wanderin' Star*, the Hampton Pilothouse, for one and a half years and went a total of 11,000 miles (900 engine hours).

Women On Board Cruising

There were some things I wished I'd known before I started long-distance boating? I wish... we'd had headsets right from the beginning! When we cruised the Loop, I saw a couple using headsets as they docked their boat. Their docking went so smoothly and the couple was actually smiling and talking to each other calmly right after docking the boat! Soon, I wandered over to chat with the wife and she told me about these headsets. She told me that many people called them "marriage savers." Instead of yelling at your spouse, who was on the bow or cockpit of your boat getting the lines ready and couldn't hear you, you could quietly talk to each other while having your hands free. As you were handling the lines, you could calmly and quietly tell the captain that your stern was ten, eight, five, or three feet away from the dock, or to bring the starboard side in closer, or that the dockmaster deserved a big (or no) tip. The headsets worked great, were inexpensive, and I'd recommend them for anyone with a boat over 22 feet. I ordered them from the Internet (cruisingsolutions.com). My husband and I love ours and would never be without them again on a bigger boat!

I wish... I'd talked to more long-distance cruisers beforehand to understand how to handle visitors better. First of all, I learned to always leave at least a week or two between guests' visits. You shouldn't pile them up back to back; you could get tired and crabby and end up not being able to enjoy your cruising life. No matter how helpful your company was, you need downtime.

Secondly, I learned to help company set their expectations correctly. Let them know that they could meet you close to a city with a major airport and that you'd do your best to be in that city when they arrived. However, due to weather or problems with the boat, you might not be able to be at the prearranged meeting spot, and they might need to take a long cab ride to wherever you were docked or anchored. Let your guests do the traveling. Do NOT allow yourselves to be pushed into getting to a location by a certain time. Safe boating doesn't allow for taking risky chances. You will also need to let your guests know where you estimate the boat will be at the end of their stay so they can make their travel plans home. It's possible you might never leave the initial meeting place because of weather or mechanical issues. You may find that that some friends/family couldn't handle that type of visit with you. But many, especially friends/family that love adventure, would understand and would find it easy to adapt to these circumstances.

I wish... I'd taken a woman's boating course sooner. Two girlfriends and I attended such a course in St. Petersburg, Florida for five days aboard a Grand Banks trawler. We took a Sea Sense Boating School course (seasenseboating.com). This school is owned, and all the classes are taught, by women. There were only four students in our group, all women. We lived aboard during the five days, and we learned an amazing amount about boating. We learned everything from reading charts, engine maintenance, docking, line handling and more. Our instructors smilingly told us not to worry about our mistakes and "There will be no yelling." I learned so much! And surprisingly I learned the most about smarter ways to handle the boat lines, something I felt I already knew.

Jan Nelson – *Wanderin' Star*

Dreams! Our cruising lifestyle started with a dream. Could we? Should we? We found that for many couples it would only be one person's dream being fulfilled, other times it would be both people's dream.

One thing I found interesting when doing the Loop was how many couples had one partner who was fairly seriously ill. It seemed like it was always the unhealthy person's dream to cruise the Loop, and the healthy spouse helped to make it possible. This demonstrated a huge commitment by the healthy spouse because they were doing the bulk of the work.

We had an interesting experience when going through one of the many locks on the river system. Of course, pleasure boats went through the locks last after the commercial and tour boats. When you locked through, the lockmaster would frequently call ahead and let the next lock know how many pleasure boats were heading their way. It usually ended up that a group of boats would move together in this fashion from one lock to the next. The lockmaster almost always waited for the slowest boat in the group, before closing the doors and proceeding with the lock through. There were a couple of days on the rivers when one boat in our group was ALWAYS last and much farther behind the rest of us. Everyone else would be all tied up at the lock and during the first few locks, we'd wonder what the hold-up was. We looked out and saw that this last boat got close to the lock and then slowed waaaaay down. They seemed to inch along, entering the lock and creeping over to the wall and finally, but slowly, tying up to the wall.

We became exasperated. Didn't they realize how many people were waiting for them? I mean, how inconsiderate! We began hoping they'd stop somewhere and exit our "group." But no, there they'd be, coming at the next lock, and they'd continue their snail's pace when entering the lock. One night, we were docked and ready to walk up to Mel's Riverdock Restaurant in Hardin, Illinois, for dinner to enjoy a piece of their famous – among boaters – gooseberry pie. We groaned as we looked out and saw the slow boat coming in. It's an unwritten law among boaters that you help an incoming boat tie up. We did – silent groan. After docking, the couple on the slow boat talked about having dinner at the restaurant. Did we want to join them? Another silent groan, but we did join them. I'm so happy I got to know them because we found out that the husband was legally blind. Can you believe it? The wife was doing everything necessary for them to cruise the Loop. She drove the boat. When they got close to the dock or marine wall, the blind husband took the helm and the wife climbed out to the edge of the boat to tie up. Not only was she ready with the lines, but she also quietly called back to him and told him which way to steer! Talk about making your spouse's dream of cruising the Loop a reality!

The Loop is within the U.S. and Canadian waterways (with optional side trips to the Bahamas). Medical facilities were usually only a few hours away. If necessary, hospital helicopters were probably only a call away from your cell phone or marine radio. We carried a huge first aid kit on our boat, plus a couple of boating medical emergency books "for dummies." There was only one time we needed a doctor, and that was when we cruised in the Caribbean. Unfortunately, a jellyfish stung Tracy and one of our guests. Luckily, Tracy's college roommate was on board, he is an M.D. and the problems were quickly dealt with. It helped to see that he read our "dummies" medical book and agreed with their instructions.

At one marina in the Caribbean, we docked next to a couple who lived aboard their sailboat and had raised their son while boating all over the Caribbean. When we chatted with them, we talked about the quality of the Caribbean medical facilities. They felt very comfortable with them. In fact, the husband had open-heart surgery in Venezuela. They said they had never been more impressed by a hospital than the one they were at in Venezuela. The surgery was a great success.

Did we encounter storms? Of course we did. Most of the time, we were tied up to a dock in a marina. We're rather cautious boaters. We'd wait a storm out for as long as it took rather than cross any open water in stormy weather. Cruising across the Gulf of Mexico, the Great Lakes, or the Gulf Stream on the way to the Bahamas, you could wait one to two weeks for the right weather window. We always waited. However, there were a couple of times we started out in calm seas and good predictions and several hours later a storm hit us out of nowhere.

That happened one time when we cruised from Guadeloupe. We started our day about 5:30 a.m. and cruised through sunny and calm waters until around noon. We were heading to St. Martin and were about halfway there when we saw the angry storm clouds rolling in from the southeast. We considered alternative plans. Soon, the winds were howling and we quickly decided to head for the closest island, which was Saba. Saba is a completely round-shaped island with no safe harbors. In the entire country, it had only six mooring lines, all on the west side of the island. As we drew near, we saw that there were six boats moored. Luckily, a huge cruiser of 100-plus feet pulled away. We grabbed their mooring line and waited out the winds for two days. We were safely protected on the west side of the island. After a few hours of settling in, we hopped into our dinghy, pulled up onto shore and started to explore the island, which is described in cruising manuals as the Shangri La of the Caribbean.

Did I get lonely? I think I did more than my husband. It was easily resolved. We had many friends and family who came to visit us while we were cruising. We had such great times with them. I also kept connected to people by e-mail and cell phone calls. I made weekly calls to my elderly father, who loved to pull out the maps and charts that I'd sent to him ahead of time so he could see exactly where we were at any moment. Website? We never intended to have a website of our travels, but so many people asked us about it, we finally started one. It was surprising to me how many people followed our travels that way! I would call someone on the cell phone, perhaps to wish him or her a happy birthday, and I would start to tell that person where we were and surprisingly they already knew! They'd seen the photos I'd posted. This was remarkable to me. In addition, we found time to fly home every month or two for important events such as weddings, funerals, special birthdays, holidays, etc.

During our many cruises, we made lots of new friends. When we cruised the Caribbean, we didn't find many boaters whom we could travel with. Why? The sailboats cruised so much slower than us that it just wasn't easy to travel with them. Most of the powerboats in the Caribbean were yachts of 100 feet or larger. We chatted with the crew, not the owners. But on the Great Loop and the Bahamas trip, it was exactly the opposite. More often than not, when we'd finished docking or anchoring for the night, another boater would stop by and say, "Happy hour on the dock about 5:30 p.m., BYOB and a snack to share." We met new boaters, heard their exciting stories, shared tips and cautionary tales or heard accounts of fun places to stop. We all laughed at everyone else's misadventures, and pretty soon it was 8:30 p.m. and we realized that we hadn't made dinner yet. Oh well, who needed dinner after all those snacks? What fun we had getting to know these other boaters. We had so much in common. We shared a mutual love of adventure and exploration. Consequently, many friendships quickly clicked and after many initial meetings we thought, "Wow, I really like these people."

I remember one happy hour like the one I described above. It was in Spanish Wells in the Bahamas, and we were aboard another person's boat munching on snacks and drinking cocktails with our newest cruising friends. After a while, another couple came aboard for the party. The husband had cruised to the Bahamas, hoping his wife would join him. The wife had finally flown in and was trying to figure out how she could stay with him and cruise. She was clearly having a hard time with it.

After she was introduced to me and heard about how long I'd been cruising, she promptly sat next to me and started drilling me with questions. "How did you do your laundry?" "Where did you buy your groceries?" "What about storms?" Every time I'd answer a new question, she'd immediately have another. I was happy to share. After a while, the questions started coming more slowly until they seemed to stop. All of a sudden, she looked at me with a GOTCHA look in her eyes, and said, "Pedicures! How do you get pedicures?" I replied, "Why, I do them myself." With surprise on her face that turned to quiet wonder, she replied, "Ohhh! I suppose I could do that."

I wish for you many wonderful days aboard your own boat! – Jan

Jan Nelson lives in Punta Gorda, Florida located on a canal connecting to the Gulf of Mexico. She enjoys Lake Superior summers in Superior, Wisconsin. Jan and husband, Tracy, have been married for 38 years and have two sons, one daughter-in-law, and two grandsons, Jacob and Max.

Before retiring, Jan and Tracy owned a technology business, which specialized in helping businesses network and maintain their computer systems, for 22 years.

For fun, Jan enjoys boating, traveling, photography, reading, music, walking, and doing any activity with her family. Jan feels that retirement is terrific, but being a grandma is absolutely the very best job in the world.

Barbara Benjamin

Vessel: M/V *Golden Lily* – 42-foot Nordic Tug Trawler
Residence: Killingworth, Connecticut
Homeport: Westbrook, Connecticut
Website: goldenlilytug.com

My husband, Jim, and I bought our first boat early in our marriage and took the 12-week Coast Guard Auxiliary course, *Boating Skills and Seamanship (BS&S)*. That summer started our boating adventures, and for ten years we boated totally on Long Island Sound. We then decided it was time to broaden our horizons, and we excitedly headed west, around New York City, and north to upstate New York, Lake Champlain, and Canada. We eventually joined the Coast Guard Auxiliary and took courses in navigation and piloting. In addition, Jim and I became instructors for boating safety classes and vessel safety check examiners.

We decided to trade in our powerboat for a 42-foot Nordic Tug trawler, which we later named *Golden Lily*. The four criteria we had for our new boat were fuel economy, living space, galley up, and easy access for our Golden Retriever, Lily. *Golden Lily* provided us with all four. The pilothouse, saloon, cabin, bridge, upper deck, cockpit, and galley provided us with plenty of room for living as well as our own individual "space." Living aboard for extended lengths of time was enjoyable for both of us. Lily was able to get off in many different docking situations: swim deck, side deck under the railing, tailgate ramp from under the ladder, and from the pilothouse gate. With Lily traveling with us these features proved helpful and in fact made this the perfect long-distance cruising boat for us. We found that we loved the long-term cruising lifestyle.

Our longest cruise at this point was the "Little Loop," which took us up the Hudson River to the Erie and Oswego Canals, across Lake Ontario, the

Rideau Canal to Ottawa, then the St. Lawrence River to the Richelieu River and south to Lake Champlain, where we then were back to familiar waters and on our way home.

It became increasingly clear to us that this was no longer enough of a challenge for us! Jim had always dreamed of doing the Great Loop. We had joined America's Great Loop Cruisers' Association (AGLCA) several years before, but I personally never thought we would ever get to do this long-distance boat trip. As I looked at the route for the Great Loop, it seemed so long, and we would be heading through so many different bodies of water, including Lake Michigan and the Gulf of Mexico. There were too many plans and preparations to make, as well as charts to buy. I couldn't imagine traveling around the eastern half of the country in a boat for a year. I just didn't know if I was up to this kind of trip.

I finally reached my 36th year of teaching elementary school, and the trip preparations were now in high gear. This is when some of my real anxiety started to build. There was so much to do to get ready for the trip. I had to complete the school year, keep teaching the children, prepare the class for state testing, pack my classroom, and get all the supplies on the boat. I had fallen in the driveway in January and had a hairline fracture in my tibia just below my knee, and Jim had three surgical procedures that year. In May, he had a setback of a medical condition, and we had to cancel our big "Going Away Party" with all our friends and family. I really didn't think we should go, and the anxiety continued to grow.

We continued to prepare for the trip anyway, and our Golden Retriever, Lily, the REAL Golden Lily, saw us loading the boat and suspected a big trip was in the near future. Lily had turned out to be a great boating dog after traveling two summers with us, but she had no idea of the trip that was in store for her this time!

The last week of school arrived, and I, in my haste, running to keep on schedule for school in the morning, broke my toe on the frame of the doorway in the cabin. I hobbled all week long, wearing Crocs, which turned out to be my footwear for the next six weeks, since I was unable to put on a shoe. Finally, my last day of school arrived and my retirement began. Jim had the OK from his doctor, and an appointment scheduled for October, when we would drive home from our planned location in Kentucky.

I was somewhat exhausted from ending a busy school year and having only five days to get our last-minute preparations done, but on a sunny day in late June, we left our slip in Westbrook, Connecticut to begin our Great Loop journey. I couldn't believe that we were actually going to do this! It still didn't seem real at first since we were still in familiar waters. However, when we reached Canada after crossing Lake Ontario and were headed towards Trenton, we were in brand-new and unfamiliar, to us, cruising territory.

As we traveled along the route, we met up with many other boaters, and most of the anxiety disappeared for the moment. I was keeping track of our journey on a Great Loop map on our website, making little red stars to show our route as we continued north. Once we reached the Georgian Bay, and the dotted stars began to reach the North Channel, I definitely knew we were on our way, and there was no turning back!

Jim and I had already worked out the docking and maneuvering of our boat during the previous years that we boated and I, as crew and line handler, was able to instinctively "feel" each situation as we approached a lock or dock. However, no docking or locking is ever quite the same. Always with a different mix of wind, current and tide, communication between captain and crew is imperative. Jim would usually dock our boat from the flybridge rather than the pilothouse because of the increased visibility from there, and we discovered hand signals, which I could easily see from the bow. We would give signals to each other on which side we would be tying to the dock. We were fortunate enough to have had people on the dock to help catch our lines in most places, but I became very good at throwing a spring line around a cleat to secure the boat. Practice makes perfect!

Many years ago, when we first cruised north and had never been in a lock before, I met a couple on the Hudson River and asked for advice on the locking process. The woman said to me, "How good is your marriage?" I answered, "What do you mean? Wonderful, of course!" But I became apprehensive about her words and wondered how our trip through the Champlain Canal would be. Luckily, we met a great couple from Canada who reassured me that it was a snap. All we had to do was put on rubber gloves, grab two hanging lines, one from the bow and one from the stern, hold the boat, and that was it, and they were right! Going through locks became a breeze.

However, new challenges always creep in to test you. We were locking down on the Erie Canal in our powerboat after the wind had picked up to 25 knots. There was no way to turn back or tie up anywhere, so we had to keep going. No help was offered at the lock, so I did my best to grab a hanging line from the bow, and Jim ran down to grab a hanging line from the stern, as was our usual procedure. The wind was so strong that neither of us could hold the boat, and it turned perpendicular to the lock walls. Jim let go and ran up to the bridge to regain control. He eventually turned the boat right and actually drove the boat into the center of the lock, back and forth slowly to keep parallel to the walls. Luckily, there were no other boats in the lock with us. Relieved by our success and quick thinking, we proceeded on our way.

We immediately questioned whether we would be able to avoid this kind of situation again as we continued on to the next lock. This lock had hanging lines that were too far apart for our boat length, and we had to grab a cable. This was our lucky break because here was the answer to our quest for a better way to secure our boat in a lock. I took one of our shorter dock lines and secured one end to the center cleat on the boat. Next, I wrapped the other end around the cable and took it back to the center cleat using a working turn. As the lock emptied, our boat stayed snug to the lock wall. There was no place for the boat to go! Jim and I both looked at each other, amazed, and said, "Wow, why didn't we think of this before?" Here was the lesson we learned as a result of that windy day experience. All those other times we strained and struggled to hold the boat when there was wind or turbulence in the lock, but with the center cleat method, we were all set!

This revelation helped us immensely with our locking skills, as on a trip like this we had many more locks to go through. I became a pro at getting the line around the cable or pole and even getting a loop around a bollard on the inland rivers with just one try. It was this learned teamwork and practice that built my confidence. In our entire boat cruising, we have traveled through 475 locks, and in spite of what the woman asked me years ago, our marriage is still wonderful!

While heading south on the Illinois River toward a lock Jim detected with our AIS System, a tow ahead of us at the next lock and, after calling the lockmaster, we found out it was scheduled to lock through before us if we didn't get there in time. Our buddy boat, which had left the anchorage earlier than us, was hoping to get there first and lock through before the tow and try to have the lock wait for us since we didn't travel as fast as them.

Two other Looper boats, which we had anchored with the night before, were already in the lock. This was the one time we kicked our Nordic Tug up to 16 knots and kept in touch with the lockmaster who kept saying, "I can only hold the lock open if I see your boat." We were coming around a curve in the river and were so close, but the trees and sharp bend obstructed his view. He said we only had a few minutes, and he would have to close the doors. It began to rain, and we would be left far behind the other boats and would have to "doodle" in the current for one to two hours by ourselves while waiting for the tow to proceed with its time consuming lock through.

The current was too strong to try to anchor, and there were two tows that were also waiting to lock through. I got on the radio and pleaded with him to wait for us because we didn't want to get left behind by our friends. He kept saying, "I'm trying to work with you, ma'am, but I need to see your boat."

"We're coming, we're coming!" I answered back.

Finally, his voice came back on the radio, "I see you! Keep coming, I'll hold the lock."

I waved to the captains of the tows as we passed them, and they gave us a thumbs-up. I know they had heard my desperate cries on the radio. Jim called on the radio to thank them. They were glad to help us. What a relief, and we thought about how kind they were to let us go ahead of them.

Another challenging moment found us in Alton, Illinois on the Mississippi River when the remnants of Hurricane Ike hit. The water level had been dropped in this area by the Core of Engineers in anticipation of the storm, and we were sitting in a marina on the bottom in a muddy bank. The rain and wind finally came, and the river flooded. We could see trees, bushes and logs floating by but the breakwater protected us. The entire marina floated up about 20 feet. Now we knew why they had dropped the water level before the storm hit.

However difficult these situations have been, we have found that boaters always seem to make the best of the circumstances. During our layover in Alton in the aftermath of Hurricane Ike, we had get-togethers, carry-in suppers and often walked to the local casino for buffet dinners. Some of us rented cars to tour St. Louis and make runs to the local Wal-Mart. Eventually, after ten days, the water level was safe for travel, and they once again opened the locks. The Loopers traveling on the river during this period of flooding became known as the "River Rats."

While on the Georgian Bay, we anchored in one of the most beautiful anchorages you could imagine. The rock islands were tall and had bent trees growing everywhere, the water was crystal clear and the sky bright blue. We were soon traveling with four other boats we had met back at the beginning of the Trent-Severn Waterway. We finally caught up with each other at Killbear Park, several miles from Parry Sound. It was so good to see them, and we were happy to be able to spend time with them, especially as we headed north to where we would be anchoring.

Hopewell Bay was our first overnight anchorage experience... ever, and I was a little nervous. But soon the other boats ahead of us got situated, and two of them had already dropped their dinghies. Before we knew it they were at our side giving us tips on how to get the anchor set properly. It took several tries because of the wind, but soon enough our anchor was secured. Next, we dropped our dinghy because we had to get Lily to shore.

After we lowered the dinghy and got underway, although the engine started up, it kept stalling, and we would drift with the current. Jim had to row back to the boat with Lily and me sitting tight. Our boat wasn't anchored close to shore, and the rowing was difficult. Our friends from North Carolina, who had a Jack Russell dog named Carley, came to the rescue. While we remained anchored out, since Bud would take Carley for a romp on the rocks three times a day and then take her back to their boat, he began to swing around to pick up Lily for her romp. When she heard the dinghy engine, her tail would start wagging, and she was clearly ready for her boat ride to shore. This was Lily's taxi service for the next four anchorages.

When we got to Drummond Island and immediately had our engine serviced. There was a problem with the carburetor, and we felt lucky to have had it fixed so promptly.

We stayed at marinas for the rest of the trip. I tried training Lily to use the K-9 Grass mat, a mat especially designed for pets to relieve themselves when it isn't possible to get to shore, and she did occasionally use it, but it wasn't guaranteed, and I didn't feel the need to stress her with it. Georgian Bay had good places to dinghy to shore, but on the Tennessee-Tombigbee Waterway and farther south, the land was swampy and full of burrs, alligators, and snakes.

Traveling with a dog, especially one as large as a Golden Retriever, means you have to be organized. Our veterinarian gave us a large bag of extra supplies for her that included several different antibiotics, bandages, tick, flea and worm preventatives, ointments, and medication for calming her if we needed. I also purchased a heavy Ruff Wear float coat for heavy seas and a lighter-weight, more flexible one for the dinghy. Muttluk dog boots are a must for long-term travel on a boat, and I wouldn't leave shore without them. They stay on and they appear to be very comfortable. Lily is proud to wear them as she prances along the dock. We came across dock situations where the metal ramps and steps were sharp and could have cut the pads on her feet. Some wooden docks had large spaces and holes where a dog's foot could easily slip through. The boots provided good protection from injury. There were also places on shore that had sand burrs; these are nasty little things that can get caught in a dog's paw and hurt. The boots came in handy on many occasions. We met lots of people who stopped to ask about these special yellow boots.

A Ruff Wear harness was something she also wore on a daily basis when getting on and off the boat. It has more support than a regular harness and had a good handle for holding or lifting her on and off without too much effort. We also have a retractable tailgate ramp that we used quite often on fixed docks and walls to help get her off.

Open-water travel on any boat trip usually puts me in an anxious mood. We had always traveled in more protected water except for Long Island Sound and our trip across Lake Ontario two years before doing the Loop. It was here, on Lake Ontario, that we encountered four-foot waves off our port beam for about four hours, although it calmed down as we came closer to the Canadian shore. We should have waited for the next day, but we were still learning about how to choose that good travel day. We had to make this crossing again, and memories of our past trip remained fresh in my mind. However, the day we crossed was the most beautiful day, nothing like we had the year before. The water was FLAT calm! Before we left on this adventure, we had mutually agreed that we would only travel on "good days," those with light wind and reasonable seas.

I would carefully check NOAA weather several times a day before we were scheduled to do any traveling, and for the most part, it was pretty accurate. Of course, there were days where the forecast was great, but it would depend on where you actually were in regards to the coastline. On Lake Michigan, as we left Charlevoix, the seas were predicted to be one-foot with wind from the east. This was perfect as we planned to travel close to the east shore. However, you take the good with the bad. As we reached Grand Traverse Bay, there was a very long easterly fetch, and we saw the boat in front of us almost disappear from view only to bob up again. We were next!

The waves had built to three to four feet. Yikes, what a ride, but it only lasted an hour, and I have to say it was actually fun! As we passed the point at the north end of Grand Traverse Bay, the water turned absolutely flat. The days on Lake Michigan were perfect as long as we watched the weather. It was reassuring to know that there were marinas and anchorages to pull into every 30 miles or so. We loved docking at the small towns where we could stop at farmers' markets, grocery shops, and get a daily ice cream cone.

When we were within a few days of our crossing to Chicago, I studied the weather report in detail for several days. We managed to get to Benton Harbor the day before the ideal forecast of waves less than one-foot, and that is just what it was the next day! I had anticipated crossing Lake Michigan and worried myself sick about it for two months, and here was a day that was a gift. The six-hour, 60-mile crossing was wonderful. I was nervous about being out in the middle of the lake with no land in sight, but we could see the water towers from Benton Harbor for miles behind us, then to our port side we could see the smokestacks from Michigan City, and at the same time could see the skyscrapers of Chicago build before us. Magnificent!

A good example of the popular boating quote "Just pick your day" was our decision to go or not go when we were in Cape May. We had two stormy days with high winds and rain. The third day had a good forecast of fair weather, but before then there was a small craft advisory in effect for seas of around four feet. Those are the days I DO NOT plan to leave the dock.

The problem was that the next day WAS the day to head up the New Jersey coast since that day the forecast was for waves of around two feet, then the weather was going to turn stormy again. Here was that weather window we wanted, but to get there and get situated for the long run to New York, we had to leave Cape May with some higher seas.

We were in luck that day. The captain on the trawler next to us was planning to stay only a few days and had rented a car. He heard my concerns and our situation and volunteered to drive me the 40 miles to Atlantic City. Jim got someone from one of the other boats we were traveling with to crew for him. I arrived in Atlantic City just a few hours before our boat and the other two that Jim was making the run with. Well, the waves Jim and the others experienced that day were over five feet. Sometimes you just have to stick with your gut feeling and do what you feel is best at the time. I am sure I would have gotten through the trip, but when my heart tells me, "DON'T GO!" I usually try to stand firm with my decision, and Jim as the captain agrees! If I hadn't gotten the ride to Atlantic City that day, we would have just waited for another day to go and enjoyed a few more days where we were.

Our journey in the fall brought the turning of the leaves on the hills as we traveled the Tennessee River to Chattanooga, Tennessee. This was a relaxing time on our boat. The days were warm with a deep blue autumn sky, calm water, and the boating was good! Of all the places on our boating trips, I remember this as one of my favorites. However, the road ahead was still a challenging one.

The mornings were cooler now and brought dense fog, making us wait longer to leave. The days were getting shorter, so there was less travel time each day, and it was a common occurrence to find ice on our bow in the morning! I was glad I bought that warm woolen hat while in Little Current, Canada and fleece gloves in Chattanooga. My heavy jacket was finally taken out of storage.

We had just left the AGLCA Rendezvous at Joe Wheeler State Park in Alabama, where we had met so many Loopers and local boaters. No matter where we now traveled, we started meeting up with someone we knew. It was hard leaving friends behind at home when we first left, and I sometimes felt homesick. However, by October we had a new group of friends. I couldn't imagine doing the Great Loop without the friendship and support of everyone we met. For example, when we had battery trouble, a short in our wiring, and a problem with our bow thruster, it wasn't long before we had a group of people at our boat to help us. There was always someone to take a walk, do laundry, share books, go shopping, ride a bike, go for breakfast, chat, laugh, and travel with.

Our crossing from Carrabelle to Steinhatchee, Florida, across 80 miles and ten hours on the Gulf of Mexico, was another one of those times we got to decide whether to go or not go. We had been traveling with friends from New Hampshire, and when we docked, we noticed there were four other Looper boats all waiting for the right weather window to leave as well. The report at our 5:30 a.m. captains' and admirals' meeting was for waves of two to three feet – not the greatest day we were told, but not the worst, and definitely do-able. So, at 6 a.m. the next day, five trawlers left for Steinhatchee.

In the beginning, the water was fairly calm, but as we ventured farther out, the wind picked up and whitecaps appeared, then more ripples and more whitecaps. One of the boats behind us called over the radio, "Hey, guys, I think it's getting a bit rough out here!" The waves very slowly grew without us realizing it, and the two to three-foot seas described in our pre-departure meeting were now hitting four, with a few five-footers mixed in and the wind kicking up to 20 knots with some stronger gusts. It wasn't dangerous, just lumpy and bumpy. Lily crawled into her spot under Jim's feet at the helm in our pilothouse and wedged her feet against the wall. I was holding tight to the little table in front of my seat eating saltines and ginger candy that I bought at the health food store for nausea. We scooted over the three footers, but it was a bit of a roller-coaster ride over the higher waves. At least they were on our bow, and we didn't roll much. As we neared the west coast of Florida, the waves began to lessen and the last two hours were much calmer.

It is highly recommended to go with other boats when doing the Gulf crossing, not only for safety, but also for the companionship of being with other people. Talking on the radio, telling a few jokes, and checking up on each other made the hours go by faster. Plus, you now had a bond with these folks, as you covered a major body of water together. As it turned out, if we had waited for the next day the seas were very calm. Oh well, you go with what you know for the moment and try to make the best decision based on what information is available at the time. However, times like that test you, make you stronger and build your confidence. I still can't believe I crossed the Gulf of Mexico! It had always been just a place on the map, but now I feel part of it.

One thing about doing a ten-hour crossing with a choppy sea is the concern about getting to the head. We were about six hours out from Carrabelle when Jim made a quick trip down below. We are lucky to be in an all-enclosed pilothouse where the steps to downstairs are close by, yet when Jim came back up, he warned me not to try going down. He has a pretty strong stomach, yet his face looked a bit white on his return. I have trouble going below if the boat is bouncing too much, and this day it was! I tried not to think about "going", but when it reached seven hours, I couldn't wait any longer. I tried going down the first set of five stairs, holding on to the railing I peeked around the corner trying to make it down the next five steps to the companionway and make a run for it, but after two more steps, I already felt queasy. I have never been seasick, but I knew if I went below at that time, I would be sick for sure.

I had to be creative, and I had to think fast! If I could only keep the horizon in view, I would be OK. From years of outdoor activities riding my horse on long trail rides, and from primitive tent camping with the Girl Scouts, a light went on. "A-HA! Why not?" I chuckled to myself. I quickly headed out to the cockpit, grabbing the rails on the ceiling of the saloon. Lily's mostly unused K-9 Grass was still sitting in the corner of the cockpit by the scupper. "Well, that's what the K-9 Grass was for, right?" I thought. The trawler following us was at least a mile and a half behind, so you have to do what you have to do, as the old saying goes! Afterwards, since the outside deck shower was right there, I did a brief hosing down and was back in my seat in a jiffy. I wouldn't recommend doing this on a regular basis, of course, and now that I think back on it, I have a good laugh over my "creativity" in this situation – it sure worked for the moment!

Getting stuck in the mud in Crystal River, Florida was an experience to remember, and we laugh about it now. I always checked with marinas before reserving a slip to make sure there was enough water for our 4.7-foot draft. We needed to stay at a marina close to the Gulf because in early December it would be near dark when we got there after a ten-hour travel day. We were assured that we would be fine. The next morning, *Golden Lily*, along with two other boats, was sitting in the mud at low tide. We could not get out! So, the next morning we were all up really early, and with the dinghy we checked out the depth of the water. One boat was able to get out first. An hour later, our friend left his slip, and we soon followed. Unfortunately, the current swept him too close to a sandbar and he went aground. By the time TowBoatU.S. came, it was too late to leave for the 70-mile trip to Tarpon Springs, Florida. Later, when the tide was at its highest, we both left and headed a few miles up the river to a marina where we actually floated at low tide.

It was necessary to leave the next day because of the rotation of the low tide. If we didn't leave early that day, we would be in Crystal River for ten days waiting for the tide to cycle back to a time where we would have daylight long enough to make the run down the river and to the Gulf and still be early enough to reach our destination before dark. Jim was in his glory as he calculated the tide charts. He called friends who had left on their boats a few days before us to find out the time they left, then he was able to calculate the time for us to leave safely with the tide. Our buddy boat left at 8:30 a.m., and we left at 9:05 a.m. They reported water depths at each buoy for us. We both made it safely down the river and to the channel in plenty of water. This was just one of those experiences you hope never happens, but when it does, you make the best out of it. Jim was able to use his technical plotting skills to plan a route and timed it to the minute, which he loves to do. Both captains and crews had a sense of accomplishment at "beating" the tide. Times like this keep your mind and skills sharp. The best part was that we made it to Tarpon Springs after a beautiful, calm day on the Gulf. We met up with four other Looper friends at the city dock and had a great dinner at a Greek restaurant – our reward after such a challenging experience.

Whenever we came to a dock or marina, both of us had our "jobs." Jim is an excellent judge of wind and current, and an excellent boat handler. We had become a good team at getting our boat secure in a slip. However, the next question was, "How do we get Lily off?" Floating docks were never a problem because we would use the swim deck. Fixed docks and walls where there was a significant tide change or docks that were narrow and short were the big issues. Most of the time we were able to get her off from the side deck. When we woke up the first morning in Clearwater, Florida to such a low tide, we realized we couldn't get her off at dead low.

We waited several hours, then put Lily's tailgate ramp under the ladder on top of the propane compartment on the cockpit and guided it to the opening in the railing and up onto the dock. She scrambled up with ease. After that we decided to get up very early the next morning while the tide was still a bit higher so she wouldn't have to wait until noon to get her walk. Lily is very agile and loved finding new ways to hop off.

This brings me to the eating part! Our propane stove is our main cooking source. I didn't want to bring my large crock-pot from home because it is just too big for storage. After being on the water for two months, I purchased a small crock-pot that I used at least once a week. This was one of the handiest ways to get a meal ready. I would start it in the morning, let it simmer all day, and by dinnertime

Barbara Benjamin – *Golden Lilly*

we would have a great meal already cooked. Meeting up with boating friends always gets a happy hour or pot luck started, not to mention experiencing the local restaurants in all those towns along the way: whitefish in the North Channel, catfish, shrimp and grits along the inland rivers, oysters in Apalachicola, and crabs in the Chesapeake Bay. Food was one of the highlights for us on our yearlong trip!

I was worried about how often we would be able to get to a grocery store, drug store, laundry as well as what would happen if we got sick. We stocked the boat with a full load of supplies when we traveled the Georgian Bay and North Channel since part of that trip was in remote areas for several days at a time. However, along most of the trip, there were always places to shop and ways to get there. We bought a shopping cart to pull behind us to carry groceries. Some marinas have courtesy cars.

Our doctors gave us antibiotics just in case we needed them, and we had prescriptions filled at our pharmacy chain when we came to a place that had one. The marina in Steinhatchee, Florida let us borrow their golf cart to go to the local grocery store. All four of us piled in, and had the ride of our lives! The town is very small and the roads quiet. We managed to stuff our grocery bags in all the nooks and crannies for our return trip back to the marina. This was one shopping spree I will remember forever!

Some of the most amazing aspects of long-term cruising, besides making so many new friends, are the constant changes of scenery, the local sights, and the new experiences as you travel. I will always remember the starry nights, the sunsets and sunrises on Georgian Bay, the granite cliffs in the North Channel, the bluffs of Lake Michigan, autumn leaves on the hills along on the Tennessee River, the fog in the morning, and the ice on our bow. I will remember the warmth of the bonfire on the rocks while anchored near the Benjamin Islands in the North Channel, the dolphins swimming next to our boat in Florida, the gentleness of the manatees, and the antics of the pelicans flying and diving for fish. Jim and I were amazed at the turquoise water of the Gulf of Mexico as we dodged hundreds of crab pots. We gazed at waterfalls, lighthouses, waves, shells on the beach, storm clouds, lake cottages dotting the shoreline, honeysuckle and butterflies in the Great Dismal Swamp, the Statue of Liberty and one of the biggest thrills of all… crossing our wake at the Battery in New York City.

A friend told me about a quote thatt will stick with me forever:

> "Lord, please keep your arm around my shoulder,
> and your hand over my mouth."

It is easier said than done, but a quote I will try to remember. I think I will always be an anxious boater, but after traveling 5,960 miles on this yearlong trip, I won't ever let anxiety take over my life. I have always anticipated most situations and challenges that have come to me on land or sea, but I have learned not to worry about them so much, and instead I try to enjoy each day to the fullest. There is always another day to travel, and if the sea conditions change for the moment, you will reach your destination soon. Have your lines and fenders ready on both sides, go slowly, hold on, speak up tactfully when necessary, and share your thoughts and feelings. Every boating day ended happily for us! Being pushed beyond my comfort zone and taking on new challenges have helped me grow not only as a boater, but also as a person.

Barbara Benjamin lives in Killingworth, Connecticut with her husband Jim and their Golden Retriever Lily. They have one married daughter. Barbara is a retired third and fourth grade teacher and a church organist. Since the Benjamins' Great Loop trip, they have found it difficult to leave the comfort of their boat. They now have plans to cruise north each summer and south to Florida in the winter. Barbara and Jim continue to enjoy the adventures of boating!

Linda Brennan

Vessel: M/V *Shore Thing* – 43-foot Californian Cockpit Motor Yacht
Residence: Groton, Connecticut
Homeport: Mumford Cove, Connecticut
Blog: shorethingyacht.blogspot.com

I began this escapade as a reluctant boater and first mate. That said, now I would not give up the experience for anything! I just loved it. My husband, Ed, decided he wanted to do the Great Loop boat trip (who ever heard of the Great Loop; is that some weird cult?) about 12 years before we started our trip. For those who don't know what the Loop is: it is a circumnavigation, by boat, of the inland waterways in the eastern half of the United States.

We have owned a few small boats (17 to 23 feet) in the New York and Connecticut area waters. We've also rented 40-foot houseboats for several years, a week at a time, in the Trent-Severn Waterway and the Rideau Canal in Canada. Just before Ed retired we bought a 1985 43-foot Californian Cockpit Motor Yacht and the longest trip we took with that boat, prior to the Loop, was for three weeks from Groton, Connecticut to Block Island, Rhode Island to Martha's Vineyard, Massachusetts. So, you can see that we didn't have much experience in long-distance cruising before we attempted this trip. I was reluctant to get on board in the beginning for many reasons.

Was I going to be capable of handling the lines (ropes), fenders (bumpers)?
I had to learn the proper names of all these things and actually do something with them. I have to admit, I'm a bit clumsy. I had visions of tripping and falling overboard! Not that I haven't tripped, but the rails have held me on board. I've been known to get one foot on the dinghy and the other on the boat and doing

a split into the water, and then my husband had to dive in to retrieve my glasses. That didn't happen on this trip… thank goodness.

Would I be able to buy groceries?
During this trip, I saw the inside of more grocery stores than I care to remember. There definitely is no lack of stores along the way and some are better than others. You can sometimes even find gourmet supplies, which is always a nice surprise. Seeing what other countries have on the shelf has been very interesting. The only time we were running low on groceries was when we stayed on anchor longer than I'd anticipated. Then the meals got a little repetitious but we didn't starve. I know what sometimes happens to me is that I overbuy, not knowing when the next grocery store will present itself. Of course, there are also many boating guides that tell you where supplies are readily available.

How was I going to cook in that small galley (kitchen)?
It turned out that I'm no worse a cook on the boat than I am at home; I'm no better either, but I've received many compliments on the meals produced from my galley. Of course, the compliments were from other boaters who were happy that they didn't have to cook themselves.

Would I be able to share such a small space with my husband?
I retired ten years before Ed, and I was used to my own time and space! As it happens, I actually can't find him sometimes on the boat. One of the messages I put in our blog from time to time is that my husband and I are still talking. I have to say that people now look for that message. In reality, I feel lucky to have had my best friend on board with me.

How would I deal with missing my family?
I knew I'd miss my family a great deal, and that has been true; but with Skype (virtual visits via computer) and physical visits from them and scheduled trips home during our trip I've managed that aspect fairly well. On Christmas morning, our kids signed on to Skype so we could watch them open their presents and converse with them. Because of Skype, we felt like we were all together for this big holiday. It felt very close to being there.

We live in a boating community on Long Island Sound. I had a lot of support for our trip even though no one else we knew in our area had heard of the Great Loop. Later I discovered that my neighbors were taking bets that I wouldn't make it. Boy, were they wrong.

However, after three weeks on the boat I did have a meltdown. I was ready to throw in the towel and give it up. We were rushing our trip to meet our kids in Waterford, New York so that they could be with us for a week. During their visit, it was very hot and humid and we were in the Erie Canal. The meltdown occurred just after our family left after spending a week on the boat with us, and all of a sudden I wasn't sure when I'd see them again. I felt that boating was all about rushing from one place to another and cooking all the time. After that difficult time, we decided to go out to dinner more often and not to rush. Both have helped to turn my attitude around. Now I don't want to get off the boat.

Being naturally shy, how would I deal with the social aspect of this trip?
My personality is quiet, private and shy, but in long-distance boating I'm seeing and meeting people all the time, having dinner with them on our boat or theirs, or at restaurants sharing boating experiences. Other boaters are very willing to share information about things that have worked for them. For instance, I thought it was interesting that those Green Bags actually do extend the freshness of vegetables and fruits. The experience of meeting all different kinds of people has made me more outgoing, and I've found it easier to come out of my shell.

Speaking about food, another item you have to be flexible about is meal planning. Some of the stores you come across, although plentiful, just don't always carry your favorite foods. It's important to be creative and try something new occasionally and expand your pallet whether cooking in or eating out.

How would I deal with bad weather?
We didn't have any discussions or steadfast rules of what we'd do in certain weather conditions before we left on our odyssey; a routine just naturally evolved as our experience grew. For instance, we were leaving Sacketts Harbor, New York, on Lake Ontario to go across to Canada and the prediction was for waves of two to four feet and winds of 12 knots. Now, in our home waters that would be an ideal day to go to Block Island, which is about 26 miles away. Well, what we didn't realize was that the period between waves was crucial – we had no clue. It was a very uncomfortable ride that we soon aborted and headed to Cape Vincent, New York instead.

As a result of that experience, we decided that we wouldn't go in those conditions again, and that has served us well. It wasn't unsafe, just uncomfortable. We're doing this to have fun, not to test our endurance for "rocky" rides.

How would we incorporate guests from home into our trip?
Wanting to meet friends and relatives on the trip and take them with you for a portion of it is always a challenge. We've found that it's great to have people share your adventure with you; trying to set a time and place is harder to arrange though – but not impossible.

I learned many things while our trip progressed. I found many happy surprises waiting for me as we became experienced long-distance boaters.

As far as spending the night docking or anchoring, I found that I preferred anchoring out. I liked being able to commune with nature while enjoying a quiet evening. Many times the sunsets or sunrises were spectacular. Sometimes we dropped the dingy and went exploring around the anchorage.

It's very easy to get going in the morning, just pull the anchor and go. You don't have to take in the electric cords and release all the lines and decide how you're going to get off the dock and hope that the winds don't pick up or change direction. After you're off the dock, then you have to get all the lines ready for the next docking event and pull in all the fenders and get them stowed. I think I'm lazy!

Actually, the easiest for me is a mooring ball, but even this isn't foolproof. One time I dropped the boathook in the water after I'd hooked the mooring pennant – luckily, I had another hook. Some good people going by in their dinghy were able to retrieve my lost boathook and return it. This also turns out to be an excellent way to meet people. Of course, we like the security of a dock when there are storms in the area. As a result, we do some of each.

One fun thing that was an unexpected benefit was the willingness of other boaters to loan their car to make trips for grocery supplies, laundry or the boat parts store. It seemed at times we'd barely docked when someone was offering their car.

Courtesy cars at marinas are a great help along the way as well. Some of the cars offered their own challenges, however. It could be worn suspensions, automatic windows not rolling up, or the brakes making loud noises, but we always made our trip safely to and from our destination. We looked at it as just another adventure.

We found very early on that we needed a means of communication between captain and crew. When I'm in the cockpit, the captain can't see me or hear me (sometimes he thinks that's a good thing). All the screaming and yelling we'd seen on other boats when trying to dock wasn't for us. We purchased a hands-free, voice-activated walkie-talkie headset with an antenna on each unit. In some places we picked up radio stations and static and the antenna kept getting in the way. We've since found a headset that is less cumbersome and doesn't seem to pick up the local radio stations. The headsets aren't foolproof, however; one time we were coming into a dock and the last thing the captain heard from me was "watch out you're going to hit..." The wire to the plug had gotten caught and pulled away from the transmitter. Fortunately, we didn't hit anything.

We enjoy golfing and have found some interesting courses right along the way. Some are better than others, but our game isn't that great anyway. One course in particular stands out in my mind. It obviously had cows on it very recently, but it was up a hill overlooking a lake, and we could look out and see our boat at anchor. What a great sight! We just dinghied in from our boat with our clubs and there were people waiting at the dock with a golf cart for us.

Sometimes we're having so much fun we wonder what we can do to help other people. There are so many opportunities for volunteering at marine exhibit centers and marine parks. There is a group that brings reading and math programs, that are being discontinued in school systems in the United States, to the Bahamas and distributes them to different islands in the Exumas.

Of course, we always hope that we won't need medical attention. It seems that it's very accessible to boaters along the waterways. Most towns have a clinic of some kind. If attended by a nurse, the nurse has access to a doctor. It really isn't a concern that has plagued me.

Probably one of the keys to having a good adventure is being flexible. You may get up one morning and think you're off to the next planned port, but the weather has changed and you just decide to wait another day or more. Usually boaters have a general plan of where they're headed – but not always. We were spending some weather delay time in Nassau in the Bahamas when I met up with a couple on a sailboat from Seattle, Washington. I asked where they were going; the answer was either South America or Philadelphia, Pennsylvania. Now this is the epitome of flexibility!

I'm very proud of meeting the perceived challenges of long-distance boating and being in a position to impart some of the things I've learned to others. I'm not exactly sure what has settled me into this new lifestyle, but I do know now that it will be very hard for me to give up – every day is a new adventure. The long-distance cruising lifestyle is addictive!

Linda Brennan resides in a shoreline community in Long Island Sound, Connecticut with Ed, her husband of 41 years. She has two grown daughters and enjoys Grandma and Grandpa Camp with her grandson.

Linda retired from the accounting field and now enjoys walking, golfing, tennis, kayaking and of course boating.

Leslie Firestone

Vessel: M/V *Grace Full* – 40-foot Present Sundeck Trawler
Residence: Lake Marion, South Carolina
Homeport: Charleston, South Carolina
Blog: gracefulljourney.blogspot.com

Have you ever had a dream that excited you beyond anything you had ever imagined but scared you so much that you didn't even want to think about it? My dream first began to take shape when I was a 58-year-old financial planner, was married to Flint Firestone for 35 years, and had just become a great-grandmother for the first time. We had lived in the Baltimore area for many years and enjoyed spending our free time cruising the Chesapeake Bay on our 22-foot Bayliner. There is nothing we liked better than to push away from the dock on a Friday evening to spend the weekend swimming, fishing, eating, drinking and relaxing as we anchored in one of our many favorite spots each night.

This particular year I found a book advertised in a magazine related to boating called *Honey, Let's Get a Boat...* by Ron and Eva Stob. It looked interesting and I thought my husband might enjoy it, so I bought it for him. The book describes a cruising trip called the Great Loop that circles the eastern half of North America. Long-distance cruising was never anything that either of us had ever aspired to, but suddenly a spark from my dream began to ignite as I thought about the possibilities. Could we do this? Would we be capable of all that would be required of us in such an undertaking?

To make this life-changing decision, we needed more information about cruising. We joined an organization called America's Great Loop Cruisers' Association (AGLCA). The Stobs set up the organization to share their experiences with other boaters who have caught the bug of cruising the Great Loop. After attending a rendezvous sponsored by AGLCA, which included both dreamers and veteran cruisers, we decided that we could make this dream a reality and began to take steps in that direction.

The next step was to figure out what kind of boat we would need. We connected with a yacht broker on Kent Island, Maryland who specialized in trawlers and we visited her often over the next three years to determine which trawler style was right for us. We poured over the offerings on *Yacht World* and went to see many of them in our area to get an idea of what we felt would suit us. Our final choice was a 40-foot sundeck trawler because we felt it would give us more living space than most of the other styles. We attended a Trawler Fest in Solomons, Maryland, where we were able to board various brands of sundeck trawlers. It was then that we finally felt it was time to purchase our boat. We called our broker when we arrived home and told her to find the boat that was just right for us.

Within two weeks, she called and said that she had found a 1987 40-foot Present sundeck trawler in Tom's River, New Jersey. We were so excited and couldn't wait to go look at it. We went up the next weekend, and as soon as we stepped aboard, we knew this was our boat. She came with everything, right down to the dishes and silverware, and was ready to cruise. Her name was *Journey*, but we decided to change it to *Grace Full*. This dream had been a "grace full" process because we were seeking God's direction each step of the way. Since it was December, we decided that we had better leave her on the hard in New Jersey for the winter. We made the long four-hour trip many times during that winter to spruce her up and replace a few items, such as the mattress, that were showing their age. It was so exciting to know that we owned our dream boat and that the first step toward the realization of our dream had been taken.

Spring finally arrived and it was time to bring our lady home. Friends drove us up to New Jersey, and we cruised Barnegat Bay with them for a couple of hours that afternoon to get a feel for how she ran. Believe me, a 40-foot trawler with two engines is very different from a 22-foot Bayliner! Our friends left us, and we had only one way to get home, and that was by boat. We spent our first night aboard and, after three tries, we finally left the dock for our maiden voyage. That trip included a storm that began to blow as we docked for the night in Cape May, New Jersey. It was necessary to stay there for two days until the winds subsided. We called work and let them know we would be late getting home. It was a good lesson in not allowing our schedule to rule our cruising. We do not go out when the seas are in any way threatening, no matter what is on the schedule. What a joy it was to finally dock our boat at her new home at Maryland Yacht Club!

Each weekend that summer, we invited a different group of friends to visit our beautiful new boat. They were vicariously living this dream through us and were just as excited as we were.

Leslie Firestone – *Grace Full*

We had lived in Maryland for 30 years and loved it, but we knew we didn't want to spend our retirement there. Once our "new" boat was home in Maryland, we felt that it was time to sell our land-based home and move aboard. Many people were shocked that we would be willing to give up our home because to them "home" meant stability, but we couldn't have been more excited. It was a very freeing experience to go through all our "stuff" and decide what was important to keep and what we could eliminate. We made many trips to the dump and the Goodwill store as we pared down to what we really needed and what would fit on a boat. We kept a few heirlooms and moved them to our son's new home in South Carolina for safekeeping. We were finally ready to list our home on the market and hoped that it wouldn't take too long to sell. We tried living on *Grace Full* on weekends and at our home during the week, but we couldn't stand being away from the boat because we felt more at home there than at our house, so we moved onto the boat full time well before our home sold. There was no question that we had made the right decision because we already loved living on the water.

Our final year at work was coming to a close, and we were within weeks of starting to cruise. We had attended the AGLCA Spring Rendezvous a month earlier and met a lot of people who would be cruising the same waters at the same time we were. It was comforting to know that other people would be experiencing this dream along with us. A used car dealer picked up our two vehicles the morning we left and gave us cash for them. We stashed it in various places throughout the boat and hopefully remembered where all those places were.

As we began cruising, it was important for us to be comfortable in our roles on board. Flint has his Coast Guard captain's license and is very adept at piloting a boat and taking care of engine maintenance. I didn't have a lot of interest in "driving" vehicles in the past, whether they were motorized, land-based vehicles or boats on the water. I was more than content to allow him to be the "Captain" and I enjoyed my role as the "First Mate." It was important that I learned to pilot our vessel in case of emergency, so we had some teaching experiences along the way on docking and operating the boat. I would also take the helm for a couple of hours during the day so Flint could have a break and relax a little.

I remember one day on the Mississippi River, I took the helm while Flint was doing some maintenance work below. I approached a tow and barge from behind and called the captain on the radio to find out how he wanted me to pass him. He indicated that there was another barge coming toward us, but that it would be OK if I passed him on the "two whistle" between the two tows. Flint came up from below just as we passed between them and, as soon as he realized that we had a tow and barge on each side of us, he said, in a voice that held a touch of hysteria, "Did he tell you to do that?"

As a financial planner, my expertise fit more in the navigation role and my husband learned "not to question the navigator" when I told him where we needed to travel to get to our destination. There wasn't much need to navigate on the Chesapeake Bay because we had traveled through most of the rivers and coves in areas familiar to us and knew them "like the back of our hand." As we prepared for our cruise, we became more adept at reading charts and purchased a new Garmin GPS, which was immensely helpful in keeping us in the deeper water and out of the shallow water. We always used both paper charts and the GPS so that if anything happened to our electronics, we would know where we were and where we were going. We purchased guidebooks for each of the areas we would be cruising in, and they were extremely helpful in choosing marinas and getting the "lay of the land" for each port. We would spend some time each evening planning our course for the next day. If we were traveling with other boats, that planning time usually included a "captain's meeting" with our friends to make sure we were all headed in the same direction.

Our skills were tested soon after we started cruising while we were traveling in the Atlantic Ocean off the coast of New Jersey. We had anchored overnight in Cape May harbor and were socked in with fog the next morning. We waited for the fog to lift before we left the harbor and entered the ocean through the inlet. It quickly became apparent that, although the fog had lifted off the land, it was still thick as soup on the ocean. We had to make the decision to turn back and wait or "go for it" and trust our GPS to guide us. We decided to move forward, and once we located our first buoy at the mouth of the inlet, we headed north to find the others along the coast.

We couldn't see past the bow so we blew a warning horn regularly and followed our GPS to each buoy. At one point, we knew we should be able to see a buoy on the port side of the bow, but as much as we squinted into the fog, we couldn't make anything out. All of a sudden it appeared within a foot of our bow and we had to adjust our direction to miss hitting it. We could see other boats on our radar and hear them sounding their horns as we all made our way up the coast. After that experience, we knew our navigational tools would safely take us anywhere we needed to go.

One of the skills we had not worked on with any great effort was the "dinghy drill." It came back to bite me a few days into our cruising experience. We anchored in a bay near Atlantic City, New Jersey and saw that the boat in front of us was flying the AGLCA burgee. We waved to them and indicated that we would be over to meet them as soon as we dumped our dinghy. Flint climbed aboard the dinghy and was starting the motor as I boarded. Rather than sit down on the swim platform and ease myself aboard, I jumped from the swim platform onto the dinghy seat and promptly catapulted over the other side and into the water – clothes, sunglasses and all. I came up under the swim platform and turned to see the lady aboard the other boat clapping and giving me a "10." I climbed aboard the dinghy and off we went to meet our new friends.

Troy, New York was the site of our first lock experience. Although we had been given some good information about how to do it, we still had some fear about how we would handle it the first time. We had purchased some round fenders because they were supposed to hold the boat off the wall better than the long fenders. I tied one on the bow and my husband tied one on the stern. We lost the stern fender on that first lock because the knot came loose, so I became the knot-tier on board from then on. Locks can be transited quite easily depending on the strength of the wind. Each time we went through one, we learned a little bit more about easing the boat to the wall and grabbing or looping the line at the proper time. It soon became old hat and our confidence increased some more.

We had planned on anchoring out half the time and using marinas for the other half. Our main objective in making that decision was to limit the financial cost at each port so we would be able to stay within our budget. We were inexperienced at anchoring this new boat, and my husband was very nervous about strong winds dragging the anchor, allowing the boat to drift out of the anchorage area. His fear, and our desire to meet new people and see new places, changed our plans significantly and we found ourselves staying at marinas most of the time. We realized that we were less likely to meet local people and enjoy the sights in each of the areas we visited if we anchored out – we didn't want to miss anything. We especially wanted to dock at a town on weekends because it was important for us to attend church services on Sunday. We would usually arrive in a port on Saturday and scope out the available churches within walking or biking distance. We didn't care what denomination they were, as we wanted to experience all types of services in various parts of the countries we visited. What a joy it was to become part of a local group of worshippers and participate with them as they read the Word and sang His praises!

Our first month of cruising was difficult emotionally because every day we had to accomplish tasks that were new to us. We would wake up in the morning with sick stomachs and question whether we could really do this long-term. Of course, when I realized that I had run out of Prilosec, I understood that the stomach trouble was probably more a medical problem than an emotional one; but we were still experiencing some trepidation about our ability to cruise and at the same time find pleasure in it. We honed our skills as we traveled each day and faced new tasks while repeating old ones. We gained confidence in our abilities with each passing day and finally reached the point that we could say with pride, "We are capable cruisers!"

Before we started cruising, we were told that the people we met along the way would be one of our greatest joys, and we definitely found that to be the case. We made some wonderful friendships with other cruisers that will last for a long time because we shared some experiences that give us an uncommon rapport. Since we made the decision to use marinas more, we also met some wonderful residents who were gracious and helpful in giving us local knowledge about their town and helped us solve some of our needs. One of our new Canadian friends showed us a way to use weather-stripping on our flybridge to funnel rain to the outside so that we could keep dryer during storms. We usually asked the locals where to eat in their town, as we wanted to experience the hometown flavor rather than the tourist flavor.

Our daughter and her husband joined us as we transited the Trent-Severn Waterway in Ontario, Canada. It was great to have four extra hands on board and the time we spent sharing new experiences was delightful. It is sometimes difficult to plan a pickup and drop-off of visitors, but it is usually worth the effort to share your cruising life with those you love.

We have been blessed with good weather during most of our cruising, but we had one experience in Canada that tested our mettle and could have been disastrous. We were anchored in Mill Lake in Ontario and enjoyed meeting some local people aboard a sailboat. We had the unique sighting of two moose feeding at the shoreline. We could see some clouds forming a storm cell to the west, so we "battened down the hatches" to prepare for the rain. As the storm came over the granite wall that lined the lake, we realized that this was more than just a thunderstorm. We were anchored next to our friend's boat, and both captains decided to start their engines in case they needed to have more control. The cell hit us with over 60 mph winds and rain that was pelting us sideways. Our boat was blown toward our friend's boat, and we were listing over 30 degrees as my husband powered up our engines in an effort to avoid them. Neither of us knew how we missed their bow and anchor line, but we were grateful to pass by them safely with about five feet to spare.

The storm lasted about 45 minutes; during that time, we tried to pull up our anchor, but the rode became jammed in the windlass. I wasn't strong enough to bring it on board by hand, so I took the helm and my husband pulled up the anchor. My job was to keep us off the rocks. When he was finally able to see the anchor, he realized that he had a "Christmas tree" of weeds attached to it that had to be cut off in order to bring it up all the way. When the wind and rain finally subsided and we were able to anchor again, we just held each other and cried. We cried because we were able to do everything we needed to do to keep safe without panicking, and because our Lord protected us during a very scary time.

Before we started cruising, we would hear "horror" stories about different cruising areas, such as the mighty Mississippi River. We realized that it was probably best not to put too much stock in these rumors and understand that everyone will have positive and negative experiences as they travel, and that their experiences won't necessarily be ours. We transited the Mississippi after it had been closed to recreational boaters for two and a half weeks due to flooding. The current was still quite strong, but we had no trouble handling the speed and enjoyed our trip down the river. The towboat captains were very helpful and responsive during our radio contacts. Other than one section of the Cal-Sag Channel near Chicago, we never had to guess how to pass a tow and barge.

Food and drink are important aspects of preparing for cruising, and before we weighed anchor we researched how other cruisers stocked their boats. Water was probably the most important drink that we planned for, as we weren't sure what the quality and purity of the drinking water would be during our travels. We purchased a Nikken Pi-Mag water filtration system that passed our water through many layers of filtering before we used it for drinking and cooking. It sat on the counter next to our sink, and we would fill the top level with water from our tank, allowing it to run through the filtering agents. We used the filtered water from the spigot at the bottom of the system as we needed it. It was cheaper than many other automatic filtering systems and served our needs very well. Beer and liquor needs were easily taken care of in most of the ports we visited, although they were very expensive in Canada. There are limitations on what amounts can be taken into Canada, and since each cruiser has had a different experience during their entry into Canada, it would be best to follow the rules.

Since we had been living aboard for a year before we started cruising, we had most of the foodstuffs we needed to cover our meals for a number of weeks. We had been told that food stores were readily available along the route we were traveling, so we didn't feel that we needed to stock a huge amount of food before we started. I was shopping in Wal-Mart one day and found Hamburger Helper on sale at ten packages for $10.00. That seemed like a good deal, and it would make a quick easy meal as we traveled, so I bought ten boxes. We had been told by long-term cruisers that bugs can be brought aboard through the cardboard that food is packaged in, so I began to transfer the contents of the Hamburger Helper packages to plastic bags when I arrived back at the boat. I cut off the portion of the boxes that indicated which variety of Hamburger Helper was in the box and included that in the plastic bag. I was proud of myself for being so organized until we were cruising and I decided to make Hamburger Helper for dinner one night. As I opened one of the plastic bags and proceeded to gather my ingredients, I realized that I had not included the directions from any of the boxes and had no idea how to prepare the meal. As we traveled throughout the coming months, I obtained the needed directions in various ways: going online and printing them, buying another box of the same variety and using my cell phone to take a picture of the directions on a box at the store. The last idea came from my daughter, but the next problem arose when we printed the directions from the picture and had no idea to what product they applied. We eventually obtained directions for all our Hamburger Helpers and enjoyed them all.

Some of our favorite venues for food along the way were the farmers' markets in the towns where we docked. They were often situated close to the marina and offered quality produce and baked goods that we thoroughly enjoyed. Each area of the country had special products that related either to the ethnicity of the area or to the available produce, such as berries, which grew there. There were often grocery stores within walking distance of the marinas and many marinas had courtesy cars that could be used to make trips for shopping farther away. "Wally World" (Wal-Mart) is a favorite of cruisers, as we could purchase just about anything we needed in one place. It was also an excellent place to get prescriptions filled because no matter where we were we could usually find a store in close proximity. We did have a problem filling prescriptions in Canada due to the fact that any prescription processed through a Canadian pharmacy has to be written by a Canadian doctor. It would be important to have your prescription needs fully covered for the time spent in Canada.

As I was thinking back over our cruising adventures and savoring the many wonderful experiences we have had, I understood even more why we named our vessel *Grace Full*. As we cruised into the New York Harbor and gazed at "The Lady" rising up from the water, we were reminded that through the grace of God, we were free and well off compared to so many others in the world. As we sat on our sundeck and watched the sun set over the water, we felt very grateful for the ability to enjoy such beauty. We have lived our dream and have grown in so many ways as we have accomplished new tasks and stretched ourselves during scary times. We are anxious to take the many lessons we have learned and the skills we have acquired to explore new waterways.

We hope to see you on the water during your cruising adventure as we all live out our dreams.

Leslie Firestone is a retired CFP® who has assisted individuals and small businesses with their financial needs for 25 years in Columbia, Maryland. She has been married to Flint Firestone, a radiologic technologist, for 41 years and has a daughter and son who have produced five grandchildren, ranging from four to 27 years of age, and almost nine great-grandchildren, ranging from infant to the age of six. The Firestones are currently living in Chapin, South Carolina and at this time are taking care of the two youngest grandchildren during the week while their mom works.

She and Flint hope to return to Alabama next year to complete their "Loop" and continue cruising until they are ready to build on their property in Wyboo Plantation on Lake Marion in South Carolina.

Angela M. Metro

Vessel: M/V *Lady Enna* – 56-foot Matthews Motor Yacht
Residence/Homeport: St. Petersburg, Florida
Blog: themetrofamily.blogspot.com

There are millions of women out there, just like you, who love the thought of long-term cruising but are holding themselves back. You're not sure if this is the right thing to do. I mean, you have a house, responsibilities, and a full life. "Cruising sounds like fun, but come on, is it really for me?" you ask. I'm here to tell you that it's an unequivocal YES! Furthermore, in this section, I will illustrate how these perceived roadblocks could be turned around, allowing you the freedom to embrace this experience.

So, with all due respect to David Letterman's Top Ten List, here's Angela's countdown for the Top Five List for long-term Women Cruisers.

Number 5 – It's emotionally exhilarating, visually spectacular, and just plain fun!
Women, by nature and stereotype I might add, are inclined toward giving and nurturing – putting aside their own interests and needs to cater more towards others. Well, this isn't the 50s "sistah" – embrace life for YOU! Cruising is a tremendous experience! It's the perfect juxtaposition of tranquil waters, dazzling vistas and the exhilaration of life. Imagine the wind messing up that perfect hairdo, and no one cares, even you!

I don't propose altering your personality, but I do suggest that if there's a tiny little seed of Sir Walter Raleigh or Christopher Columbus inside of you... let it out! There is a way to successfully balance your nurturing side with the explorer in you.

If you don't have the urge to discover new continents, even seeing familiar places from the water is stimulating. That change of perspective allows you to see "the same old places" in a new and invigorating way. For example, I once lived near Annapolis, Maryland for several years, but when we pulled into the city by boat recently, it was as if we were coming into a new place. Ever the tour guide, I told Nick, my husband, "The Naval Academy is just a couple of blocks off the main downtown area." To which he answered, "Look, it's right there!" Of course, my perspective had been from land, and now we were coming in from the water. It felt like we were entering a new place, which made it just as much fun for me to explore as for the rest of my family.

Admittedly, there's comfort in living the same life and the same Friday night activity with the same friends – knowing which stores have just the right bargain and when to find them. However, the contrast between that and the true excitement of the unknown is an experience which will lift and transport you. Those comforts will seem all the more precious while allowing you the thrill of the novel. You can still keep the same Friday night activity (maybe it's happy hour or pot luck or a new restaurant), but it can be in a different place each week with fascinating new people, each with their own adventures to share. Just imagine how fun and invigorating those conversations will be!

Adulthood is not just about paying bills, working, and being serious. It's about the freedom, the logic, and the maturity to make what you want of your life. If you have any water-related wanderlust, it's time to experience the pure joy of the open waters!

Number 4 – Don't wait!

"I have a job. I have two kids. I am the vice president of the Parents' Association. I run the Cub Scout troop. I have responsibilities. I can't just chuck it all and sail the high seas." That was me, and I suspect it sounds very much like you too. Land lives are very full. I certainly don't suggest that you simply disappear one day and your relatives put your picture on the side of a milk carton. Create an exit strategy, one that might take a year or even two, to work through these various responsibilities. When Nick and I finally decided to pull the trigger, as it were, it took us a full 12 months to pull away from shore.

The school positions were the easiest to pass on to others. I finished my volunteer jobs and ensured they were covered (and don't kid yourself, there's always another volunteer waiting in the wings). My work had always been done virtually, so that simply continued without interruption. My husband's work, however, was a bit more challenging. He manages a software support group and "virtual employee" was a term his boss was uncomfortable with despite the fact that it's a technology organization. Luckily, the company later came out with a company-wide virtual employee policy, which has allowed Nick to keep his job while we were underway, ensuring our income and our benefits stayed the same. Another item off our exit checklist!

The hardest part was the kids. Don't get me wrong, we knew this experience would be one of the most valuable of their lives, but it was really hard for them to leave their friends. It was the educational part that concerned us. Friends we knew could be kept in constant contact by phone, e-mail, and our blog site. Taking on the task of educating our children, however, was daunting, but we were determined to figure it out. I researched some of the available curriculums as well as looked into buying the kids' current curriculum that they were already using in school. I asked the tough question, and luckily the school in which they were enrolled at the time gave us the go-ahead to use their curriculum and allowed our children to be virtual students. We were assigned a teacher, given the curriculum, and were provided with a learning timeline. It couldn't have worked out better for us! My point is you never know what may work out with a little time, effort and determination.

Our exit strategy also included fixing up the boat we currently lived on full time, taking care of repairs, updating electronics and charting mechanisms (electronic and paper), securing everything inside and spiffing up the exterior. We joined, and carefully watched, cruisers' forums and searched every place else we could to learn about the journey we were going to undertake.

Yes, it took a year, but we finally made it, and the effort was absolutely worth it! Don't wait for "someday." Start today!

Number 3 – We women really need you out there!

In my 11 years of living on a boat, I have learned that boating is a last vestige of male domination. To be blunt, men rule out there on the waters and women are the minority. We've made some great footholds in sailing – when a boating magazine runs an article on women in boating, it's filled with world-class women sailors (You GO girl!) – but there are fewer female powerboat captains or even powerful voices for women in motorboating. The ads in many boating magazines still portray women draped over boats in skimpy bikinis. (I've even seen one ad with topless women in bikini bottoms advertising bottom paint colors – arghh!)

There have also been recent strides made by boat manufacturers who are finally getting the input of the female involved in the boat-buying process. Boats are finally being built knowing that the galley is not a cubby for cooks but an integral part of the interior which adds to the quality of lifestyle, that the closet space needs to be bigger than a six-inch side opening in which to shove clothes, and that heads are more than just places to "relieve" oneself.

We need you. Women need to be vocal. We need to know the industry. Be able to talk "shop" with men – know and use boating terms like beam, draft, LOA/LOW, what types of anchors there are, and much more. The only way to feel comfortable with something new is to learn it and embrace it.

Number 2 – Let go!

You don't really need those three sets of dishes, do you? And what about all those knick-knacks?

Honestly, there's a freedom in letting go of your "stuff" when living on a boat. By the time you're ready to cruise, most people have amassed enough stuff in their homes that going through it all becomes a Herculean effort. "Someday, I'm going to de-clutter and get rid of all this!" As is usually the case with "somedays," though... they rarely come. Until now!

Now, I'm not suggesting you have some yard sale with people haggling over your son's first woodshop piece. Keep the things that are precious. But don't try to bring them on your boat – your boat is your refuge, a place where freedom reigns – not only freedom on the water but also freedom from the clutter of your lives that will keep you from exploring.

I was like many of my friends who swear they can't go one day without stopping at the grocery store, Target, or even the mall. Once you're cruising, you'd be surprised at how little you actually need. Boaters are open-minded people whose priorities are more about the experience and less about what one wears. Food becomes part of the social event and not the centerpiece. And those things that sit on shelves and look pretty, well, they'll just end up toppled over by some wave. It's so much easier to not have them. So, let go, be free!

The Number 1 thing about women and long-distance cruising is... Learn to drive the boat!

Driving a car is easy and second nature to most people. However, if you try to remember back when you were 16 and just learning how to operate this complex and potentially dangerous machine, you were scared, right? Not only did you have to figure out the machine itself but how to operate it in traffic and, of course, not kill anyone at a busy intersection.

For some reason, however, I've noticed that women are either hesitant or simply not interested in getting behind the wheel of a boat. Is it age that decreases our drive to... well, drive? Most women will take the helm for a few minutes to relieve their captain, but I'm talking about the real captaining. It's just plain common sense that there are two people able to operate the vessel for any emergency situations that might arise. (Ever hear of a plane being flown by ONE pilot? Nope, there's ALWAYS a co-pilot who can take over if necessary.)

When Nick and I first began cruising, we took the traditional roles of his being the captain and steering the boat while I handled the lines. We always argued because I never got the right order of the lines for the wind, the current, or the particular driving situation. At one point, he drove the boat into the slip, got down from the pilothouse house (while the boat was still running), and took the lines from me. That was it – the pilot should NEVER leave the steering station until the boat is secure! I take the helm now whenever we dock while Nick handles the lines. Just between you and me... docking the boat is ever so much easier than doing the lines: you get to stay comfortable in the often climate-controlled pilothouse, physically it takes less strength, and since everyone is amazed that a women just docked the boat, you'll get cheers from those catching the lines from the dock as you pull in. Your partner will also be proud of you and will brag to the other boaters.

Take a class (there are many), practice (we would go out, pick some piece of floating debris, and I would practice backing or maneuvering up to it), and have some driving fun. Let your inner 16-year-old relive the pride of successfully operating a motor vehicle!

Angela M. Metro is a long-term boater having lived aboard for 11 years with her husband Nick and their two children. They have a 1979 56-foot Matthews Motor Yacht called *Lady Enna*, which is going through a major (five years and counting) renovation while they're cruising. Currently they are on a voyage traversing the east coast of the United States incorporating their homeschooling curriculum into the travels with their children.

If you have children aboard, we would love to hear from you! (themetrofamily.blogspot.com)

Sharon Larrison Stepniewski

Vessel: M/V *Finally Fun* – 50-Foot DeFever Motor Yacht
Residence: Full-Time Cruiser
Homeport: Clearwater, Florida
Website: finallyfun.talkspot.com

FINALLY FUN... and more!

Take one triple Type A personality and one Type C or C minus personality, blend together in a marriage and let the YING-YANG begin. One party is at full tilt with a "go for it" attitude, and the other is more hesitant but game to "maybe try it." Throw in the decision to charter a boat – a trawler no less – what IS a trawler anyways? None of us knew, but with a little bit of exaggeration on our boating resumes and a "just do it" attitude, we found ourselves aboard a 48-foot trawler with a group of fun-loving friends cruising in the British Virgin Islands seven years ago.

The YANG (Type C personality) smuggled aboard a large number of books in order to kill time during what he thought would be a very boring vacation aboard this slow trawler thing. The YING (Triple Type A) brought aboard a list of 1,000-plus places to see and snorkel which, in hindsight, might have been a little ambitious for this ten-day period. YING and YANG survived the trip, as did the rest of the "crew" of fun-loving friends, cruising successfully by ourselves without a real captain aboard. Kicking and screaming and hating to leave, the group of us sadly flew back to the States after the best ever vacation aboard this trawler "thing."

Sometime during the five more trawler charter trips back to the British Virgin Islands and one charter trip to Belize, YING and YANG began dreaming about plotting a new, totally unanticipated and unexpected course for their lives. Why NOT cruise full time? Why NOT live aboard a trawler? Why NOT explore the unknown?

The Preparation

Given our limited boating experience, our rationale was to prepare thoroughly in order to minimize risk, thereby potentially saving the (yet to be purchased) boat, our lives and certainly our marriage. We discovered the world of cruising and the resources available to one that wants to learn and, most importantly, to learn from the experiences of others.

We attended numerous Trawler Fests as well as participated in various and sundry boating courses sponsored by Trawler Fest or by the U.S. Coast Guard Auxiliary. These courses increased our knowledge base and our confidence. Diesel repair, navigation, weather, ship's systems from stem to stern, and even such courses as how to keep one's boat clean began to make sense, or at least some sort of sense to us as time went on. We planned our vacations around the Trawler Fests and other boat shows, which allowed us to physically climb aboard, touch and poke around in a large number of trawlers of all sizes, makes and models – all with various characteristics and with price ranges as vast as the Atlantic Ocean. After several years of comparing and contrasting boats, we were able to develop a very realistic "must-have, non-negotiable" list of features and a "nice to have but could live without" list of criteria. This focused approach ultimately led us to our 50-foot DeFever Motor Yacht. Planning and preparation then began in earnest for YING (myself) and YANG (Andy).

There is NEVER a perfect time to cast off – much like there is NEVER a perfect time to have a child, sometimes one must just "GO FOR IT" (here speaks YING again).

With a strong belief in never wanting to look back and say, "I WISH I HAD…" I wish I had done this or I wish I had done that, I woke up one morning to two very loud thoughts reverberating in my brain. (1) I realized that my spouse and I were not getting any younger and that one needs reasonably good health to cruise. (2) That somewhere along the line I had lost sight of the fact that even though I believed in "Working to Live" and not in "Living to Work," my life was consumed by work and there was no hope in sight of turning that around. The decision to retire early a year ahead of my personal timeline was quick and easy to make. It came as a shock to many, including my YANG spouse, who had already retired, his being much (grin) older than I. This was also surprising to my children and certainly to my colleagues at work.

The Reality

There was a lot of activity among the fun-loving friends and family as they took bets. (1) How long would YING and YANG last aboard a boat? (2) How long it would be before one threw the other overboard? (3) How many times would YING have to pace on the boat deck every day?

In spite of the misgivings of those close to us, we purchased our dream boat and began the preparation to move aboard as quickly as possible.

In reality, the first thing we learned is that there is no QUICKLY in anything dealing with a boat. Commissioning the boat took months longer than we thought, and the only QUICKLY was how rapidly our funds poured out of our savings account in amounts far beyond what we had originally budgeted for.

Transitioning to life aboard was easy – it took me (YING) a full 30 seconds to switch from corporate high heels to flip-flops. and Andy (YANG) a little longer as he transitioned our land life to water (i.e. moving all financial transactions online, etc.). We named our boat *Finally Fun* to represent the closing of many of life's chapters, including moving from gainful employment to retirement from the pharmaceutical industry (YING) and from the U.S. Air Force and from various distribution companies (YANG) and from the daily challenges and rewards of hands-on parenting six children (three hers and three his). We hoped no one would take offense to the boat's name.

In reality, operating this 50-foot, three-story DeFever Trawler that weighs 60,000 pounds and does not have brakes was and is still certainly a LOT harder than in theory. We are basically a self-contained little city, producing our own power with a John Deere 300 hp twin turbocharged engines, a generator and an inverter to make things operate at all times. We handle our own waste, using pump-out stations along the way or, if in other countries such as the Bahamas or the British Virgin Islands, we churn and spew it out via macerator pumps – their choice, not ours! We compact our own trash. We store 375 gallons of water that pump on demand just like at home. We make our own water when needed via a desalination and reverse osmosis process. The 1,000 gallons of diesel fuel on board would allow us to cruise around the world if we choose – hence the term "Passagemaker" which is commonly used to describe these long-range trawler "things."

Life is not tough living aboard *Finally Fun* with its central vacuum system, full-sized front-loader washing machine that uses only 15 gallons of water and a full-sized dryer. The icemaker on the aft deck keeps up with demand and is a luxury I would hate to give up. We filter our drinking water and icemaker line three times before consumption and with two drawer-sized refrigerators and two freezers aboard, the wine stays chilled and Andy has his ice cream. A small refrigerator on the flybridge eliminates the risk of a beer or coke getting warm while being brought up from the galley. Given the choice between home-cooked meals with fresh herbs or no food, Andy capitulated and allowed my dirt and plants to come aboard. *Fox News* and Bill O'Reilly ring in my ears 24/7 thanks (or no thanks) to satellite TV and satellite radio. Funny, on land, I never had a trash compactor, a king-size bed nor even a central vac! In short, a cruising lifestyle does not mean having to do without. I equate our boating lifestyle to a floating RV when describing our new way of living to non-boater friends. The added benefit is that we always have a room with a water view!

Our Voyage Begins

We moved aboard once the weather in the Annapolis, Maryland area, where we purchased the boat, warmed up enough. Then we began the "shake down" process while becoming familiar with the boat and developing and improving our skills. Practicing in the Chesapeake Bay was a wonderful experience with its forgiving soft mud bottom, the beautiful scenery and the many rivers and creeks to explore. We especially enjoyed exploring numerous little maritime communities such as Oxford, St. Michaels, Smith and Tangier Islands, as well as the larger cities of Baltimore and Annapolis.

We usually managed to get the boat in and out of slips in those places without too much banging and smacking; we learned to anchor safely and recognize what makes a safe anchorage; we learned to tie knots and secure lines and figure out, for the most part, the mysterious innards of this trawler "thing."

The Women's Only weeklong class I took at the Sea Sense Boating School with three other women and a female captain (Captain Patty Moore) in preparation for this lifestyle raised my confidence level and my skills. Learning to physically operate a trawler by myself, dock it, turn it, keep it on a straight course, even check the oil and other mysterious stuff in the engine room was easy in hindsight. After all, that was NOT my boat I was aiming at a dock!

I give full credit to YANG – that calm Type C personality who handles this boat quite well, even docking aft in! Well, most of the time. With an eye to saving our boat and certainly for saving the marriage, YANG purchased radio headsets for each of us so we could communicate during docking and other maneuvers when we cannot hear and/or see each other. However, folks on the adjacent docks and waterway and in nearby condos need to go elsewhere for their entertainment now that we are wearing the headsets. The screaming, shouting of *?#!!&#@*% and the one-finger hand signals are no more. Now, only WE hear the verbalizations, which from time to time still include the *?#!!&#@*%!

We laughed a lot over wine each evening as we reminisced about the day's events, and were always grateful to have "survived" another day underway. It took almost a year, however, before we actually had a toast to ourselves on the proficiency of our new skill sets!

Round and Round She Goes

With no scheduled end date or planned destinations yet to be determined, the expression "Round and round she goes and where she stops, nobody knows" is an apt description of what the cruising lifestyle is all about. Every day on the water is another day of beauty, another day of adventure, and another day of skill building and gratitude for all life has to offer.

We remained in the Chesapeake Bay long enough to watch the summer season change to fall before heading south through the Dismal Swamp and on down the Intracoastal Waterway (ICW) to Florida. Our confidence much greater, we cruised to the Abacos, Bahamas for much of the winter. Spring found us cruising back up the same route, this time all the way to New York City and on up the Hudson River and through much of the Erie Canal, before crossing Lake Ontario north to the Canadian Rideau Canal. This "Triangle Loop" took us farther north to Ottawa, then east along the Ottawa River to Montreal and over to Sorel, Canada before ultimately turning southward to Lake Champlain and the Champlain Canal.

Finally, back in the United States, we will retrace our route back to South Florida to the Keys so that we can bask in the warm winter sunshine until spring. As it begins to really warm up in the Keys and the south in general, we will head back north to complete our Loop via the Great Lakes, Chicago and cruise through the great state of Alabama to the Gulf of Mexico and finally to Clearwater, Florida, our homeport. Then its back to what has become my favorite expression, "Round and round she goes and where she stops, nobody knows." I (YING) definitely have dreams for exotic places much farther away, but YANG isn't quite so willing just yet (my emphasis on the just yet, not his). We will see...

I learned a lot while becoming a long-distance cruiser.

Prepare. Prepare
The time we spent at the various Trawler Fests and boat shows, including the charter trips, was invaluable in helping us decide whether this would be a viable lifestyle for us. Contrast our experience to that of a couple we met at an America's Great Loop Cruisers' Association (AGLCA) meeting. This couple had sold their business, their home and most of their possessions, and had been cruising aboard their new boat for only THREE DAYS when he announced publicly at this meeting that their boat was for sale. She hated it all. He stood there, nearly in tears, as were many of us in the audience. Preparation will greatly increase one's satisfaction with the entire process and lessen the number of surprises along the way.

Home is a Place
Like a turtle, home surrounds me. Wherever I am, is home. Home is simply a place. Memories, not things, are what sustain me. Every day is a new adventure, a new challenge, a new experience, a new satisfaction. Every day is a new beauty to behold... sunsets, sunrises, ripples and flashes across the water. Magnificent birds, the playful dolphin dancing in our wake, the "so ugly she's beautiful" manatee and her baby, the flying fish across our bow and the numerous charming and quaint towns and villages all along the waterways reinforce my belief that every day is a wondrous gift of life.

Checking the anchor in the middle of the night is a much-anticipated special moment. The darkened scenery, lit by more stars than I ever knew existed, is mysterious and noisy with the sounds of the night, of the birds, owls, and splashing fish never heard in the daytime. Looking over the rail into the night and the water, some fish often sparkle and shine from below with phosphorous flashing lights. Although this anchor check is certainly not necessary, it has become my own personal "duty," and I don't even need an alarm to wake me!

Our children, family members and friends have embraced our new lifestyle and eagerly schedule their vacations around our cruising plans. Grown children and friends sharing wine over a sunset in a locale new to us all; grandchildren gleefully jumping off the deck into the water below; grandchildren gaining new skills as they master knots and the wheel; a grandchild learning to walk as the saloon cabin goes back and forth are yet more lasting memories for us all.

Camaraderie and Friendships
Instant friendships, albeit some fleeting, has been one of the most rewarding benefits of our new cruising lifestyle. Sharing advice, sharing tools, hands-on assistance when needed no matter the hour or the place make one feel secure and never lonely. Common interests – i.e. the boat – quickly bring on an invite, "come on over" whether the invite is via VHF radio or a personal meeting on a dock, dink or on land. The further exchange of stories, escapades, places to see and places to go make for fun evenings, more great memories and some lasting friendships. There is truly a universal "boating community" and it is wherever there are two or more boats in one place.

Closeness and Teamwork
Living together in 50 feet of space became a non-issue very quickly. As a couple, we function as a true team now with a common goal, rather than two people in separate orbs that overlapped on occasion.

For example, when cruising down much of the ICW, you cannot "wander" six inches one way or the other or you run the risk of running aground or worse. It is harder than it looks to stay in the middle, requiring both of us at the helm: one at the wheel and the other with one eye looking ahead and one eye on the depth sounder. Every time the one at the wheel takes eyes off the centerline to look around, the boat strays left or right, and respiration stops in response to the shrill screech from the other.

We have a captain, and on occasion, an admiral on board. These roles seem to flex, depending upon moods or sense of urgency. Our children have given us two T-shirts emblazoned with "Don't Yell at Me!" and the other, "I'm Not Yelling At You!" which are interchangeable depending upon one's mood and/or sense of humor and which, when worn to the flybridge, break the tension on a bad day.

As to closeness, we often go to bed much earlier than we ever had previously. We are exhausted either from tension or simply from a long day on the water. Boater's midnight often strikes at 9:30 p.m.

Next Steps
We gravitated toward our strengths when assuming roles when we moved aboard. As the YING, I handle the overall planning and all the details associated

with planning such as food, places to stay, anchorages, etc. while YANG double-checks weather, the charts and details of navigation. We share time at the wheel when underway.

We do have a twofold goal now that we have completed a full year on the water: (1) to be able to anticipate each other's moves as we launch or dock and (2) to be interchangeable in skill sets for safety's sake. We have gotten better in the anticipation phase and that alone says a LOT! However, we have evolved into some stereotypical thinking with him handling the boat in close quarters and docking while I handle the lines. I am considering investing in a Women Only refresher course to practice close-quarter maneuvering rather than one of us spending that money on a lawyer if HE has to teach me! Would YOU let your husband teach you to drive a boat?

> "I would rather regret the things I have done than the things I have not."
> — LUCILLE BALL

Far more often than men, women seem willing to walk away from their dreams. Call it stereotypical thinking, call it perceived role modeling, call it simply letting the male spouse make the life decisions, call it whatever you wish, but more often it is the male who has the boating and cruising dream and the supportive female partner follows along.

However, what if the roles are reversed and it is YOU, the female, who secretly harbors this dream of cruising off into the sunset? On the other hand, what if it is the male with the dream and the female is struggling with his idea of a daring life plan?

A few suggestions to either one of you or to both of you, whichever the case may be:

1. **Take your somewhat elusive dream of life aboard a boat and break it down into manageable pieces.** Our successful transition to a cruising lifestyle was, in hindsight, due to our careful preparation. Contrast our experience with that of the couple who sold everything, moved aboard and discovered rather promptly that this was not for them!

2. **Explore the cruising lifestyle as a couple.** Attend Trawler Fests and other similar boating conferences, attend boat shows, talk and listen to boaters who already embrace this lifestyle. Spend time at the AGLCA Rendezvous meetings, receptions and cocktail hours, ask questions and listen! Charter a boat several times – whether it is in the U.S. or elsewhere.

3. **Have little to no boating experience? Hire a captain along with the charter boat (not many more $$$ in the total cost).** See how you like being aboard for a week or two at a time. You will meet men and women of all spectrums doing what they love and you will also learn that it was one of them that started talking about a change in lifestyle, not necessarily both of them had the dream. If you are with a captain aboard, pick his brain and learn from him, be hands-on throughout your charter.

4. **Be willing to take a risk!** Get out of your comfort zone. Don't be the individual who will not take the chance they wanted to take, who doesn't take a risk, or who is afraid to fail or worse. Don't keep on doing what you have been doing and have to face yourself in the mirror much later in life, perhaps too late in life – "I wonder what my life would have been like if I had tried the cruising lifestyle?"

5. **Don't wonder. Don't regret. Don't ever have to say, "I wish I had…"**

Just Do It!

Sharon Fellows Larrison Stepniewski, aboard the 50-foot DeFever Motor Yacht *Finally Fun*, learned to pack before she learned to walk. The daughter and later the wife of career military men, and later, due to her career, Sharon never lived in any one place long, including two tours in Germany and one in Okinawa.

Two sailboats and two small powerboats over the years whetted her appetite to be on the water. That love of the water, combined with her upbringing and wanderlust personality, brought her to the live-aboard dream.

Retiring as a vice president of Sales at Novartis Pharmaceuticals Corporation, Sharon continues to share her vision with others – that vision now, however, is focused on life after work… Finally Fun!

Doris Prichard

Vessel: M/V *Segue* – 43-foot Californian Cockpit Motor Yacht
Residence: Knoxville, Tennessee
Homeport: Fort Loudon Marina, Lenoir City, Tennessee
Website: seguevoyage.com

A Woman's Perspective

For years, my husband, Wayne, and I have lived and boated on Lakes Loudon and Tellico in Tennessee... and when we vacation it's usually somewhere by the water. Wayne has always loved boats, and his business was boat related. We both liked the idea of traveling on the boat for an extended period of time, so it came as a logical progression for us to want to spend a year traveling on the Great Loop.

    We'd talked about "doing the Loop" for years, but finally decided to actively start planning the trip when I retired. That's when the research began! We decided that we'd need a larger boat for this trip. We subscribed to magazines like *PassageMaker*, *Southern Boating*, and *Sea Magazine* to start our learning process. We traveled to boat shows and attended a couple of Trawler Fests. (Trawler Fests, sponsored by *PassageMaker*, are a combination boat show with learning opportunities, as they host classes on topics of interest to boaters.) These events helped us learn more about the variety of boats available, and gave us an opportunity to swap information with other boaters that were already cruising.

    From this invaluable initial research, we decided that we wanted a used, trawler-style boat that we could work on for a few years while Wayne was still involved in his business. Never having owned a boat over 20 feet, we decided it might be wise to charter a larger boat and see what the reality would be like. So, we chartered an older Grand Banks trawler on the Gulf Coast of Florida for four days and three nights, and the experience was invaluable. The charter company gave us a couple of hours of instruction and turned us loose. Not only did we learn that we'd probably do just fine handling a larger boat, but we came away knowing a lot more about what we wanted in a boat. We wanted a queen-size bed (or larger), a covered deck for rainy days, a galley that was separate from the living area, two engines, and a cockpit on the back so we could access the dingy easily.

Returning to Knoxville after the charter trip, we started our search for the right boat for us. We identified a design called a cockpit motor yacht that seemed to have the right layout. We contacted a local boat broker and asked him to do some investigating for us. Within a week, or so, he'd found a boat in our locale, an older Californian trawler that fit our wants and needs. We liked the boat, but were concerned that some modifications that were already made for the boat (an enclosed back deck) might not work well for us. It was then that Wayne remembered "meeting" a different Californian in the Knoxville area. He called the owner, who had moved out of state, to talk about the modified Californian we were considering. Much to our delight, we learned that the owner was ready to sell his own Californian! The boat was still in Knoxville, so we immediately arranged to go see the vessel.

It was love at second sight! (Wayne had loved it when he saw it the first time!) We made a deal and became the proud owners of a boat for the Loop. A 43-foot, 1982 Californian Cockpit Motor Yacht, *Segue* signified our transition from work to retirement and from land to water.

Over the next four years as we refurbished the boat, we focused our research activities more on the Great Loop trip. We joined the America's Great Loop Cruisers' Association (AGLCA – greatloop.org). In addition to attending a couple of their meetings, we started monitoring e-mail discussion list groups sponsored by AGLCA and other cruising boater groups such as the Great Loop List, Trawlers & Trawlering (trawlersandtrawlering.com), and Trawler Crawler (trawlercrawler.net).

We'd heard about a couple who live in the Knoxville area, Rob and Eva Stob, who had written a book about doing the Great Loop titled *Honey, Let's Get a Boat...* We got a copy and read it through, stoking the flames even more. We even went over to a local public library to hear Rob and Eva talk about their adventure in person. We were chomping at the bit to get on with it!

Once we were both retired, we knew it was time to make our move. During the months leading up to our October departure we fine-tuned the boat, took a navigation class from the Knoxville Power Squadron, gathered supplies, planned our route, found a house sitter, and forwarded our mail. We were going away for a year, and there was a lot to take care of. Friends asked why we weren't going to "try it out first" for a couple of months to see how we liked life on the water. See, we'd never traveled farther than Chattanooga before this trip. We decided it was just as much trouble to close up the house for a couple of months as it was for a couple of years and we were determined to do the Loop. Now!

We set a departure date and took off in mid-October, looking forward to the show of fall color as we made our way down the Tennessee River.

Our exuberance was dampened only one day into the trip when the fuel tank started leaking. It would have to be replaced, and our trip was going to have to wait a couple of months until the boatyard could fit us into their schedule. We just couldn't bear the thought of going back to our house and undoing every plan we'd set in place for the year, so we quietly made our way back to Knoxville, got our car, and set out on a road trip to visit some of the places we planned to see by water. One month later, we went home for Thanksgiving so we could monitor the repair process daily.

Mid-December we struck out again on the Great Loop. Yes, the fall color was gone... and the weather as we made our way to the Gulf was rainy and cold, but we were on our way!

Our Great Loop trip took us from Fort Loudon Lake, Knoxville, Tennessee, to Mobile, Key West, up the East Coast to New York City, then to Canada (including Montreal, Ottawa, Georgian Bay and the North Channel of Lake Huron), across Lake Michigan to Chicago, and down a system of six rivers back to Knoxville. It was a yearlong journey of 6,800 miles, 128 locks and 4400 gallons of diesel fuel.

Traveling with us on this trip was our two-year-old miniature schnauzer, Lucy. When planning for the Loop trip, we had to take Lucy's needs into consideration as well. One of the AGLCA Rendezvous we attended had a great session on traveling with pets, and we got a lot of good information and ideas there.

Lucy's a reluctant swimmer, so we bought her a life jacket with a "handle" on top to make getting her on and off the boat easier. Our vet was very enthusiastic about the trip and worked up a first aid kit for her that included an antibiotic, eardrops, antihistamine, a motion sickness remedy, and other medications she thought might come in handy. Lucy's vaccinations were all updated, and (knowing we would be going into Canada) we got a certificate signed to that effect.

Obviously one of our concerns for Lucy was whether we'd be able to get her to shore every morning and evening for a "bio-break." The vet assured us that she wouldn't hurt herself if she had to wait and that eventually she'd relieve herself on the boat. Lucy was trained as a puppy to use a dog litter box, but we didn't like keeping it in the house and let those skills die. When we started the trip we revived the litter box idea, but Lucy wasn't buying it. Could we talk her into using what we jokingly referred to as the "poop" deck, i.e. cockpit?

At one point on our trip down the Tennessee-Tombigbee Waterway, in December, we found ourselves anchored in an area with "sucky mud" on the banks and couldn't take Lucy ashore. What would normally have been a one-night stay turned into a three-night sojourn because of bad weather. Lucy wouldn't "go." We put her out on the back deck (in the rain and cold) and peeked at her from the saloon window. Nothing. Then 36 hours after we anchored she finally succumbed to nature's call, and we ALL breathed a sigh of relief!

There were other times on the trip when she couldn't be taken to shore (the Everglades come to mind... reptiles in the water and all), and we learned that she really could go a long time and that she really would eventually relieve herself on the boat.

I'll admit that I had some concerns about the trip initially. Wayne and I have been married for 40 years. (In fact, we spent our 40th year together doing this trip!) Wayne retired in April, and I had been retired for several years. In all of our years together we'd never spent even a month together 24/7... not that that's unusual for a couple that both have careers. Anyway, I just wondered whether we would end up driving each other crazy after a few months.

Wayne wasn't concerned. Moreover, in retrospect, it wasn't a problem. There were two things we did to make it easier on each other. First, we bought the "marriage savers," the headphones that allow the captain and crew to communicate without shouting as you're docking. Second, and this was Wayne's idea, we agreed to "be nice to each other." Sounds simple, but it worked. Oh, there were times when alarm would creep into our voices as we surveyed a new problem. But the words, now almost a whispered chant in our heads, "Let's be nice to each other," would make us realize we were unintentionally working up to more than a hearty discussion! All told, it was a wonderful year spent together, and we made some great memories.

Another concern I had was that I'd get bored. I brought books (I'd say between us we probably had close to 50 or more), my watercolor paints, and a variety of papers, several needlework projects, some quilting, my portable sewing machine. Need I go on?

Looking back on it that is the craziest thing I could have worried about! I think it stems from the idea we had that one of us would be piloting the boat while the other would be eating bon-bons and reading on the back deck. Well, that's not how it was for us. Most days found us both sitting up on the bridge, one guiding the boat and watching the electronic charts while the other kept up with the paper charts. We both liked the view from the bridge, and we just felt better most times having four eyes on the course.

I'd been painting watercolors for a couple of years before we started the trip, and I was concerned that I'd regress. So, I signed up for a weeklong class while we were in Sarasota. (The Art Center is within walking distance of the marina downtown.) Then when we were in Vergennes, Vermont, I met an artist in his gallery, and we started talking about watercolor. He invited me to join him and a small group of painters he met with weekly. What a nice experience!

From then on, I made a point to talk with local gallery owners to find out about painting groups in the area.

I'd wondered about how easily we could get to a grocery store on the trip. I bet every Looper boat has at least two cans of beans in the pantry that have never been touched but represent the two meals we could have in that dire event we had nothing else to eat! I also had a couple of bags of dry tortellini that made it all the way around the Loop without being touched!

Actually, getting food wasn't a problem for us. Most Loopers would probably agree that food and drink are plentiful on the Loop. Obviously, keeping produce and frozen foods stocked was more a challenge than the dry goods, but we were usually only a day away from anything we really wanted or needed. I did use those Green Bags on the trip to extend the life of produce. We came to love the frozen bags of pasta already put together and ready for the microwave. That and whatever fresh vegetables we had around would make a meal. Our favorite thing was to eat lunch onshore and eat a light supper.

Our only grandson was under the age of two when we left, and I was a little worried he'd forget who we were! We talked weekly with our son and his family, but the telephone seemed such an abstract form of communication for the little guy. We eventually got a webcam for the computer (as did our son) so we could have our Sunday morning conferences with accompanying video. We also had them come visit us during the trip, and we took time out to go visit them.

Speaking of visitors, we invited a number of couples to come join us along the trip at various points. While we loved sharing the experience firsthand with our friends and relatives, we quickly learned that committing to be at a particular place on a particular date was not easy. Sometimes it meant we rushed through an area of the trip to be sure we were where we needed to be for the rendezvous. You just never know when the mood will strike you to dally in an anchorage for a few days longer because the weather's so nice, or on the flipside, being stuck in the same anchorage because of high winds or nasty weather. On the other hand, maybe you wanted to stay the weekend in a little town to catch the local art-in-the-park you just found out was coming up. On our next trip like this we'll probably take a "catch us if you can" attitude about visitors.

A typical travel day for us was to wake up around 7 a.m. and take our time to get going. We'd sit around checking e-mail and catching up on the news until we decided (or Lucy demanded) that it was time to get going. We were usually on our way by 8:30 or 9 a.m. and would try to end the travel day around 1 or 2 p.m. During the evening, we took time to plan out the next day's run and plot the course on the electronic charts.

Wayne handled the boat most often when docking or going through locks. In between, we took regular turns at the wheel. We spent a couple of weeks in Sarasota, and while we were there we watched a group of women on the trawler next to us learn boating skills from Sea Sense Boating School (seasenseboating.com). On talking with the captain, we found out that Sea Sense is a sailing and powerboat school for women (or private courses, on your own boat, for couples, families or groups). I mentioned to Wayne that I'd love to do that sometime, and we ended up hiring her for a day of schooling.

It was a great experience for me. Captain Patti Moore sat with me most of the time at the helm while Wayne handled the lines. She never panicked (even when I did!) and never made a nervous move. I practiced bringing the boat to a stop and holding it in place, coming alongside a dock (I found out that rub rails are made to let you "bounce" off of things), docking in a slip (stern in and bow in), and so much more. She helped us find the pivot point on the boat to make it easier to get in the right position before pulling into a slip. One of the most useful things she did was to help Wayne and me learn how to communicate in the process. Instead of saying, "Put the starboard engine in reverse," we learned to say, "the stern needs to be closer to the dock."

The other great piece of advice Patti gave us was to grab a line with your knuckles on top of the line, not under. Try it sometime! When you grab a line to pull like this, your legs automatically get into the effort, saving you a possible back strain.

You know the old adage, though: "use it or lose it." I had a couple of opportunities to dock the boat before we started a long stint of anchoring and mooring. By the time the next opportunity rolled around I wasn't feeling as secure with my skills and deferred to Wayne. I'll work on it this summer at the marina, during the week when not as many people are there, but only if the winds are calm.

Calm winds. Yes, we had them on the trip, most times. Other times, not so much. We learned during the first couple of months what our limits were as far as winds and waves were concerned. We stayed put if the winds were over ten mph or the waves were over three feet. Weather Underground has a marine forecast that we used a lot and the "good" waves were pink in color. We were happy when we saw pink in the forecast! We learned too that if we decided to go in spite of the conditions we could speed up, raise or lower the bow, or change direction slightly to make the ride more comfortable. Lake Michigan challenged us this way. We rarely had an optimal travel day on that lake.

We learned so much on this trip! Figuring out where we wanted to go and how we wanted to get there was one of the most rewarding activities for both of us. Wayne and I often traveled by ourselves because we enjoy the adventure of making our own way, setting our own course and speed. Not that there weren't times when we gladly went with one "buddy boat" or more when we felt the weather conditions warranted it.

There were also some challenging times, like the day we ran aground on the Tennessee-Tombigbee Waterway after trying (unsuccessfully) to anchor in a little cove. "BoatU.S. will help us," we thought. Oops! No cell phone connection. OK, we hailed the closest lock on the radio and had the lockmaster call for us. A little while later he came back saying there were no BoatU.S. locations within 50 miles. Did we want someone to come from Demopolis or Jackson, Alabama? "Demopolis," we said, since that was the direction we were headed.

We tried to get off the ground again and finally wiggled free. By this time it was getting to be late in the day, and there was nowhere to anchor or tie up for the night. We decided to go all the way to Demopolis and run a couple of hours after dark. We had some ambient light to go by and stayed fixed on the radar screen. We made it to a marina safe and sound, but we were both exhausted!

This whole experience taught us a couple of things. First, always have some backup plans if your goal is to anchor out. Have in mind a couple of spots, just in case the first doesn't work for some reason. Second, at all costs avoid trying to navigate into an unfamiliar marina at night. Getting into an unfamiliar marina can be tricky in the day: take away your ability to see place marks and it becomes really dangerous.

The funniest thing that happened to us is amusing only in retrospect. At the time, it was scary! We were moored at the marina in Sarasota visiting with a dear friend who'd brought his grandson over to see the boat. Little Bobby, we'll call him, was four years old and very adventurous. "Would you like to see the engine room, Bobby?" "You bet!" So, Wayne was giving him the tour, showing him the controls, how to operate the toilets, etc. Wayne, our friend, and Bobby were all down in the saloon standing near the pilot station when Bobby quickly turned the ignition key and pushed the throttle forward. We were tied to the dock, but the boat was ready to go on! Wayne quickly pulled the throttle back and turned off the ignition. When they got off the boat our neighbor in the marina said, "Was that as exciting for you as it was for me?" Lesson learned: don't leave the keys in the ignition with kids around!

One of the most rewarding aspects of this trip was that we became confident in our roles (me as crew and Wayne as captain). Every marina is just a little bit different in terms of approach and docking than the ones you've been to before. Every day offers its own unique blend of wind, waves, traffic and hazards. We learned something new almost every day about handling the boat or navigating. We also learned so much about the boat and what it could and couldn't do. I can see why people would do the Loop twice. You learn so much on the first go-round it would be a much easier and a less stressful trip the second time around.

Because we took this trip, we now have boating friends in all parts of the United States and Canada. Some of these friends we still correspond with on a monthly basis, and others less often. We've continued to make friends after returning to Knoxville and meeting people who are planning to do the trip soon. We sent an article in to the local newspaper and have spoken to several groups about the adventure since our return.

What would we do differently if we were to do the Loop again? For our first trip, I'd have to say it was just about perfect. On a second trip, however, knowing what we know, more intimately now of locations on the Loop, we'd probably leave off some destinations and pick up (or stay longer) in others that were more interesting to us. We'd make some modifications to the boat before the second trip. We'd install an autopilot for those long runs, add a small freezer for extra food storage, and swap out the carpet for hardwood floors inside. We'd also do some work on the galley to get rid of our old Princess stove and replace that with a flat cooking surface and build more storage for cookware. I'd like to say I'd take fewer clothes... but, hey, we had the space and you just NEVER KNOW when you might want to wear that special outfit. On a side note, earrings, ladies, make great souvenirs, and they take up very little space.

One of the most important things we learned on this trip is that there is no one "best" way to do it. Your plan can be a personal one; you can vary the route, the time and the expense. You can also decide when you want to travel with a group of boats or when by yourself. We just want others to know, those who've dreamed about doing this sort of trip, that there are organizations and individuals out there to help you plan and execute the journey. No matter your method, it really can be "the trip of a lifetime."

Addendum, a year later:
Our big "aha" moment has come. We are realizing now – almost a year after our trip is over – what an impact this trip has had on us and how we now want to live our lives.

Adjusting back to life on land hasn't been easy for us. We liked not receiving mail every day and limiting our spending to things we could fit on the boat. Ideally, we could have stayed on the boat and kept going, but our obligations and expectations at home were calling.

This month we sold our house on the lake and have just made an offer on a 1700 sq. ft. home in a development that will allow us to "lock and leave" when we want to travel and not have to worry about the upkeep. We're cutting our space down drastically, which will mean we need to get rid of some things we've been carrying around for a while and not really using. (I used to go to estate sales every weekend. Need I say more?)

What we've learned on this trip is that it's who you're with and what you're doing that counted for us... not where we're living or what we have in the way of the possessions that surround us. We've always thought this, but when we lived a year without all this "stuff," we found another level of contentment we hadn't known before.

Already we feel freer and more at peace than we have in years. Our goal is to minimize our expenditures, whether of time or money, to the necessities of life so we can spend time and money on the activities we enjoy.
See you on the water!

Doris Prichard – *Segue*

Doris Prichard lives with her husband, Wayne, and their miniature Schnauzer, Lucy, in Knoxville, Tennessee. A retired librarian, Doris is now spending most of her time painting and drawing while planning the next boat trip!

Darcy Searl

Vessel: M/V *Just Us* – 42-foot Carver Motor Yacht
Residence: Roswell, Georgia
Homeport: Goose Pond Marina – Scottsboro, Alabama
Website: justusboating.com

This is an Adventure, Not a Vacation

"I want to be down there looking up, not up here looking down." These were the words from my husband, Ken, as we sat on the deck of our weekend cottage atop Sand Mountain, Alabama overlooking the magnificent Tennessee River. As we continued to watch boats cruise by during their seasonal migration south on the river system, we noticed that they all flew the distinctive white burgee on the bow of their boats and it intrigued us. The Great Loop Adventure was something we had heard about from boating friends while spending time on Lake Lanier in Georgia, where we had a 70-foot Summerset Houseboat. Many of our friends had already done the Loop, and we could not ask enough questions about this boat trip. "Remember this is an adventure, not a vacation," our friends would say. Ken and I began formulating a plan that would enable us to do this trip, maintain our business and keep our personal lives too.

Right away, we had some concerns. The first one being that we are still working and own a financial planning and money management firm that we were not ready to give up. How do we create a new business model that would allow us travel AND maintain a high level of service for our clients? The second of our concerns was that we had a daughter in high school with two years left before graduation. That at least gave us a timeline, as there could be no leaving before our baby graduated from high school and was out of the nest – so to speak. The third was that we needed to simplify our lives. We owned too much stuff and life was getting very complicated.

Ken said, "My father died at the age I am now, and I don't want to wait and be too old to do this trip AND I'm tired of going around and around Lake Lanier." I was thrilled at the idea of traveling on a boat again, as I grew up in southern Louisiana on the "bayou." My father was a commercial fisherman and owned a fleet of shrimp boats. Many of my childhood summers were spent out in the Gulf of Mexico not seeing land for weeks. I don't get seasick and open water travel was never a concern for me.

So, we set a time frame to depart in October following our daughter's high school graduation in May and sending her away to college in September. Problem number two tentatively solved. With your children, nothing is ever set in stone.

Then we started selling much of our stuff. The late comedian George Carlin said, " It is all your stuff that controls you." We sold the mountain cottage, followed by the jet ski, the 17-foot ski boat and then the 70-foot Lake Lanier houseboat all to the dismay of our six children, who thought we were crazy. We decided to keep our main house in Georgia and hire a house sitter to care for our 13-year-old dog, Beau. You can sell a lot of things, but you can't sell your dog. He had been an excellent boat dog for many years but arthritis and age would make this type of long-distance boat trip impossible for him.

We began looking for our "Looper Boat" and started the process of changing our business model for our firm. We decided that investing in better technology would be the answer and give us the freedom to achieve our goal of "staying connected." Our new financial planning software was web-hosted so we could conduct business anywhere we could get an Internet and cell phone connection. This software was so efficient that we were able to reduce staff and kept only four planners in our group. Learning this complex system took some time, but it was well worth the effort, and we still use it today even after finishing our trip.

Our lease was up in our large office space just in time to move Ken and me to our new home office – in the future we would rent conference room space nearby to meet clients when necessary. The other two planners in our group decided to work in a different location. The plan was coming together and problem one, keeping the business running while we traveled, looked doable.

Now, a more concentrated effort to find the boat began. We researched all different types of boats and traveled far and wide to find just the boat for "us." We read many blogs and websites of other Loopers who wrote daily accounts of their trip. We made a list of what was important to "us." During one of these trips, we sat in a bar (some our best decisions happen in bars) in Charleston, South Carolina, reviewing our list of growing requirements for the perfect boat. Who will we want to travel with us, how many staterooms must we have, what size boat will be comfortable, and what engines and generator combination will meet our needs? With each question we would end with "but most of the time it will be "just us." Thus, we named the boat *Just Us* before we even found a boat. Pleased with ourselves for coming up with a name for the boat we didn't even own yet, we rushed home to tell our kids. They didn't like the name because it didn't include "them." So we settled on a more inclusive name *"Just Us and Sometimes Them."*

After a year of searching, we decided on a 1989 42-foot Carver aft cabin motor yacht with twin Caterpillar diesel engines. We found her on Lake Guntersville on the Tennessee River in Alabama. She had been in fresh water and under cover most of her life. She was in excellent condition with a recent interior refurbishing. She was very comfortable and roomy with a 15-foot beam. She had two staterooms with head and shower in each. The guest stateroom and head was important to us. Having "Them" on board can get a little too cozy with everyone having to use the same head. The galley had an eat-in settee and tons of storage plus a pantry closet. The master stateroom was large enough to have a walk around bed and lots of storage and an en suite head. The aft deck was roomy enough to entertain several guests for the famous "cocktail hour." SOLD!

We took possession of the boat in March and planned to depart in October. That gave us only eight months to get used to the boat and prepare and outfit it for the trip. Soon after we bought the boat, it seemed like all the electronics failed. They certainly were dated technology and expensive to update. We became familiar with the expression B.O.A.T., standing for "Break Out Another Thousand." You just hate to break out so many thousands in a row. In eight months time we replaced, or added, an all-new Ray Marine chart plotter, radar, depth finder, KVH satellite TV, dinghy and outboard motor, inverter and other miscellaneous items.

Just as we thought things were coming together and we would make our deadline to leave by October 30, Hurricane Katrina hit New Orleans and my parents' home was flooded. My parents called for help, and we packed our truck with as much food and supplies as we could and made the ten-hour drive (we normally made it in eight). We spent a week ripping out walls and throwing out furniture in 100-degree heat. Ken can fix anything, but getting materials was almost impossible in the aftermath of this disaster, so we drove home and tried to decide if we should cancel our planned trip to help my parents.

My parents assured us that they had things under control and for us to "GO." In talking with others who have done the Loop, there always seemed to be a reason NOT to go. I am here to tell you that, "if there is a will, there's a way." With the help of some great friends, we departed at the end of October, as scheduled, after a going-away breakfast given by our dock neighbors. We wondered if it was a "bon voyage" or "glad they are gone" breakfast. It must have been the former because four of them leaped on board and claimed they were going with us. They did too for 40 miles! Seems they had taken a car downriver the day before in preparation for this little joke. So, our solo trip actually began once they departed.

Ken and I have always worked well together, and we quickly fell into the daily routine of taking care of our responsibilities. We knew Ken was to captain the boat... and I, the "admiral," (along with being the navigator, deckhand and chef) would oversee all other operations. Since we worked in our business while we traveled, it wasn't uncommon for one of us to be piloting the boat while the other was on the cell phone with a client or working on the computer.

The KVH satellite TV stayed on the financial channels all day so we knew what was happening in the financial world. We tried to plan our travels so we would reach our next destination by early afternoon. This gave us time to secure the boat, work for an hour or two and then explore the town. We had originally planned to anchor out quite often but found ourselves going into marinas far more often than anchoring out for several reasons.

First, we enjoyed meeting other Loopers. We would walk around a marina in search of the white "Great Loop Burgee" flown by other Loopers. When we met up with a few it felt like we had found family. We would invite them to join us to walk around the town or meet for cocktails at five. Ken called me "Julie, the cruise director" (remember the old "Love Boat" TV series?). I guess that dates him.

Second, we really wanted to see the towns, visit the museums, taste the food and learn about the culture in the area. We carried bikes on our boat so we had wheels to get around in a limited fashion. We won't talk about how many times I fell off my bike. Ouch!

The third reason was that the captain slept better when tied to a piece of wood. While anchoring out, he would be up with every sound to check if we were dragging anchor. This made for a rather grumpy captain in the morning. Keeping the captain happy by being tied up to a dock at a marina always makes for a good day.

We had several friends and family join us throughout our journey, and we loved sharing this special time with them. I think it is always important to set clear expectations before guests join you to travel. We simply tell them our much-used line, "This is an adventure not a vacation." We always communicated the fact that our boat was a "working boat" and everyone had duties. It could be helping with meal preparation, cleaning, watching for crab pots and debris, driving the boat, handling dock lines, getting through locks, etc. It is also important to establish any financial arrangements. Do you expect your guests to help with food cost, fuel, marina fees, etc? In addition to chores, I found out that one of the hardest aspects of having guests was the ability to arrange for a good meeting place. Where do they meet you and when? How long will they travel with you and how will they get back to their car or other modes of transportation? We discovered that any guest joining us needed to be as open as possible with their travel schedule. We also discovered that each time we traveled, despite iffy weather and against our better judgement, to make some deadline, we deeply regretted that decision afterwards.

During our trip we made some life-long friendships from all parts of the world. We were so blessed to have met and become fast friends with so many people. If you ask almost anyone that has done the Loop, they will tell you that making friends is one of the highlights of a trip like this. I feel I must caution that though you meet so many people, not everyone is a compatible match. One such occurrence happened to us while we traveled with three other boats that had already formed a "buddy boat system" before we met up with them. We were in a lock system that grouped boats together so you started and ended your travel day together. After about the third day we decided that we didn't want to "play" with them anymore. We stayed another day where we were and allowed them to move ahead. Enough said, that is the beauty of this kind of travel, you have many choices.

Our travels took us over the entire Great Loop route in addition to a couple of side trips, one week in Key West, 40 days in the Abaco Islands, Bahamas, the Tennessee River and Georgian Bay, Canada. We traversed Georgian Bay one and a half times with friends who lived on the bay and took us to all of their special places where most Loopers never go. Georgian Bay and the North Channel are beautiful places.

I am often asked what my favorite place was. To say I have a favorite place is like saying I have a favorite child. However, the single moment that I will always treasure was when we passed the Statue of Liberty in New York Harbor in our own boat. We count our blessings that we have the freedom to live the life we choose. Another special place for us was Ellis Island, on the Hudson River. Ken's mother had come through there when she came to the United States from Scotland as a 12-year-old child.

It took us almost two years to complete our trip due to our particular circumstances. Because we were still working, we needed to go home at the end of each quarter for billing, quarter-end reports and meetings with clients. Sometimes we rented cars, flew or even managed, with the help of friends, to use our own car to get home. I also think that our knowing we were to be home every three months helped give me a sense of staying connected to family, friends and our house.

We had originally planned to do the Great Loop in one year. However, when we got to New York heavy rains caused flooding and damaged several of the locks on the Erie Canal. The repairs weren't scheduled to be completed for several months, which closed our travel window to be out of the northern section of the Loop by Labor Day. We had the boat hauled out of the water, winterized and stored for 11 months in upstate New York. We were very disappointed and sad that we had to leave our boat across country and be landlubbers for almost a year. We reminded ourselves that "this was an adventure not a vacation" and remaining flexible makes for a better experience.

As things worked out, it was better we were home during that time as we had many personal issues that would require our presence. Ken needed surgery. Then Ken's mother passed away, then our dog, Beau, also passed away. It wasn't just raining in our lives, it was pouring. Being home also gave us time to tend to business issues and service our clients. I think one of the important lessons we learned along the way was to remain flexible. Before we started the trip we heard people say, "Don't have a schedule." Ken and I are both big planners by personality (that is also what we do for a living) so it doesn't come naturally for us to "go with the flow." There are many things that happen that are out of your control when traveling on a boat, so it is important to adjust and make a decision quickly. Ken and I never really argue... we debate. I have tremendous trust and respect in Ken's abilities and decisions; however, we approached this journey with equality and his trust and respect for me helped make us good partners. Working as a team definitely made for better days once we established and verbalized that mutual respect for each other.

I think one of my nemeses of traveling on a boat was the laundry. However, as trivial as that sounds, doing laundry is one of my least favorite things to do. Our boat came equipped with a Splendide washer/dryer combo unit. The washer worked great but used a lot of water and the dryer didn't work that well. The process took all day to do one batch of clothes and required that we have the generator running or be plugged in at a marina. When we arrived at a marina, we worked at our business for an hour or two and then wanted to tour the town, not sit at the dock and do laundry.

So my answer to this was, (a) encourage Ken to wear a pair of shorts for more than one day, (b) stay an extra day in port at least once a week to get chores done which included grocery shopping, laundry and getting my nails done. We prefer this all be accomplished in an interesting town with shops, restaurants and amenities within walking distance of the marina. We have been known to rent a car to get around to visit other areas. Splitting the cost of a car with another boater worked well too. Having Enterprise Rental Car "come pick you up" was sometimes just the right ticket.

Yes, you read correctly "getting my nails done." The one thing I was determined to keep as some semblance of my former self (before boat travel) was to keep my nails up and wear make-up every day. I rode my bike as far as five miles to get to a nail saloon once. Crazy? Yes, but for me it was comforting. I ALWAYS wore gloves when handling a dock line, which protected my hands and nails and gave me more grip and strength. I wore very light make-up, most of which was for sunscreen protection.

I think if you ask almost any female boater, you will find that there is a different preference on laundry, housekeeping, storage and what is important to them. I think the important thing is to identify what is important to YOU and think through some creative ways to make it work so your trip is enjoyable to YOU.

Some additional suggestions would be to:

1. **Ask a lot of questions.** When you are unsure, ask. The boating community is very helpful and generous with sharing information and their own experiences.

2. **Purchase or borrow the cruise guides, in addition to your charts, of all the areas you will be traveling.** The information in these cruise guides is invaluable to help you make decisions on trip planning and places you want to visit.

3. **Keep a road atlas on your boat.** When you travel by water, you do not always know what county you are in when the local weather reports give severe weather warnings. Also, the atlas is helpful when giving directions to your visitors and judging distance to nearby towns, in addition to being handy for those car rentals. Some people even take a portable GPS with them to use in rental cars when traveling some distance.

4. **Purchase a pair of communication headsets (marriage savers).** When we were coming into a dock, lock or anchorage, we always wore our headsets. Once I left the helm, Ken and I could not "see" each other, and I have a hearing loss in one ear. Yelling on top of the noise of the engines and the possibility of miscommunication does not make for a good docking experience.

5. **Become a member of America's Great Loop Cruisers' Association (AGLCA – greatloop.org) if you plan to do the Great Loop.** The information and support received through this organization and its members is invaluable.

My wish to all who are considering doing the Loop, or other long-distance cruising, is that you actually do it. I've probably heard dozens of people say "It's my dream to do the Loop" for every one I've heard from that has actually done it. Enjoy the experience, the people, the places, and most of all enjoy yourself. Just remember – "This is an adventure, not a vacation."

Darcy Searl is President of Financial Consultants Group, Inc., a financial planning and investment firm specializing in helping women with their financial needs.

Her hobbies include boating, cooking, reading and spending time with her friends, three children, three stepchildren, five grandchildren and one great-granddaughter.

Elvie (Elvina) **Short**

Vessel: M/V *Roy El'* – 44-foot Gulfstar
Residence/Homeport: Hampstead, North Carolina
Website: liveaboarddream.com

What an exciting life I have been fortunate to have, living aboard our boat *Roy El'* for six years. Our daring change in lifestyle began 12 years ago before my husband, Roy, and I retired. We decided to sell our 32-foot Bayliner Express Cruiser to start looking for a boat that we could cruise and live aboard. We sold our home and bought a condo on a golf course and got rid of lots of our "stuff." Then five years later we found the 1978 44-foot Gulfstar, which has become our home on the water, we named her *Roy El'*, which is a combination of Roy's name and mine. Our daughter said that when the houses got smaller and the boats got bigger, she knew we were serious and she was in deep trouble. We now have no house or car.

    The first four months of our live-aboard life, we wintered in Charleston, South Carolina at the Charleston City Marina. We had no house then, but we still had our car, so we were able to shop for what we needed to make our Gulfstar our home. We continued to get rid of things we thought we needed but found that we really didn't need. This was a good shakedown period. It gave us a chance to get used to living aboard a boat, and we still were only three hours from our daughter, son-in-law and grandkids. I was still working, doing consultant jobs, one of which was in Charleston.

    We really didn't have any plans as to where we wanted to cruise when we first moved aboard. Then four years later, for Christmas, my brother-in-law Rick, who lives in Nashville, Tennessee, gave us all the river charts for the Tennessee-

Tombigbee Waterway, Cumberland and Tennessee Rivers. Finally, we had a goal, and in May of that year, we left Charleston heading south to Florida and then north towards the river system. That summer, we spent several months at Cedar Creek Yacht Club above Nashville. From Nashville, we cruised on to the America's Great Loop Cruisers' Association (AGLCA) Rendezvous. The stories we heard and the people we met inspired us to take the next step and do the "Great Loop!"

Over the next year, we cruised back through Florida, up the East Coast to New York City, up the Hudson River, through the Erie Canal and across Lake Ontario to Canada and through the Trent-Severn Waterway. We then continued our journey on to Georgian Bay, North Channel, down Lake Michigan, along parts of the Illinois, Mississippi, and Ohio rivers, then finally back to the Cumberland River in Tennessee, where we had started.

We have cruised over 20,000 miles while doing not only the Loop but going to the Bahamas twice, spending one summer in the Chesapeake, two winters in Fort Myers, Florida and one winter in Panama City Beach, Florida.

We have learned many valuable lessons while living aboard and cruising. Getting to really know my mate is one of the valuable experiences that I cherish. While living in such close quarters and spending most of the time together, you and your partner have to learn to give and take so much more than with a traditional lifestyle. I learned more about my husband while living aboard than I had known about him in all the years we were married and still working. Our lives were so fast-paced back then. Now we have lots of time to talk and learn more about each other. Romance is sweeter and our communication on every level has increased significantly.

The people we meet while cruising have become very important in our lives. We not only learn from other boaters about new places to go and sites to experience, but we also learn practical information as well. Boaters are a special bunch of people, and they will do anything to help each other. About half the time, we cruise with one or more other boats. The remainder of the time we cruise alone. I love both types of cruising. Playing Greedy together, learning new card games, playing Sequence or just sitting on the aft deck enjoying music and visiting are some of the best memories we have made with other boaters. I found that it makes no difference if you are on a small cruiser or a large yacht; you are all on the water together enjoying what it has to offer.

One of the most shocking things I have discovered is how much I enjoy living aboard. In the beginning, I actually thought I was just going along with what Roy wanted to do, and when he got tired of it, we would be back on land. Well, I found out that I simply love it!

I only have three things I require on the boat. I must have a sewing machine, a laptop computer and a Yamaha Keyboard. We took all of these with us, and I put all three of them to good use. Friends and family ask me, "Don't you get bored? What do you do all day?" Playing my keyboard is therapy for me. Sewing is relaxing and rewarding. Having a hobby that I can enjoy while on the boat fills my time, is relaxing, and can bring a sense of accomplishment and satisfaction.

The first couple of years we cruised somewhere almost every day so we never had time to get bored. Planning our next day or week's trip is always a new learning experience for us. We value all of the other boaters' input and also use as many cruising guides and charts as we can. Deciding where to go, to anchor or go to a marina, to eat on board or try a local restaurant, to visit a museum or historical site, is challenging and exciting. We enjoy making these decisions together based on our research and interests.

I am a fair-weather boater. We try never to be on a schedule because that may cause us to cruise in questionable weather, which can sometimes mean trouble. If the weather is forecast to be miserable or unsafe, we simply stay where we are. We feel life is too short to put ourselves in situations that are not fun or maybe even risky. Cruising, sometimes 40 miles a day, is what we find most enjoyable. Pulling anchor early or leaving a marina early is our choice. If bad weather is coming, it usually hits after lunch. We like to be anchored or tied to a dock by two or three o'clock in the afternoon. This way we can enjoy the rest of the day exploring and enjoying our surroundings.

Our grandchildren, a boy and a girl, have cruised with us for two to three weeks every summer since five years after we got the boat. They have learned to read charts, spot buoys, and assist while going through locks. They have visited many museums and places of interest with us including: West Point, New York on the Hudson River, and the Naval Academy in Annapolis, Maryland. They were with us when we went through New York Harbor past the Statue of Liberty. It was a cloudy, foggy day and as the mirage came to reality, my granddaughter, 11 at the time said, "I think I'm going to cry." They love to fish, jump off the swim platform to swim, drive the dinghy, go exploring and just enjoy anchoring and spending time with us. We have made so many memories with them that will stay with them forever.

We have cruised up and down the 450-mile Tennessee-Tombigbee Waterway six times. One of the most enjoyable cruises was when there were four Looper boats cruising together: *Sonsie*, a 42-foot Symbol; *Windless*, a 42-foot Monk; *Little T*, a 24-foot Rosbourgh; and *Roy El'*, our 44-foot Gulfstar. We would send the little boat in to check the depth and determine where we were all going to anchor. Then one of the larger boats would go into the anchorage and drop their anchor. Then we would all raft up off that boat. We took turns cooking so only one boat had to prepare a meal at night. Sometimes our flotilla had to put out a second anchor. The camaraderie we enjoyed and the fun evenings will never be forgotten. Being with friends makes a boring trip very exciting. We cruised together all the way down to Tarpon Springs, Florida.

Women On Board Cruising

I love to cook and find that entertaining on our boat is lots of fun. I would not be without my pressure cooker, my crock-pot, or my toaster oven. The crock-pot and toaster oven draw very low amps, so they will run on the inverter (if you have one – if not, consider adding this unit to your boat, it will make life so much easier). If you haven't tried the Green Bags, they really work. I put my fruits and vegetables in them and they last an extra week at least. Casseroles or one-dish meals are just as enjoyable with friends as a five-course meal. Potlucks are very popular with boaters, and I have increased my recipe box with some awesome recipes other cooks have shared with me as a result of these potlucks.

Storage on a boat is another challenge. We woman love our clothes and shoes, don't we? I probably have 30 pairs of shoes on board right now. We put a shoe garage in our stateroom that serves as a vanity with a mirror as well. I put my seasonal clothes in vacuum bags and then store them behind the drawers next to the hull of the boat where there is usually enough space. Another tip: I seemed to never have a box on hand when I needed one to mail things to folks, so I collected several sizes of boxes, flattened them and stored them under my mattress in the forward stateroom. Now, I always have a box when I need it. We also built bookshelves behind our steps going down to our saloon. The steps going down from our saloon to the galley are now a pantry for my canned goods. Not all boats can accommodate adding the extra storage, but lots of them can.

I love to sew, so we built a table between the V-berths in the forward stateroom. The berth still comes down when we need to use it for guests, but the rest of the time the table holds my sewing machine or my laptop when I use it as an office. We also added a folding chair in that stateroom. The extra chair comes in handy for overflow of guest seating on the aft deck. I also sew for other boaters, mending canvas, sewing zippers into enclosures, mending dingy covers and all kinds of tasks that need to be done with a sewing machine.

There is always something new to experience every day when cruising on a boat. We have been on our boat for six years and are still learning how some things work or finding new ways to do things. The waterways and shorelines change with the seasons. The Tennessee River, Little Tennessee and Cumberland Rivers have some of the most beautiful shorelines you will ever see. We try to research beforehand what each place we visit is known for and then try to make sure we experience whatever that special something is while in that port. When we went to Watts Bar Lake, we visited the Y12 Museum in Oakridge, Tennessee. It was there where we learned the true history of the making of the atomic bomb. It was so interesting we went back a second time. Roy and I decided we must have slept through our history classes in school because we sure learned an awful lot more about the history of our country when we did the Great Loop.

The education, experiences and memories I have obtained while living aboard far surpass what my working life gave me. The relaxation on the water, lack of stress, God's nature and then the many friendships are what makes this boating lifestyle so much fun and immensely rewarding.

Elvie Short retired from the New York Times Company as a systems analyst, doing installations of software in the 26 newspapers that they owned.

She comes from a large family of ten and is second to the youngest. Elvie learned to cook and sew at a very early age in Oklahoma, her birthplace. She lived in California for 20 years and then North Carolina for 30 years.

She believes that you can never compare places or experiences, as they are all great for what they each have to offer or the lessons they teach. Elvie and her husband, Roy, still enjoy living on their boat *Roy El'*.

Barbara Doyle

Vessel: M/V *MemoryMaker too* – 30-foot Rinker Powerboat
Residence/Homeport: Jacksonville, Florida
Website: cruisingthegreatloop.com

In my experience, many women who spend long periods of time on their boat are in large trawlers or sailboats with many of the conveniences of home. Our boat, *MemoryMaker too*, is a 270 Rinker powerboat. It has the bare necessities for cruising, not lots of extras. We have traveled thousands of miles aboard smaller boats that were even more sparsely equipped and enjoyed every minute of it. We did the Great Loop trip in a 30-foot cabin cruiser that traveled comfortably at 30 miles per hour, and I am here to tell you that we smelled lots of roses along the way.

I am a college professor and not as yet retired. I have several months off during the summer months, nearly a month at Christmas, and a week during the spring (spring break). We like to spend that time aboard our boat. Fortunately, my husband, David, has been semi-retired for several years. He still manages our rental property business but can mostly take care of business with the aid of a phone and a computer. His philosophy, which I admire, has always been to enjoy life as it is happening. He is not one of those boaters who say, "Someday! Someday, we are going to make that voyage." As opposed to waiting for a time when we are both fully retired, we both enjoy boating now while we are still young, agile, and healthy enough to jump around and handle the boat.

We take advantage of what we have and make the best of it. We are trying to live out our dreams. As Mark Twain said, "Twenty years from now you will be more disappointed by the things that you did not do than by the ones you did do." So, throw off the bowlines. Sail away from the safe harbor. Catch the trade winds in your sails. Explore. Dream. Discover.

Boating was not part of my childhood. It was not until after I married that I had an opportunity to experience the enjoyment of being on the water. Some 25 years ago, my father-in-law brought the family's old boat to our house and wanted to know if we might get some use out of it. It was a 15-foot Starcraft aluminum runabout. Boy, did we ever enjoy using that boat. We lived in Kentucky, close to several large manmade lakes. Every chance we got, we would head out on the water in that boat. The boat, of course, was not large enough to overnight on, so we would pack a cooler and tent on the boat, pull up on a bank or into a camping area and set up the tent. The next day we would do more boating.

As time passed, we kept venturing farther and farther from home. I guess that is when I first got the bug. I so enjoyed the serenity and peacefulness of finding a little cove that was all ours for the night.

Looking back on it now, it was a lot of work. Sometimes we would carry all of our gear up a tall embankment. Sometimes we would get caught out in a rainstorm and get soaked, as we had no bimini top to keep us dry, but we always got so much pleasure from these outings. We loved finding and exploring new areas.

We would watch the fish jump early in the morning and watch the birds fly by in the evening as they went to roost. We would lie in the tent and listen to the frogs and crickets chirping in the quietness of the night. Back then, we did lots of swimming in the freshwater lake, some water-skiing and lots of sunbathing.

We used that 15-foot boat for about five years and then moved to northeast Florida. We wanted to do more boating and wanted to be able to spend nights on the boat as opposed to doing the camping drill. So, we purchased a 21-foot Donzi with a little cuddy cabin and started boating on the St. Johns River near Jacksonville, Florida.

We soon became familiar with a busy area, where many boaters spent weekends, Silver Glen Springs. Silver Glen, or "The Springs" as locals call it, is off Lake George down the St. Johns River, south of Palatka, about halfway between Jacksonville and Sanford. Silver Glen pumps out 65 million gallons of crystal-clear fresh water every day, creating a large boil on the water's surface. You see lots of wildlife at the springs. It is not uncommon to see otters feasting on fish, mullets jumping four and five times to clean their gills, ospreys with their young ones resting in a nest on top of a tall tree or diving into the water to snatch up a fish. You are able to see striped bass swim right by your feet in the crystal-clear water and blue herons and egrets perched on old logs or cypress trees that extend out into the water.

Occasionally you will see an alligator sunning on one of the logs near the bank. We, like so many other boaters in that area, anchored our boats out in front of the boil in waist-deep, crystal-clear water. On holiday weekends, hundreds of boats anchor at the mouth of the boil. Even today, we consider

Barbara Doyle – *MemoryMaker Too*

Silver Glen one of nature's best presents – it is one of the prettiest areas we have encountered during our boating adventures.

For several years, this is how we would spend our summers and weekends. We would take the four-hour boat ride from Jacksonville down to Silver Glen Springs, spend a few weeks or sometimes just a weekend, and return back by boat. With the bigger boat, instead of packing camping gear we were able to pack our coolers and sleep and eat on the boat. We made lots of new boating friends at Silver Glen. These are friends who we still communicate with today. Some traveled many more miles than we did, but we all shared a common love for spending time on our boats.

Most of our Jacksonville boating friends would trailer their boats to Silver Glen. We didn't because we enjoyed the cruise. We wanted to be on the boat as much as possible. I recall on one of our trips to Silver Glen we took a side trip through Dunn Creek and then into Murphy Creek, south of Palatka, Florida. We saw something swimming in the waters in front of us. As we got closer to it, we could tell it was a confused raccoon. It kept changing directions in the water. We stopped moving forward in the boat and watched it for several minutes. It would swim for ten feet toward the bank and then change directions. It did this several times, and we were starting to be concerned that it was going to drown if we didn't do something. David slowly brought the boat between the raccoon and one side of the bank – encouraging it to finish swimming to the other side. When it made it to the bank, it just collapsed. It lay stretched out looking back at us as if it was totally worn out. We both felt like we had saved that little guy. It is encounters with nature like this that brings big smiles to both our faces as we share these incredible boating times together.

Thanksgiving weekend, while we still had the 21-foot Donzi, we were in downtown Jacksonville watching the annual Christmas boat parade. We had been talking about taking a trip and decided instead of doing a cruise on one of the commercial cruise ships, we would take our 21-foot boat and do our own cruise. So, we went to the local boat store and bought a compass, charts, and a handheld VHF radio and started planning the trip. We packed up the boat and rode it from Jacksonville to Key West, Florida, a 500-plus-mile trip. It took us three days to travel down the Intracoastal Waterway (ICW) to Key West. I still recall the anxiety I felt when we left Miami and headed out into Biscayne Bay, hoping that we would be able to follow the compass reading and then the excitement I felt when we found the marker that the compass reading had directed us to. We spent about three weeks over the Christmas holiday taking this trip on the boat.

I rarely drive the boat, but on that return trip from Key West back into Jacksonville we were in the St. Johns River, almost back to our homeport. David had gone down below into the cabin to use the head, and I was at the helm when I saw the blue lights on the water patrol boat heading quickly toward us. It was drizzling rain and very cold. The fenders were hanging from his boat. He powered right up to our boat very quickly and tied his lines to our cleat. He did not seem to be in a very good mood and proceeded to yell that he wanted to see our fish.

About this time, David came barreling out of the cabin wanting to know why I had stopped so suddenly. It turned out the officer was a fish and game agent checking fishermen's catch. After a few minutes of conversation with him, David informed him we were on our way back from Key West and that we had NOT trailored the boat down but had powered it and spent every night on the boat. As he untied from us and left as quickly as he had approached, his statement was something like "you did that trip in this boat – have a good day." I am sure he felt we were a little crazy.

Over the years, that is the kind of comment we have received when we tell people about our boating adventures. Many people do not believe we are able to do the cruising that we do in boats of this size.

David is the adventurer. He loves exploring new areas – especially by water. I am usually less thrilled about new challenges, but really thankful (after we do it) that he pushes us to experience new places, to go to different ports of call, or visit new towns along the waterway.

I handle the lines, and when we approach a dock, I make sure fenders and lines are ready. When we depart, I take them off and stow them away. I also take care of the isinglass. Since David does practically all of the driving, I try to contribute by calling myself the "isinglass lady." I put the curtains up and down as needed. I also take care of logging our adventures. I write narratives of our daily activities and keep up with our expenditures. I usually write a short book with every outing. I figure one day when we no longer want to cruise, I will pull out my books/logs and re-live some of our past adventures. I am also the photographer, and I take lots of pictures. During our Loop trip, I uploaded over a thousand pictures and maintained a blog on our website (cruisingthegreatloop.com).

I also play a big role with the navigation. We now have a GPS on the boat, but we still keep paper charts of everywhere we travel. When we are traveling through new areas or waterways that are somewhat challenging, I follow our route with the paper charts. I am also more electronically inclined than David, so I tend to be the one that puts routes into the GPS if they are needed. David could handle our boat by himself, and as I do not enjoy driving, I only drive when he needs a short break. He is the one that gets us into marinas or through tight spots; I contribute by keeping a watch out when we are underway.

We have cruised all over Florida. We have cruised down the east coast of Florida from Jacksonville to Key West many times, as well as having cruised across the state through the Okeechobee Waterway repeatedly in addition to having traveled along the west coast of Florida. We enjoyed cruising up and down the St. Johns River, going all the way to Sanford several times. Finally, we have completed the Loop, boating into Canada as part of our Loop route, and have explored a number of inland lakes.

As I mentioned, I am a college professor and was completing a yearlong sabbatical about five years ago when David decided that that year was going to be the year we did the Loop. The Loop had been a dream of his for many years. By the time we were ready to leave, I was almost as excited about the adventure as he was. We had been riding on a 27-foot Chris-Craft cuddy cabin boat for about ten years, and we could not stand up in the cabin. We did many extended trips on it but felt we wanted something a little larger to do the Loop. So, we went to the boat show in Miami that spring and picked out a new boat – a 270 Rinker Fiesta Vee. We named her the *MemoryMaker*. Even though the *MemoryMaker* was only about 30 feet long from the tip of the anchor to the end of the swim platform, it had a fairly large cockpit with a full canvas/isinglass enclosure. You could also stand up in the cabin. It had a one-burner stove, microwave, portable toaster oven, small bathroom, queen aft berth, TV and a table that could be lowered for a second berth. It also had quite a bit of storage space. David had a special bar made for the back of the boat so we could carry two bicycles. We carry bikes on board our boat for land excursions, and we rarely sit idle when we are in port.

It was May 3rd when we departed Jacksonville, Florida to do the Loop. We arrived back home in Jacksonville exactly 15 weeks after we left, completing the Loop adventure during a summer vacation. We traveled over 5000 miles.

While we were in Michigan one of our stops was in Grand Haven where we had a chance to have visits from David's family. We were even able to have our 102-year-old grandmother on board.

We encountered several challenges along the way, including waiting out hurricanes Cindy and Dennis in Mississippi on the Tennessee-Tombigbee Waterway. Fortunately, since our boat traveled at a fairly fast speed, we were able to get across some of the "big waters" quickly. The bikes that we had on the back of the boat, combined with the capability of traveling across the water a little faster, enabled us to do an incredible amount of exploring in the time that we had available.

We met a lot of boaters while we were doing the Loop. We anchored out only one night during the entire 15 weeks. We enjoy staying at marinas, walking the docks, and getting a chance to talk to locals and other traveling boaters. You see a different side of a town when you visit it by water. The only traffic we had to contend with was bicycle related. We like to find out what the locals feel makes their town special. We also feel you get a sense of the area from the dining options. One of our favorite lines we asked locals was: "If you were going to go out to dinner tonight, where would you eat?"

During our trip, I did very little cooking on board. We would have breakfast on the boat and then usually get off for a late lunch/early dinner. To cut down on expenses, we often shared an entrée. Locals love to share their stories and tell you where the best place to eat is located.

We had people tell us that unless you have at least a year to do the Loop, you shouldn't attempt it. Of course, we do not agree with that statement. Sure, we would have enjoyed having more time, but we just didn't have it. Instead of waiting until we had more time or a larger boat, we took the plunge and made some of the best memories of our life – we were able to live out our dream. David sometimes says that we kind of did a preview trip of the Loop doing it the way we did, but we had a chance to explore a number of areas and decide which towns and ports we wanted to come back to another time and do more extensive exploring.

This summer we had a conference to attend in Washington, D.C., so instead of flying or driving from Jacksonville to D.C., we took the boat. Our adventure kept us on the water for a little over two months. We were able to explore the Potomac River and stop at many of the marinas we did not get a chance to enjoy when we did the Loop. On this trip, we had a different boat. It is the same size; David calls it a twin to the one we used for our Loop trip. We named this boat *MemoryMaker too*; it is also a 270 Rinker.

Today our boating is much different from our early boating. While I still enjoy being out in the fresh air, I am now more of a shade seeker. I no longer sunbathe, and I rarely swim in the water, but I still enjoy the wildlife. Boating offers opportunities to explore areas that we would never have found by land, it also enables us to meet a lot of people and hear a lot of stories. It has opened up an adventurous spot in my heart. We hope to spend many more years on board our boat. We are trying to live our dreams in the moment. We both live by the philosophy that "today is the first day of the rest of our lives." We are trying to make our dreams come true NOW by living life to its fullest. I challenge you to do the same!

Barbara Doyle is a Professor of Computing Sciences at Jacksonville University. She has taught at the university level for over 25 years. She has a Ph.D. from Florida Institute of Technology, an M.S. from the University of Evansville, and a B.S. from the University of Kentucky. She is the author of several programming books, including *C# Programming: From Problem Analysis to Program Design*. She also serves as a Commissioner for the Accreditation Board (ABET), which is recognized as the accrediting agency for university and college level programs in computer science, applied science, engineering and technology.

Nancy Ojard

Vessel: M/V *Proud Heritage* – 43-foot Albin Sundeck Motor Yacht
Current Vessel: M/V *Superior Lady* – 55-foot Ocean Alexander Motor Yacht
Residence: Knife River, Minnesota
Homeport: Pike's Bay Marina, Bayfield, Wisconsin

Life On Board – In the Beginning

I now describe myself as a boater; however, that has not always been the case. My husband, Rich, and I boat on Lake Superior out of Pike's Bay Marina near Bayfield, Wisconsin. I grew up on the beautiful rugged North Shore of Lake Superior in a shipping port-town of Two Harbors, Minnesota. Two Harbors is sandwiched between Lake Superior, the largest freshwater lake in the world by surface area, and the remote Boundary Waters Canoe Area bordering Canada.

Living around and on the water is a way of life in northern Minnesota. My childhood and teen years were spent enjoying the inland lakes, either swimming, water-skiing or going off on canoe and camping trips in the Boundary Waters. My definition of boating was a canoe or water-ski boat.

Rich grew up seven miles down the shore from Two Harbors in Knife River, Minnesota. His childhood playground was Lake Superior, where he played in the surf and took overnight camping boat trips up and down the shore. The son of a commercial fisherman, Rich had old wooden skiffs to play with from an early age. Boating was a way of life for his family as well.

When we started dating, a picnic on the shores of Lake Superior with an old 20-foot inboard fishing skiff as transportation was a typical summer date. We borrowed Rich's dad's 36-foot Trojan for our honeymoon to the beautiful, and at that time secluded, Apostle Islands off Bayfield, Wisconsin. Boating was an unspoken part of our wedding vows, yet I still wouldn't have been able to describe myself as a boater. Lake Superior, the largest of the five Great Lakes, is beautifully clear, cold and clean. It is also very moody. The lake can be calm with warm weather. It can have light breezes one minute while switching rapidly, only ten minutes later, with fog and a 20-degree drop in temperature. It can blow at 25 knots raising whitecaps on the lake. Lake Superior is a lake to RESPECT, and that is the message I grew up with. However, Rich respects the lake more with a sense of challenge than fear. Piloting a boat is second nature for him.

Our first boat together was a 1947 23-foot Chris Craft that was soon traded for a 26-foot Chris Craft. At six months old, our oldest son, Nels, experienced his first of many boat trips across Lake Superior from our home in Knife River to Lake Superior's South Shore. When Bjorn, our youngest son, was born, we traded in the 26-foot Chris Craft for a 29-foot Erickson sailboat. This was our first experience with sailing, as all boats previously had been powerboats. From then on, all of our summer family vacations were spent on sailing trips either to the Apostle Islands or to the Upper Peninsula of Michigan.

We have fond memories of most of those vacations. However, there were times when the fog rolled in, bringing crashing waves and flapping canvas as we tried to haul in the sails. The boys and I were seasick and all I wanted to do was get off the boat and walk to shore. Needless to say, that wasn't an option. During our early years of boating as a family, my enthusiasm for the pastime did not match my husband's. Boating with little kids has its stresses and for me safety was the primary stressor. However, every time we survived a bad-weather experience, it gave me more confidence. I knew that a good boat could take more than I could. So, when we found ourselves in foul-weather situations again, I began to think more about persevering instead of survival or toleration.

After eight years of sailing, we decided to go back to power boating. Rich fell in love with a 32-foot Grand Banks. Making a move from a sailboat to a trawler was an easy transition for me. We still didn't go anywhere fast at eight knots, but it was a lot faster than sailing, and we went in a straight line. This opened up our vacation cruising grounds to the northern shores of Lake Superior and the Canadian islands. Boating in remote wilderness areas of Canada is like taking your living room into the Boundary Waters. It's a camping experience with hot running water and showers. The beautiful natural inlets and harbors along these waters are the most remote and spectacular boating that we've experienced. Few U.S. boaters venture past Isle Royale and still fewer past Thunder Bay, Canada, but those that do come back awestruck. Needless to say, it's our favorite boating grounds.

Planning meals for a two-week boating vacation for a family of four in a remote wilderness can be a challenge, especially if the captain doesn't like to fish. Planning for fuel and water stops was also important, but the extra preparation was worth the trip. These two-week extended trips wetted our appetite to try other cruising grounds. Rich started floating the idea of some day doing the Great Loop boat trip.

We had learned of this route, affectionately called the "Loop," that allows boaters to circumnavigate the eastern part of the United States. As our boys grew out of their teens and began college, we knew we would not be able to afford to do such a trip for a number of years, but the seed had been planted and it started to germinate.

The Seed Grows
We purchased a 43-foot Albin Motor Trawler with a semi-displacement hull and christened her *Proud Heritage*. It was a huge jump in size for us but perfect for our cruising needs. Her spacious staterooms, master and VIP, each had their own head, which made for privacy both for us and for our guests. A flybridge and covered sundeck made her the perfect long-distance cruising vessel for us. We'd sold our Grand Banks to a recently retired couple who wanted to do the Loop trip with the boat. I thought to myself, "If this couple, who are just getting into boating, plan to do the Loop, why couldn't we?"

Rich and I decided to set a five-year goal to do the Loop. As we've learned, in making any dream become a reality, you have to act and plan as if your dream will happen. Financially it seemed doable if we saved for the next five years. We reasoned that within four years, Nels and Bjorn would both be out of college and without their tuition fees, we'd then have a huge increase in our take-home pay and extra money to do the trip. In the meantime, we planned on doing boating trips that would help us experience similar situations to the Loop and prepare us for the "Big Trip."

Our first extended cruise took us out of Lake Superior to Canada's North Channel and Georgian Bay of Lake Huron. The scenery was spectacular! The pink granite cliffs defining the North Channel sparkle when the sun hits them. The breathtaking scenery of Georgian Bay's 30,000 islands combined with the challenge of following the charts and channel markers that define the "small craft route" was quite an adrenaline rush.

As we headed up the Trent-Severn Waterway to Port Severn, Ontario, we had our first locking experience. All hands were on deck as we prepared ourselves for the unknown. It went without a hitch, and the crew felt very proud of themselves for surviving their first lock. Farther up the Trent-Severn Waterway a ship lift ferried *PH* and crew over a dam at the Big Chute Marine Railway. The incline is a pretty amazing engineering feat. We watched our 43-foot boat being lifted out of the water, carried by rail over the top of the dam, (making cars on the road stop as our boat passed in front of them) and then floated again on the other side of the dam. This is an awesome sight and quite amazing to experience on board a boat.

Our next extended boating opportunity came about quite unexpectedly. We got a phone call from the couple who purchased our 32-foot Grand Banks. They had begun their Loop trip and asked Rich and I if we would be interested in joining them on *Lucky Maru* as they headed down the Tennessee River. We jumped at the chance to spend five days cruising through the Kentucky Lakes and Tennessee River. This was our first river boating experience. Sharing the waterway with commercial tows is not for the faint of heart and learning the language of towboat captains is not only challenging but essential.

It was during this trip that I realized how remote boating could be. It dawned on me that if I were going to go on this Loop boat trip, I better know more about how the boat systems work and feel comfortable in operating a boat. I decided to take a Sea Sense class, a boating class taught by women for women, with some of my boating friends. This was money well spent!

The class I attended was held on the coastal waters of Florida near Sarasota. We spent five days on a Grand Banks trawler with Patti, our instructor. She taught us how to operate, maintain, dock and navigate a 42-foot powerboat.

I learned more in that five-day class than I had during all the previous years of boating with Rich. The engine room had been an intimidating place for me, but during the class I took the big step in to the dark engine room and practiced basic engine maintenance procedures through hands-on experience. I learned about the basic systems of the boat and how they work, as well as some basic troubleshooting strategies. I learned to maneuver and dock a 42-foot boat using twin engines, and I picked up new line-handling techniques for both leaving and coming into a dock. The most important thing I took away was the confidence that in an emergency I could handle the boat on my own. Since Rich was always "the boat guy," I had left boat handling, engine maintenance and navigating up to him. I now better understood the weight of responsibility that Rich experienced during our boating trips.

After the Sea Sense class, I felt I could be a true partner in our boating experiences. I had been a passenger in our previous trips, but came home from those classes feeling like a BOATER! Finally, I felt ready to do the Loop.

The Trip Begins

Rich and I made plans to do the Loop trip on *PH* over a two-year period. We planned on doing the trip in two segments. The first half would bring us from Bayfield, Wisconsin through Lake Superior and the Soo Locks; then along the eastern shores of Lake Michigan; down to Chicago; following the Illinois, Missouri, Mississippi, Cumberland, Tennessee Rivers and the Tennessee-Tombigbee Waterway to the Black Warrior River and finally out to the Gulf of Mexico, leaving *PH* in Florida for the first winter.

Our plan was to complete the second half of the Loop in the spring of the next year by heading around the tip of Florida and cruising the Intracoastal Waterway (ICW) up the East Coast to New York City. Here we planned to take the Hudson River to the Erie Canal and Oswego Canal, crossing Lake Ontario into Canada. We'd work our way across Ontario via the Trent-Severn Waterway to Georgian Bay and the North Channel. Taking a hard right, we'd then head through the Soo Locks and back to our home waters of Lake Superior.

In our planning, we talked about how nice it would be to have others join us on portions of the trip. We have a relaxed approach to having guests on board. It's understood that we will not be waiting on them and everyone pitches in to help when possible. We've enjoyed sharing our boating adventures with others in the past and thought it would be fun to share this experience as well. So, we let our family and friends know that they were welcome to join us on any part of the trip; however, we impressed upon them that finding transportation to and from whatever port we happened to land in during their stay on board was their responsibility. Unexpected weather can impact planned destinations and remote river towns can be a long way from airports or other modes of transportation.

Before we left on our trip, we read where it's important to discuss financial expectations with potential guests. Being people of Scandinavian heritage, we aren't comfortable with this approach and tend to ask people we really know well to be guests for a week or longer. Almost without exception, our guests offer to either help with paying fuel costs, marina fees, or offer to treat us to a dinner out. On-board food and liquor costs are split equally and any out-of-the-ordinary boat repair expenditures are our responsibility. We've found it best to not have more than one couple for an extended period of time. Even though the boat was big enough for more guests, the extra stuff that goes along with the extra people adds to the clutter. Our on board motto is "a clean boat is a happy boat!"

We made arrangements with our employers to be gone for three months for each half of the trip. I took a combination of vacation and a leave of absence for the first half of the trip. Rich, as part owner of an engineering firm in Duluth, made arrangements with his partner to continue working during the trip, staying connected to work by cell phone and computer. Having that connection to home was important to both of us. It was important to Rich so he could continue to work, and it was important for me to keep in touch with our family and friends.

Other arrangements for our departure included figuring out what to do with mail over the period of time we were gone. We set up automatic bill paying for our regular monthly bills and made arrangements for periodic guests to deliver mail when they joined us. Rich and I decided that taking our dog on the trip would be too complicated, so we arranged for a friend to take care of our dog while we were away. Rich added additional navigational equipment to *PH* while I started planning for additional on-board boat supplies. By the spring of the year we planned to leave, we were coming down the home stretch and felt all of our planning put us in good shape for the upcoming Loop trip. But as we all know... life happens!

Our oldest son, Nels, got engaged. He and Sara decided to get married during a period right after we had planned on leaving on the "Big Trip." As parents of the groom, we realized our actual presence was not necessary in the wedding planning process; however, it was important for us to figure out how to get to the wedding, in Iowa, while cruising down the river system. We spent some time calculating where we expected to be on our trip and decided St. Louis, Missouri would be a good place to leave *PH* and drive to Iowa for the wedding.

Women On Board Cruising

As the day for our departure came closer, I started to get a little nervous about what we were actually undertaking. Some simple yet very helpful advice from a fellow boater was to "take one day at a time." This puts the trip in a daily perspective and therefore makes it not so overwhelming. We left Pike's Bay Marina in Bayfield, Wisconsin in mid-August and began our trek across Lake Superior, most of which was familiar cruising grounds for us. Our trip was on a pretty tight time schedule, so we soon developed a daily cruising routine and responsibilities. Rich, the captain of the ship, navigated and piloted the boat and maintained the boat's systems. As first mate, my role was to coordinate the day-to-day on-board activities, deck work, meals, and general maintenance. Food, meals and happy hour were an important part of our cruising experience.

A typical day cruising started with a half-hour walk for me while Rich checked the weather, and did the engine checks and maintenance. When I got back, we cast off and enjoyed our morning coffee and breakfast on the flybridge while firming up our cruising plans for the day. After breakfast we each had our own personal time. I cleaned up breakfast dishes, and if the day was nice, did morning stretches on the bow of the boat, enjoying the scenery as we cruised. Rich did his morning work phone calls while piloting the boat. Running a business from the flybridge of your boat equates to great office accommodations. I usually relieved Rich on the bridge for a couple of hours in the morning and then it was time to think about lunch, which was again served underway on the flybridge. Of course, all this time we were soaking in the surrounding scenery.

Rich and I typically anchor out while cruising in Lake Superior; however, during our Loop trip we preferred to be in a marina for the night. It gave us the chance to stretch our legs and to explore new territory. Our goal was to be in port by about 3 p.m. By the time the lines were all secured and we had checked in at the office, it was usually 4 p.m. This gave us some time to explore the town where we'd landed and replenish groceries or other supplies if needed.

We brought bikes on the trip, which was a great way to get some exercise while exploring new territory. They also provided us with land transportation if a marina courtesy car wasn't available. Many marinas on the rivers in the South had a car available for transient boaters, so we took advantage of those circumstances and made sure to get extra supplies for our pantry.

Rich and I prefer having dinner on board. We enjoy the marina view off our back deck and I can really get creative putting meals together while we're cruising. Of course, it's also great to have an evening out, and we probably ate at local restaurants a couple times a week.

For the most part, cruising is a very relaxing experience. Seeing the country from the waterways is quite a unique experience. Traveling by boat, at least in *PH*, a motor trawler, makes you slow down. Traveling at an average speed of ten miles an hour allows for an appreciation of the sights and scenery along the way. It also gave us a great perspective of the "inner workings" of our country's transportation system. We all learned in our early history classes how important water transportation was for the settlement of our country. Towns were built and grew up around lakes, rivers and waterways. However, our perception of commercial transportation over the years has changed. Rail, highway and air have become the most visible form of travel and transporting goods. Most people, including us, forget that the Great Lakes, along with the rivers and waterways, serve as a main connecting artery for our cities and towns throughout the country. Waterways have and still do provide transportation for many of our goods today.

Commercial freighters, tows or military vessels all take precedence over pleasure boats when it comes to navigating on the waterways. We learned the rules and language used when it comes to passing tows on the river or preparing to go through a lock. It goes without saying that knowing canal markings and navigational aids are essential.

Experiences Along the Way
Rich and I met some wonderful people on our adventure. We identified boaters doing the Loop on the river system by the Looper burgee flying on the bow of their vessel. *PH* traveled with other boaters on and off during the trip, meeting up with them at locks, marinas or towns farther along the way. *PH* hung out at a dock near St. Louis while we went to our son's wedding and became the boat noted by other boaters on the river for "the couple who went to their son's wedding by boat."

Stories, adventures and experiences get passed on from boater to boater at locks and happy hour marina gatherings. These stories are a way for boaters living a transient lifestyle to connect with people they might not otherwise get to know. It becomes a boating community where people help each other and look out for one another. Good friendships are developed not necessarily on past history but on common boating experiences. We all shared a historical memory with one of our boating friends on *Magenta* on 9/11.

We woke up to a gorgeous fall day. Katydids were chatting and the herons and gulls were enjoying an early morning fish breakfast. *PH* and *Magenta* slipped out of the marina about 7:45 a.m., becoming a part of the early morning river life. As she made her way down stream to the Dresden Lock and Dam on the Illinois River, her trip meter rolled to the 1000-mile mark.

After going about one mile we pulled into our first lock of the day, the lock tenders were waiting for us and once again we locked right through. We were enjoying the serene river scenery when we got a call from Rich's office informing us that the New York Twin Towers and the Pentagon had been hit with hijacked commercial planes. We were stunned! Shocked and grief stricken, we listened as Peter Jennings detailed the day's events on the radio.

How could this happen? It felt surreal. We were experiencing an absolutely calm picture-perfect day. The birds and scenery were spectacular. How could all this chaos be happening?

We listened as it was announced that all planes were ordered to land. Being

Women On Board Cruising

only about 50 miles south of Chicago, airplane contrails crisscrossed the sky overhead. Later in the day, the sky too was quiet. We were probably the only form of transportation moving that day, and we weren't so sure that the locks wouldn't be shut down.

At about 1 p.m. we learned the lock system would remain open, and we locked through in silence. We listened to the radio all day and no longer felt like we were getting away from the world. Dad called and told us, "Come home, it's war!" But there would be no way to come home; airports were closed, planes were grounded, car rentals nonexistent, Greyhound bus stations all closed down. We were in the middle of the country's heartland with power and chemical plants lining the banks of the Illinois River, could these also be targets?

At about 4:30 p.m. we heard that President Bush would be flying from Omaha, Nebraska to Washington, D.C. We looked up a few minutes later and saw a single jet stream heading east with four jets following close behind. It was probably Air Force One carrying the President. We sent a prayer to the heavens for his safe return to Washington.

PH pulled into a city dock at Hennepin, Illinois with *Magenta* at her side. We consoled each other as we discussed the day's events and then decided to walk to a local bar and watch the news on TV. It was awful to see those towers collapse. A guy came into the bar and said the price of gas had gone up to $4.00 per gallon. We wondered if we would be able to continue our trip.

Back at the boat we made supper and went to bed, both wondering what the night or morning would bring.

Traveling down a remote section of the Tennessee-Tombigbee Waterway, I learned the importance of identifying channel makers. Knowing channel and buoy markers is important. Going upriver the buoys markers are red on the starboard side and green on the port side. It's just the opposite when you're heading downriver. "Red, right returning" is the phrase to remember when going upriver. We had just left the Tennessee River, traveling upstream with red markers on the right. When you enter the Tennessee-Tombigbee Waterway, the boat is traveling downstream so the buoys marking the channel changed from red on the right to green on the right.

I had taken my turn at the helm and was looking for the next mile marker and had just spotted it when we both noticed a different sound from *PH*'s wake. We looked back and Rich called "green on the right!" I had forgotten we were now going downriver and the buoys had changed. We were plowing through mud 20 feet outside the marked channel... and the wake was lapping on the shallows! Thankfully, *PH* had enough forward momentum to squeak back into the deeper eight-foot channel. Whew, no damage except my pride and my shaking knees. Not a great place to get stuck with little or no boat traffic! Rich gave the helm back to me with the words "green on the right" echoing in my head throughout the day.

Rich and I finished the first half of the Loop in October of the first year as

Nancy Ojard – *Proud Heritage/Superior Lady*

planned. We left *PH* safely tucked away at a marina in Fort Myers, Florida while we headed to Minnesota for the winter. Other boater friends thought we were crazy, but we had bills to pay and jobs that would enable us to pay for the next half of our trip. It was very hard for me to sit in a cubical after having a fresh breeze on my cheek every day for the previous three months, and I anxiously looked forward to our return trip. By the time we left to pick up *PH* in April of the next year, I had decided to leave my job for good.

When we returned, we took *PH* out of boat storage in Fort Myers and cruised her down Florida's Gulf Coast to Key West. Then we rounded the bend up Florida's east coast, continuing to follow the ICW up the east coast of the U.S., stopping along the way at the historic cites of St. Augustine, Florida; Savanna, Georgia; Charleston, South Carolina; Wrightsville Beach, North Carolina; and Norfolk, Virginia.

At Savanna, Rich and I took another detour, flying to Minnesota to attend our youngest son Bjorn's graduation from the University of Minnesota and to meet his girlfriend and future wife, Nikki.

While cruising can be a very relaxing experience, you always need to be aware of your surroundings and be ready for the unexpected. When traveling by water you usually find yourself coming right into the heart of towns and major cities. That's especially true traveling up the East Coast on the ICW. One minute you're cruising backwaters and marshes watching dolphins jumping your wake and seabirds diving near your boat. Then, right around the bend, you're in a major shipping port with a variety of channel markers and of course shipping vessels. Situations can turn from calm to chaos in a short period of time.

Somewhere between Daytona and St. Augustine, Florida, we met up with a towboat traveling north. Tows are not common on the ICW, but with our river experience, we felt like experts in the art of passing tows. However, with a narrow channel and the moderate boat traffic, this was a different situation. We followed the tow for a while, waited for a straight stretch of water, and then radioed the captain requesting a starboard pass. As we pulled alongside the tow, Rich kicked up the throttle. Halfway through the pass we realized we were being sucked into the mud and were now stuck! *PH*'s wake hit us, then the tow's wake hit us, and *PH* turned on her side! It happened in a matter of seconds, but the sinking feeling felt like it would never go away. As both wakes passed, *PH* righted herself, but we were firmly in the mud! Lots of thoughts go through your head at a time like this, i.e. glad we got the BoatU.S. towing insurance; hope the bottom is OK; did we get mud in the fuel, in the engines? And just plain… "OH SHIT!" Collecting himself, Rich turned the engines back on and proceeded to try and back *PH* out of the mud. To our amazement, she pulled herself out!

With prayers answered and legs shaking, we crept back into the channel. Once again, we approached the tow and radioed the captain for a pass, this time on the port side. He told us to stay close to him (I mean within spitting distance) as we passed; we heaved a sigh of relief as we pulled away from that tow. Miles later on the channel, we passed a large abandoned pleasure craft, on her side in the mud with water lapping on her side, there but for the grace of God... We safely pulled into the St. Augustine Municipal Marina at about 3 p.m. and had a stiff gin and tonic!

We experienced a different kind of "Calm to Chaos" while entering Norfolk Harbor later in our trip.

There are two locks in the Dismal Swamp system, and they only open at 8:30 a.m., 10 a.m. and 1 p.m. In order for *PH* to make it through the 15-mile Dismal Swamp Canal, she would have to be underway just after sunrise. So, on Tuesday, we were up with the birds. *PH* crept out of her berth and headed up the bay leading to the channel and to South Mills Lock. A morning fog clung to *PH* as she navigated the channel markers.

We enjoyed a beautiful sunrise and breakfast on the flybridge as *PH* made her way to the lock in time for the first opening and then proceeded into the Dismal Swamp. Trees overhang the waterway and Virginia creeping ivy covers the banks of this historic canal. It was a peaceful and relaxing way to spend the morning and early afternoon.

With Deep Creek Lock in sight, *PH* and crew prepared for her last locking experience of the day. As *PH* locked through, the lockmaster informed us, "There are more military personnel in the next ten miles than there are in the whole world!" Literally, around the next bend *PH* chugged into the heart of the hustle and bustle of Norfolk Harbor. Boy, were we caught off-guard and what a wake-up call! Norfolk's waterfront is an amazing array of Navy battle and supply ships and a plethora of aircraft carriers. All kinds of impressive ships everywhere... Yikes!

We also had some hair-raising experiences that taught us that things might not be what they seem.

We got an early start Thursday and Captain Rich nosed *PH* into Norfolk's busy harbor. Even in the early morning the harbor was bustling. It was amazing how close pleasure boats could get to these war machines! With a constant eye on the buoys and chart, Captain Rich maneuvered *PH* through the channel... anxious to leave war games to other mariners.

PH headed for the open waters of Chesapeake Bay. As she made her way through the harbor we were keenly aware of the Coast Guard's radio broadcast warning boaters to stay clear of an incoming naval warship. We scanned the horizon, looking for a large battleship and channel markers but only saw fishing and clam boats. The broadcast became louder and more frequent so we knew we were close, but we still couldn't see anything. Rich was checking the charts to locate the next channel marker. He thought he saw it in the distance and pointed *PH*'s bow in that direction. A sailboat decided Captain Rich looked like he knew where to go, so he followed *PH* out of the channel. Oops, his mistake!

Then we saw it! Coast Guard and Navy gunner ships escorting a Triton submarine! We were close enough to feel its huge wake... but thankfully not close enough to be "taken off to jail for six years or pay a $250,000 fine," as was irritably proclaimed by the military broadcaster. That experience started the morning off with a shot of adrenaline that woke us up more than strong coffee ever could.

Later that morning, we saw another military ship off in the distance, but it looked like it was anchored. It turned out to be a Victory ship that had been grounded for fighter pilot target practice. Our son, Nels, was at the helm as fighter pilots dove for the target and then shot straight up over that target. We read in the guidebook just about that time that, "If planes are flying maneuvers overhead, adjust your course out of the area!" Guess what we did?

Cruising can bring you to unique places, Tangier Island, for instance, is a remote island in the middle of the Chesapeake Bay. We had heard that the residents of Tangier are "watermen" and they trap crabs for a living. So, we decided to take an afternoon and visit this island. We found that the people on Tangier are so isolated that they still speak Elizabethan English. Their accent sounded like Elisa's from *My Fair Lady* with lots of OOWs and HEYs.

The only part of the Loop where we had to travel in the Atlantic Ocean was between Cape May, New Jersey and the New York Harbor. I wasn't looking forward to this part of the trip, as neither of us had ever boated in the Atlantic.

After touring historic Cape May on our bikes and enjoying a seafood platter on the docks, we headed to bed. We wanted to get an early morning start for our 115-mile run "outside" to Sandy Hook. The alarm rang at 5:30 a.m. and we were ready to go by 6 a.m. The harbor was socked in with heavy fog, but the forecast was for only early morning fog and 5-15 mph winds with two to four-foot waves building from the southeast. We decided to go, hoping the fog would lift as the sun came up.

PH followed a fisherman out the channel into the Atlantic Ocean, Rich set waypoints on the GPS, and I stowed stuff in preparation for heavy seas. By 7 a.m., we were cruising into the Atlantic about two miles offshore. I had steeled myself for a 12 to 13-hour day and had my seasick wristbands on, not knowing what to expect with ocean swells. After a few miles, the sun did its work and the fog lifted. We could see Atlantic and Ocean Cities. It looked like the shore was one constant city. At the first turning buoy, we slipped back into a cloud of fog. I ran a compass course with our autopilot from the flybridge while Rich watched the radar below and blew the horn about every three minutes. The waves and fog became hypnotic, so we were glad when it lifted and we were cruising in sunshine again. However, we kept going in and out of fog patches. About halfway into the trip the dense fog still would not leave us completely, so for five hours we ran on *PH*'s GPS waypoints, time, speed and distance. A couple of hours out from Sandy Hook we switched positions. I read the radar screen with Rich as pilot and lookout.

I had never used the radar before but after a quick lesson, I could distinguish wave noise from boat traffic and buoys. The radar screen has a large compass divided into concentric circles, with each circle (depending on the screen setting) a quarter mile. *PH* was in the center of the bull's eye (the center of our universe) with a straight line indicating objects directly in our path.

Coming into Sandy Hook, New York Harbor, I could see we were coming up on a number of small steady dots, it was something to see. "Rich, we have boats dead ahead and five degrees off the starboard bow. They're less than a half-mile... less than a quarter-mile... better blow the horn... NOW!" I pulled open the door and saw a small fishing boat just off our starboard side... and another only feet away on the port side. I was staring at the radar screen looking for more dots, and a streak of sun was blinding the screen. I looked up to see where the sun was coming from... the fog had lifted and I could finally see a bazillion small fishing boats bobbing all around and in front of us! The fog had lifted!

Joining Rich on the flybridge later, we marveled that we hadn't hit anyone. Rich asked for a scotch and I had one too. I don't even drink scotch!

We made it to the anchorage in Kills Harbors off of Staten Island and joined a million other boats. Just as we got the anchor set, we heard "May Day, May Day" on the radio. "A @#?&#! pilot boat just hit me and took off my bow!" the guy screamed. "I repeat, I have no bow!" It could have been us out there.

We had grilled cheese sandwiches and Manhattan clam chowder for supper. Grilled cheese for the comfort food and clam chowder to celebrate the fact New York City was just across the bay and the Atlantic was well behind us!

There is nothing like taking your vessel into New York Harbor! Cruising by the Statue of Liberty and Ellis Island sent shivers up my spine. I couldn't help but think about how our grandparents must have felt entering this harbor after weeks of crossing the Atlantic from Sweden and Norway. We spent a couple of days sightseeing by taking the subway under the river across to New York City. *PH* was docked across from Manhattan at Liberty Island on the New Jersey side of the Hudson River. We didn't even miss the traffic jams and enjoyed getting in and out of the City by subway.

Heading up the Hudson River and through the Erie Canal, we pointed *PH's* bow north and west for home. Crossing Lake Ontario and locking through 40-plus historic locks on the Trent-Severn Waterway, she made her way west through Ontario, Canada. In the familiar and beautiful Georgian Bay and North Channel off Lake Huron, we knew our cruising adventure included one more lock at Sault Sainte Marie, Michigan and then into our home waters of Lake Superior.

PH and her crew pulled up to our dock at Pike's Bay Marina in Bayfield, Wisconsin in early July of our second year doing the Loop. Rich and I shared a celebratory glass of champagne with a transient boater passing through the area. It seemed an appropriate homecoming! We had traveled close to six months and approximately 6,000 miles at an average speed of ten knots.

Nancy Ojard – *Proud Heritage/Superior Lady*

In the process, we gained a tremendous appreciation for the beauty of our country and her waterways!

Rich and I would love to spend more time cruising. We both agreed that we did the Loop trip too fast. However, taking that slice of time out our life to do the trip was a gift to ourselves that we will never regret.

A few years later, Rich and I sold *PH* and purchased a 55-foot Ocean Alexander in Fort Myers, Florida and christened her the *Superior Lady*. Our intent in purchasing this new boat was to share our passion of boating with our grandchildren. We also hope to be fortunate enough to take her on additional cruising adventures and maybe even a repeat of the Loop for us in the future.

Cruising and living on board a boat is an amazing experience! I've found that cruising has helped me to see the world from a different perspective, and it has given me a greater appreciation for the beauty of our country and her history. In some ways it may have even defined me, even if that wasn't my intent. The people, places, experiences and memories have become so much a part of how I now look at life. This may be what it really means to be a BOATER and I wholeheartedly encourage you to take the plunge.

Nancy Ojard, (alias – NanSea when boating) lives with her husband, Rich, in Knife River, Minnesota. They have been boating as a couple for the past 35 years. Over that period of time they have owned both power and sailboats with Lake Superior as their main cruising grounds. Nancy took a five-day Sea Sense Power Boating Class. Two years later Nancy and Rich embarked on the Great Loop in their 43-foot Albin Sundeck Motor Yacht *Proud Heritage* and completed the trip two years later.

Six years after their Loop the Ojards purchased their current boat, a 55-foot Ocean Alexander Motor Yacht, *Superior Lady*, and cruised the Apostle Islands and other Lake Superior cruising grounds out of their homeport in Pike's Bay Marina outside of Bayfield, Wisconsin. Nancy currently works part-time for the Two Harbors Area Chamber in Two Harbors, Minnesota.

Hawaii is an island state, thousands of miles from anywhere. It's as if we are in a boat, caught in treacherous waters, needing to set sail for a better place. If I were to chart a course north, but you insisted on going south, then we would go nowhere. We would stay stuck exactly where we started.
— Linda Lingle

Whoever embarks with a woman embarks with a storm; but they are themselves the safety boats.
— Houssaye

ACKNOWLEDGEMENTS

First and foremost, I want to give my heartfelt thanks and appreciation to all the passionate and engaging women boaters who joined me in sharing our experiences in this book. It truly may never have come to fruition if these 24 women had not responded so quickly to the many questions and concerns I frequently bothered them with. I also have to say that I was quite astounded by the quality of chapters submitted to me, many by women who are not necessarily writers. I was very happy to see, not only the humor these women were able to share, but also in some cases a genuine vulnerability came through and I know these writing styles will be greatly appreciated by our readers.

My gratitude also to Bernadette Bernon (BoatU.S. Magazine) for her ongoing encouragement in our writing endeavors over the last two years. Her suggestions and support mean a lot to both myself and to Jim. I also want to thank Patti Moore (Sea Sense Boating School) for, not only being a source and solution for many women who sought education through her organization to better their skills, but for offering to help in spreading the word about the book. I was so surprised to see how many women mentioned her in their chapters, which gave me the idea to contact Patti to see if she would read and review the book for us. A big thanks to Christy Martin (Life On The Water Magazine) for not only being an advocate and a promoter for women on the water, but for sharing her thoughts on the book in her review.

My dear friend Diane Wade, who calls herself the "Cheerful Volunteer," took on the painstaking job of proofreading the book during its final go round. My sincere thanks go out to you Diane; I owe you a big one.

Last, but NEVER least, thanks to my dear, patient and supportive husband, Jim, who encouraged me from the very beginning. When I was struggling with whether to take on this project or not to the very end, he quietly took on many of the "pink" jobs so that I could focus on the task at hand.

HELPFUL LINKS

ASSOCIATIONS
America's Great Loop Cruisers' Association... greatloop.org
Marine Trawler Owners Association .... mtoa.net
The Salty Southwest Cruisers' Net .... cruisersnet.net
Trawlers & Trawlering .... trawlersandtrawlering.com
Cruising the ICW .... cruisingtheicw.com

CRUISING GUIDES
Dozier's Waterway Guide .... waterwayguide.com
Skipper Bob Publications................................ skipperbob.net
Claiborne Young's Cruising Guides................ cruisersnet.net
Fred Myer Cruise Guides .... greatloopcruising.com
Active Captain... activecaptain.com

WEATHER
NOAA Marine Forecast.................................... nws.noaa.gov/om/marine/home.htm
National Weather Service .... weather.gov
Sail Flow .... sailflow.com
iKiTESURF.. ikitesurf.com
PassageWeather .... passageweather.com
Weather Underground..................................... wunderground.com
WindMapper .... windmapper.com
Weather Office (Canadian Weather)............... weatheroffice.gc.ca
Crown Weather Services .... crownweather.com
GribUS... grib.us
BuoyWeather .... buoyweather.com

WOMEN
BoatU.S. Women in Boating .... boatus.com/women
Women On Board Cruising............................. womenonboardcruising.com

FAMILIES
Kids Aboard... kidsaboard.com

TRAINING
Sea Sense Boating School .... seasenseboating.com
Sistership Sailing School................................. sailsistership.com
America's Boating Course .... americasboatingcourse.com

MISCELLEANEOUS
Skype... skype.com
Grog's Animated Knots .... animatedknots.com

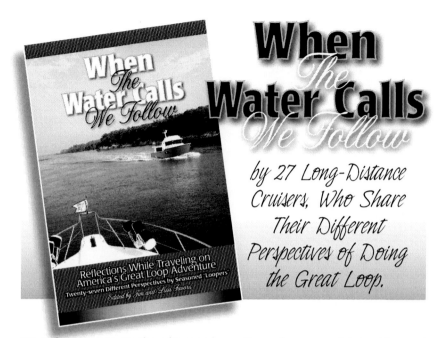

When The Water Calls We Follow

by 27 Long-Distance Cruisers, Who Share Their Different Perspectives of Doing the Great Loop.

Jim and Lisa Favors are the editors and co-authors of a very useful, inspiring, and entertaining new book, "When The Water Calls...We Follow," about the Great American Loop adventure. During their first voyage, the Favors knew of only one other couple about to embark on a "Loop". So, while they'd researched the route, got their boat shipshape, and organized their personal lives, they had no real picture of what or whom they'd encounter on this adventure.

What they found was that Loopers were as varied as the members of any large family. They'd all left behind the self-importance of their home and working life. It didn't matter where they came from, where they worked, or what their social, economic, or educational background was, the camaraderie of this family was akin to belonging to a benevolent civic organization – all willing to help each other and expecting nothing in return.

"We asked other boaters we met to share their varied and insightful experiences with us," said Jim Favors, "and tell us stories about what has made this trip valuable to them."

"With this book," said Lisa Favors, "we hoped to create a vehicle for people either considering this trip, or just curious about it, to have a better sense of what a journey like this can entail. The American Great Loop Adventure is more about the day-to-day journey, relationships, communing with nature, and most definitely not about the final destination or even the itinerary. This trip has the ability to enhance and enriche the lives of those with a taste for adventure, and a heart ripe for surprises, both large and small."

– BERNADETTE BERNON, *BoatU.S. Magazine* and *Cruising World*

Favors Ventures, LLC • 216 pages • Photos Throughout

For More Information or to Order a Copy:
favorsventures.com
info@favorsventures.com